Japan, Race and Equality

The Nissan Institute/Routledge Japanese Studies Series

Other titles in the series:

The Myth of Japanese Uniqueness, *Peter Dale*
The Emperor's Adviser: Saionji Kinmochi and Pre-war Japanese Politics, *Lesley Connors*
A History of Japanese Economic Thought, *Tessa Morris-Suzuki*
The Establishment of the Japanese Constitutional System, *Junji Banno, translated by J.A.A. Stockwin*
Industrial Relations in Japan: the Peripheral Workforce, *Norma Chalmers*
Banking Policy in Japan: American Efforts at Reform During the Occupation, *William M. Tsutsui*
Education Reform in Japan, *Leonard Schoppa*
How the Japanese Learn to Work, *Ronald P. Dore and Mari Sako*
Japanese Economic Development: Theory and Practice, *Penelope Francks*
Japan and Protection: The Growth of Protectionist Sentiment and the Japanese Response, *Syed Javed Marwood*
The Soil, by Nagastsuka Takashi: a Portrait of Rural Life in Meiji Japan, *translated and with an introduction by Ann Waswo*
Biotechnology in Japan, *Malcolm Brock*
Britain's Educational Reform: a Comparison with Japan, *Mike Howarth*
Language and the Modern State: the Reform of Written Japanese, *Nanette Twine*
Industrial Harmony in Modern Japan: the Invention of a Tradition, *W. Dean Kinzley*
Japanese Science Fiction: a View of a Changing Society, *Robert Matthew*
The Japanese Numbers Game: the Use and Understanding of Numbers in Modern Japan, *Thomas Crump*
Ideology and Practice in Modern Japan, *Roger Goodman and Kirsten Refsing*
Technology and Industrial Development in pre-War Japan, *Yukiko Fukasaku*
Japan's Early Parliaments 1890–1905, *Andres Fraser, R.H.P. Mason and Philip Mitchell*
Japan's Foreign Aid Challenge, *Alan Rix*
Emperor Hirohito and Showa Japan, *Stephen S. Large*
Japan: Beyond the End of History, *David Williams*
Ceremony and Ritual in Japan: Religious Practices in an Industrialized Society, *Jan van Bremen and D. P. Martinez*
Understanding Japanese Society: Second Edition, *Joy Hendry*
The Fantastic in Modern Japanese Literature: The Subversion of Modernity, *Susan J. Napier*
Militarization and Demilitarization in Contemporary Japan, *Glenn D. Hook*
Growing a Japanese Science City: Communication in Scientific Research, *James W. Dearing*
Architecture and Authority in Japan, *William H. Coaldrake*
Women's *Gidayū* and the Japanese Theatre Tradition, *A. Kimi Coaldrake*
Democracy in Post-war Japan, *Rikki Kersten*
Treacherous Women of Imperial Japan, *Hélène Bowen Raddeker*
Japanese-German Business Relations, *Akira Kudo*

Japan, Race and Equality

The Racial Equality Proposal of 1919

Naoko Shimazu

ROUTLEDGE

London and New York

First published 1998
by Routledge
2 Park Square, Milton Park, Abingdon, Oxon, OX14 4RN

Simultaneously published in the USA and Canada
by Routledge
270 Madison Ave, New York NY 10016

Transferred to Digital Printing 2009

Typeset in Times by Routledge

British Library Cataloguing in Publication Data
A catalogue record for this book is available from the British Library

Library of Congress Cataloguing in Publication Data
Japan, race and equality: the racial equality proposal of 1919/
Naoko Shimazu.
(Nissan Institute/Routledge Japanese studies series).
Includes bibliographical references and index.
I1. Japan–Foreign relations–1912–1945. 2. World War,
1914–1918–Diplomatic history. 3. Japanese–Ethic Identity. I. Title.
II. Series.
DS885.48.S56 1998 97–35427
327. 52 – dc21 CIP

ISBN10: 0–415–17207–1 (hbk)
ISBN10: 0–415–49735–3 (pbk)

ISBN13: 978–0–415–17207–3 (hbk)
ISBN13: 978–0–415–49735–0 (pbk)

Publisher's Note
The publisher has gone to great lengths to ensure the quality of this reprint but points out that some imperfections in the original may be apparent.

To my parents

Contents

Series editor's preface

> 'we are a people whose glorious history will bear to be held up to the gaze of Western nations. We have learned a great many things from the West, but there are some instances of our having outstripped our tutors.'

So wrote Count Okuma in *Fifty Years of New Japan*, published in 1910, some five years after Japan had emerged victorious in the Russo-Japanese war. Over the 87 years that have elapsed since those words were written, the history of Japan's relations with the rest of the world has passed through phases more turbulent than Okuma could probably have imagined. The tragic and terrible history of the 1930s and 1940s gave way, however, to decades in which the Japanese forged an amazing (and often deserved) reputation for economic development and efficiency. The idea of the Japanese outstripping their tutors is no longer as exotic as it must have sounded to an English-speaking readership in 1910, but its content has been radically changed with the passage of time. Japan has been widely accused by some Americans and others of exploiting American goodwill and soft attitudes since the 1950s in such a way as to maximise ruthlessly the interests of Japanese corporations and the Japanese economy in general. Whatever the truth of these accusations, during the late 1990s many influential Japanese have been moving to the view that forces of globalisation leave Japan little choice in terms of national interest but to move towards a more open, less controlled, form of economic, political and social order. Entrenched resistance to such a fundamental systemic change remains strong, but the balance of influences is shifting significantly. How the Japanese seek to resolve the dilemma of how far they can preserve a distinctive Japanese identity and practice in an increasingly globalising world is fascinating to watch.

The Nissan Institute/Routledge Japanese Studies Series seeks to foster an informed and balanced, but not uncritical, understanding of Japan. One of its main aims is to show the depth and variety of Japanese institutions, practices and ideas. Another is, by using comparison, to see what lessons, positive and negative, can be drawn for other parts of the world. The tendency in commentary on Japan to resort to outdated, ill-informed or sensational stereotypes still remains, and needs to be combated.

It is not perhaps widely remembered nowadays that Japan proposed a racial equality clause at the Versailles Peace Conference in 1919. The initiative failed in large part as a result of determined opposition from Great Britain and her Dominions, spearheaded by the vitriolic Prime Minister of Australia, William Morris Hughes, fanatical defender of the White Australia Policy. Among other reasons, it also failed because President Woodrow Wilson of the United States regarded establishment of the League of Nations (which the US subsequently failed to join) as having higher priority than a clause outlawing racial inequality. In this luminous study, Dr Shimazu shows that a principle that would be practically non-controversial in the 1990s seemed extraordinary and even threatening to the major powers in the very different, imperialistic, world that existed decades earlier. At the same time, for Japan, torn between the idea of being a leader in Asia and the idea of being one of the 'western' imperialist powers, the clause was hardly conceived as a way of giving equality to all races. Rather, its purpose was to assert equality of status for Japan in the ranks of the major powers. In Dr Shimazu's words, Japan was 'an arrogant yet insecure power, dismissive of yet sensitive to international opinion'. Together with other snubs from the Western world, such as the Triple Intervention which followed the Japanese victory in the Sino-Japanese war of 1894–5, the rejection of the racial equality clause in 1919 may well be seen as a trigger for the chain of events that led to Japanese militarisation and international aggression two decades later. On the other hand, Dr Shimazu persuasively argues that the Japanese attempt, however self-serving, to promote a racial equality principle after the end of the First World War, made it much easier to embed such a principle into the Charter of the United Nations after the ending of a second world conflict even more destructive than the first.

J.A.A. Stockwin

Acknowledgements

This book is based on my doctoral thesis submitted to the University of Oxford in 1995. I have restructured the thesis substantially in order to focus more sharply on my particular approach to the topic. I am indebted to many friends and colleagues. My deep gratitude goes to my supervisors who, at various stages, gave me encouragement, support and advice. They were Dr John Darwin and Dr Andy Hurrell, both of Nuffield College, Oxford, Professor Benedict Kingsbury, now at Duke University, and Dr Ann Waswo of the Nissan Institute, Oxford. I would like to make a special mention of Professor Banno Junji of the Institute of Social Science at the University of Tokyo, to whom I owe the greatest intellectual debt. His critical and imaginative approach to political history has inspired me deeply over the years. He also enabled me to spend four months in the summer of 1987 as Foreign Research Scholar at the Institute of Social Science. At Oxford, the Nissan Institute has always made me feel welcome, and I would especially like to extend my thanks to Professor Arthur Stockwin, Dr Roger Goodman and Ms Diana Dick. My examiners, Professor Ian Nish of the London School of Economics, and Dr Rosemary Foot of St Antony's College, gave me excellent comments and suggestions, which I was able to include before publication. Last, but not least, all the 'suffering' one has to go through in completing a book would not have been possible without the support of my many good friends. In particular, I would like to mention Erica Benner, Antony Best, Harumi Goto-Shibata, Masa Okano, Andreas Osiander and Paola Rota. Many thanks are especially due to John Driffill.

As this is an historical study, I have had to rely on primary sources from many libraries and archives. I would like to express my gratitude to them for allowing me to use the sources especially from the following institutions: the Diplomatic Record Office of the Japanese Foreign

Ministry, the National Diet Library, the University of Tokyo Library, the Public Record Office in Kew Gardens, House of Lords Record Office, the British Library, the Bodleian Library, the University of Cambridge Library, the National Archives in Washington D.C., the Library of Congress, Seeley G. Mudd Manuscript Library at Princeton University, Manuscripts and Archives at Yale University, and Rare Book and Manuscript Library at Columbia University. In accordance with normal Japanese practice, Japanese names have been rendered with the family name preceding the given name. Also some key Japanese words have been used in the text in order to give more accurate nuances but in such cases, the English equivalents are provided in parenthesis.

N.S.
London, 1997

Introduction

Japan attended the Paris Peace Conference of 1919 as one of the five great powers, and as the only non-Western great power. It was the culmination of a half century of intensive national effort to create a modern state, since the Meiji Restoration of 1868 when Japan discarded its late-feudal past. In retrospect, the presence of Japan in the Hall of Mirrors at Versailles, signing the Treaty of Versailles on 28 June 1919 with all the powers and looking very much part of the international scene, was a truly astonishing feat. Only fifty years before, it would have been impossible to imagine the Japan that we saw in 1919.

In principle, therefore, Japan was a paragon of success, proud and content with its newly acquired position of great eminence. Although Japan's rise may appear to have been successfully and effortlessly carried out, there inevitably existed internal and external tensions surrounding its emergence as a great power. As the Paris Peace Conference showed, the 'world' of 1919 was still dominated by the Western imperial powers, and Japan's position within it was unique. Japan was not only the only non-Western great power, but also the only one of the five non-Western powers to attend the conference.[1] In this sense, Japan's participation was highly significant because it was the only power in the non-Western world which could possibly make any impact on the conference and the world thereafter.

Many of the decisions taken at the Paris Peace Conference of 1919 were to have a lasting impact on various aspects of twentieth-century history. Possibly the most successful idea to emerge from the conference was the principle of self-determination, advocated by President Woodrow Wilson. However, the whole peace process was complicated by the fact that underneath the surface of 'new' diplomacy, as propounded by Wilson, there lay the methods and interests of the old, exercised fully by the great powers. The 'world' was in a state of flux, as not only was the old European *status quo* being threatened by the

American 'new' diplomacy, but both Europeans and Americans felt threatened by the rise of revolutionary socialism in the Soviet Union. It was in this international environment, where contrary forces were at work, that the principle of racial equality emerged for the first time. This study is about understanding the rise and fall of the racial equality proposal of 1919, from the perspectives of the three protagonists – the Japanese who proposed it, and the British and Americans who opposed it. Moreover, it is about understanding the principle of racial equality as it stood at the time.

The picture of Japan painted in this study is a subtle and complex one. It shows Japan as an arrogant, yet insecure power, dismissive of, yet sensitive to international opinion. Domestically, there was a wealth of conflicting visions of Japan's role in Asia, in terms of its status as either the leader of Asia or as one of the 'Western' imperial powers. Because the racial equality proposal revealed more of the side of Japan which had not been adequately explored in the past, it provides an insight into how the Japanese themselves perceived their identity as being inherently dialectical, as both a 'Western' and an 'Asian' great power. Indeed, one of the most potent messages to emerge from the ensuing analysis is the uncertain nature of Japan's international status. In 1919, Japan still had not gained enough political confidence or military strength to act more independently of the Western imperial powers. Therefore, Japanese politics of the time generally consisted of reconciling the contradictory forces of pro-Westerners and 'independent' minded pan-Asianists. Importantly, the racial equality proposal was one issue which revealed such internal contradictions.

For Japan, the desire to gain 'equality with the West' had been one of the consistent national imperatives since the 1850s when the 'unequal' treaties were signed.[2] One of the major tasks of the Meiji government after 1868 was to revise these 'unequal' treaties, in order to gain 'equality' with the Western powers. After several unsuccessful attempts, beginning in 1878, the Japanese government finally managed to revise the 'unequal' treaties in 1894, taking effect from 1899. It has been argued that the pursuit of pragmatic concerns and concrete goals came to characterise Japanese foreign policy, which lacked an 'ideological backbone'.[3] However, though the means of achieving the objective of the unequal treaties revision involved a pragmatic process, it can be argued also that the underlying motivation to achieve that objective must have been dominated by a deeper need to prove that Japan was not 'less' than the West, but equal to it. Seen in this light, the notion of Japan's 'equality with the West' was a highly significant underlying 'ideological' force in its thinking on foreign relations from the inception of modern Japanese foreign policy. From this historical perspective, it may not be too surprising that it was the Japanese who submitted the racial equality proposal in 1919.

In the past, the question of why the Japanese government submitted the racial equality proposal at the peace conference has attracted some scholarly attention. From the standpoint of Japanese history, the proposal stands out as an aberration in Japanese foreign policy for having insisted on the acceptance of an international principle at a major international conference. One of the major tasks of this study, then, is to attempt to understand 'why' the Japanese submitted the proposal. In this sense, this study is about the history of Japan around the time of the peace conference. In spite of the existence of many excellent general works on the Paris Peace Conference,[4] there has been no sizeable study on Japan's participation from the Japanese perspective. This study hopes to fill in, albeit in a small way, a gap in the existing literature on Japan's emergence as a great power and its participation at the Paris Peace Conference.

Moreover, this study is also one of diplomacy, since many of the key observations made in the context of the racial equality negotiations have some relevance as to how diplomacy was conducted generally at the peace conference. The racial equality proposal illustrates a typical case of great power diplomacy at work where the primacy of *realpolitik* had set the tone for deliberations, negotiations and decisions on many vital issues. Since diplomacy, by definition, cannot be a one-way process, it is necessary to understand why the Japanese proposal was defeated by Britain and the United States as a principle unsuitable to be part of the covenant of the League of Nations. This sets in context the second major task of this study which is to explain the Anglo-American responses to the Japanese proposal. Only by understanding the international as well as national positions held by the three protagonists can we hope to reach a satisfactory, comprehensive understanding of this issue. In so doing, this study shows that the diplomacy surrounding the racial equality proposal was complicated by many layers of misapprehension on all sides. None of the protagonists had a neatly confined single perspective on the racial equality issue because, in most cases, there existed many diverse and often conflicting perspectives within the seemingly united national front. Hence, it is necessary to identify the separate strands, and to give appropriate weighting in terms of the ultimate decisions made by each state. In the end, the most noticeable commonality in the position taken by the protagonists is that each acted according to the perceived threat or gain to its national interests.

Lastly, this study is about the evolution of the principle of racial equality. This was how the topic germinated initially, as it seemed strange that racial equality should be discarded in 1919, only to be fêted as being fundamentally crucial to the peace and stability of the international system in the United Nations Charter only some twenty-six years later. Evidently, what happened in the interwar period and the Second World War had a profound effect on the mores of society at both national and international levels, causing a radical change in attitudes towards some ideas which had previously appeared unimportant and even marginal. In this sense, the proposal of 1919 can be seen as the first major stage of the development of racial equality as a general principle of international importance. As the perspective taken here is not theoretical but historical, it will focus on understanding how contemporaries understood the term in 1919. The findings presented in the ensuing chapters may disappoint some purists, who may wish to believe that the Japanese had valiantly attempted to fight off Western racism by demanding universal racial equality. But there was little unselfish idealism displayed by any of the main players in this story. Hence, it will not be possible to reach a 'heroic' conclusion, but instead a more sober one. It will be shown that the principle of racial equality, as we conceive of it today in the universalist sense, was not even the issue at stake during the racial equality negotiations. Nonetheless, it cannot be denied that this is an important revelation as it brings us closer to understanding the values which governed the international society of 1919.

Methodologically, this study attempts to redress what is perceived to be an incomplete picture of the story presented in the existing literature. It seems that much of the existing literature on the racial equality proposal adopts a certain analytical position in examining the issue. For instance, one Japanese scholar has argued that the proposal was submitted to resolve the anti-Japanese immigration problems in the Anglo-Saxon territories by inserting a racial equality clause into the covenant of the League of Nations.[5] However, this view was evidently adopted as a result of the type of original sources consulted. Another scholar has looked at the issue from the angle of Australian immigration.[6] Yet another analysed the issue from the perspective of racial prejudice and racism.[7] Then there have been those who have taken interest in the issue from the perspective of some of the contemporary Japanese personalities involved in the racial equality debate in 1919.[8] The most comprehensive study from the Japanese perspective published thus far has been an article by an international lawyer who attempted to look at the issue without any obvious analytical bias.[9] As many previous scholars have tended to approach the study of the proposal from a certain angle, they have invariably produced findings apparently cogent to their analytical positions. This has resulted in the lack of a systematic, full-length study. Moreover, many of the works have tended to make generalisations without making substantive elaborations, and to be too uncritical of the perspectives of previous scholars. Therefore, this is an attempt to provide a more holistic treatment of the subject by analysing the history of the proposal, as far as practicable, in its totality. Above all, it is a critical study which questions all the assumptions hitherto made about the proposal and, in turn, seeks to present an alternative set of explanations which have been subjected to a more rigorous analytical test in the light of the much larger pool of primary sources consulted.

In order to have a systematic approach to examining the three countries, an overall analytical framework based on five categories of possible explanations was constructed and applied. These explanations provide satisfactory coverage of all the possible factors which are needed in analysing Japanese motivations and Anglo-American responses. The five explanations can be broadly categorised as follows: immigration, universal principle, great power status, domestic politics and politics of bargaining at the peace conference. It is necessary to specify what the terms of each of these explanations are, and how they applied to each country. The analysis of all the explanations will show that no single explanation, but rather a combination of explanations is needed to understand the respective positions taken by Japan, Britain and the United States on the racial equality proposal.

First, there is the immigration explanation which would argue that the Japanese government had submitted the racial equality proposal to resolve the long-standing Japanese immigration problems in the United States and the British Dominions. This was a pragmatic interpretation of the Japanese proposal which underlined how preoccupied the great powers were at the time with practical problems of immigration. In order to understand whether this had any part in explaining the Japanese motivations, it is necessary to investigate the link between the racial equality proposal and immigration in terms of how the proposal was formulated as a result of the perceived correlation between the two issues. In analysing how the explanation is applicable to the British position, it is necessary first to understand why the proposal was interpreted by the British government as implying immigration, and then why it was particularly important for Australia. Similarly, for the American position, an analysis will be made of the history of Japanese immigration in the United States in terms of how this affected the politics of immigration during the racial equality negotiation at the peace conference.

Immigration is the dominant explanation given in the existing literature on the racial equality proposal. Among Japanese scholars, the immigration factor is seen to explain the political origins of the racial equality proposal. For instance, Ikei Masaru argued that the proposal was intended to resolve the immigration problems.[10] Onuma was also led to conclude that the political origins of the proposal must have derived from the national interest in resolving Japanese immigration problems.[11] Fitzhardinge, who discussed the racial equality proposal from the perspective of Australian Premier Billy Hughes, also discussed the proposal as an 'immigration' proposal.[12] It will be argued that the importance of immigration lay in its symbolic value and that the Japanese government wanted to resolve the immigration problems because that was seen as part of the 'diplomacy of saving face' (*memmoku gaikō*).[13] In spite of its importance, however, this study will reveal that immigration was not the only explanation of the proposal but one of many, in terms of understanding both the Japanese motivations and the Anglo-American responses.

Second, there is the explanation which claims that the racial equality proposal was a demand for a universal principle of racial equality. This would argue that it was the intention of the Japanese government to use the peace conference as the opportunity of instituting formally the idea of universal racial equality which had been developing within Japanese foreign policy thinking. Accordingly, the proposal was an expression by the Japanese government of their belief in the universal principle of racial equality of all peoples. In terms of analysing the Anglo-American responses, it would similarly argue that Britain and the United States perceived the Japanese proposal as demanding universal racial equality, and that the proposal was based on idealistic and altruistic motives.

This explanation, which appears to be the most obvious, is widely quoted in literature, especially among international relations writers, and this is due to the fact that universal principles are considered to be an essential element of the study of the European expansion of international society.[14] For instance, this is how the English School interpreted the Japanese proposal:

> Japan proposed that the clause in the League of Nations Covenant providing for religious equality should be broadened to embrace racial equality. The principle of the equality of all men might have been taken to mean all men, yellow and even black, as well as white,

> but the consequences of such a doctrine for the domestic policies of the powers – the treatment of the negroes in the United States, the 'White Australian policy' – militated against its acceptance.[15]

Another scholar went even further on similar grounds to claim that it was a 'human rights' proposal.[16] Ikei argues that Japan, as one of five great powers, attempted to represent the interests of the yellow race through the proposal.[17] What is attempted in this study is to gain an insight into how Japan, Britain and the United States approached the racial equality proposal as a demand of principle. The analysis of the proposal suggests that the racial equality proposal of 1919, in spite of these assumptions and extrapolations, was not really about universal racial equality. In this sense, it concurs with the view of Onuma that the racial equality proposal was not about universal racial equality, but an interesting case whereby Japan seemingly took an important international initiative to change the existing international order without ever having any awareness or intention of doing so.[18]

The third explanation claims that the racial equality proposal was motivated by Japan's insecurity as a non-white great power and its desire to secure its great power status in the future international organisation. It introduces a new element into the criteria for what constituted 'great power', because what the Japanese attempted to do was to claim great power equality on the basis of racial equality. This explanation suggests that the basic criteria of great power status identified by the English School of Martin Wight and Hedley Bull may have been too Eurocentric in its assumptions.[19] It will argue that Japan, coming from the non-Western tradition, had a different agenda in submitting the proposal deriving from a different perspective on international relations. This explanation was not applicable to the Anglo-American responses.

In the existing literature, this explanation has been suggested, fleetingly by Russell Fifield, that the Japanese wanted to establish their position definitively as a great power and hence the proposal was a sincere manifestation of this desire.[20] Fifield argues that Japan had wanted to establish its status by submitting a proposal such as universal racial equality which would be commensurate with its great power status. Unfortunately, he did not elaborate this claim. Onuma examined Japan's historical experience as a non-white great power, and while he seems to imply that great power status was an important factor, he did not specifically refer to it as a category.[21] Overall, there has not been enough serious consideration given to this explanation, possibly because this factor appeared more implicit than explicit. This study will emphasise great power status as the most important analytical factor in explaining the Japanese motivations.

Fourthly, the domestic politics explanation argues that it is necessary to understand the proposal in relation to the domestic political constraints of the respective countries. Since the category of domestic politics is too wide, we focus here on that aspect of domestic politics which had a direct relevance to the racial equality proposal. In the case of Japan, the explanation would argue that the proposal was related to the domestic politics surrounding the League of Nations, and more precisely, Prime Minister Hara's pro-League politics. Although the response of the Japanese public to the racial equality proposal has been analysed in the Japanese works[22], the domestic political explanation, especially in terms of the governmental response to the League of Nations, has been largely overlooked. This study will argue that the domestic political factor was important in understanding the Japanese government's attitude to the League of Nations and, concomitantly, the racial equality proposal which came as part and parcel of its League policy. In the case of the British Empire delegation, it will be argued that the importance of the proposal to Australia's domestic politics, particularly in terms of its perceived threat to the 'White Australia' policy, was the reason for the Australian opposition. As for the Americans, the explanation argues that domestic partisan politics, as manifested in the anti-League and anti-Wilson movement in the United States, had a limited role in explaining the American position. Contrary to the interpretation that President Wilson was affected by the domestic anti-Wilson lobby which resulted in him changing his attitude towards the racial equality proposal,[23] it will be shown that the domestic political factor was not as decisive as it seemed.

Fifthly, there is the politics of bargaining explanation, which claims that the proposal was used as part of the bargaining made to achieve other ends at the peace conference. This is a *realpolitik* view of the proposal. This explanation applies most readily in understanding the American positions, though it was not at all applicable in understanding the Japanese and British positions. At the first level, there was a group within the American delegation which suspected the Japanese government of having deliberately constructed the proposal as a political ploy to obtain Shantung. This argument, known as the 'bargaining chip' theory, was one of the key interpretations given to the proposal by the contemporaries in the American delegation at Paris.[24] The second level of this explanation argues that President Wilson had used his opposition to the proposal indirectly to attain his objective of establishing the League of Nations. Therefore, Wilson had made an implicit trade-off by sacrificing the Japanese proposal in order to salvage his ultimate priority, the League of Nations. This is a completely novel perspective from which to explain the American position.

Although the framework consisting of the five explanatory factors listed above was used duly in the process of reaching the conclusions presented in this study, we are not testing the applicability of each factor here. This is because not all factors are of equal importance and relevance in each case. Hence, this study represents the finalised version of the analysis. For instance, although the possibility of all the five explanations in explaining the Japanese motivations have been considered, we focus here on the relevant three, that is, great power status, immigration and domestic politics, out of the possible five (the remaining two are universal principle and politics of bargaining), because the other two were simply not relevant. Similarly, in the case of Britain, we discuss the immigration and domestic politics factors because they were central to explaining the British opposition. For the American case, three explanatory categories will be addressed – immigration, domestic politics and politics of bargaining at the peace conference. Having said that, the explanation based on racial equality as a universal principle is so fundamental to our understanding of the principle today that an attempt has been made to address the question whenever suitable within the analysis.

At this juncture, it may be necessary to explain why the decision was made to leave out a discussion of the responses of the other great powers, namely France and Italy, and to concentrate on Britain and the United States. Admittedly, including France and Italy would provide an interesting contrast, as both supported the proposal. France declared that it was impossible not to accept the Japanese proposal because it was 'an indisputable principle of justice'.[25] The French were sympathetic to the Japanese proposal because they perceived of it as a demand of universal principle, and saw hypocrisy in the American determination to create the League of Nations based on international justice while refusing racial equality on the grounds of Japanese immigration.[26] The Italians, represented in the League of Nations Commission by Prime Minister Vittorio Orlando, were similarly supportive of the racial equality proposal mainly because its spirit was perceived as in 'harmony' with the new organisation.[27] Although France and Italy supported the Japanese proposal, they were 'uncommitted' supporters, while the British and Americans were 'committed' opponents. Therefore, the degree of their interest in the issue was marginal throughout the negotiation, and this is reflected in the amount of material available on the topic, both in terms of primary and secondary sources. Moreover, the fact that Japan considered Britain and the United States to be the two key Western powers in this period, especially after the Bolshevik revolution of 1917, implies that more insight can be gained by focusing on the Anglo-American responses. Hence it was considered best to leave out the Italian and French responses, as it would not have been possible to give them the same coverage and depth of analysis. Needless to say, some materials on the French and Italian perspectives have been incorporated whenever appropriate; similarly, Chinese reactions to the proposal have also been incorporated whenever appropriate.

The structure of this study is as follows. Chapter 1 provides a detailed account of the negotiations of the racial equality proposal in the League of Nations Commission at the Paris Peace Conference. It is mainly chronological and largely descriptive, as its principal purpose is to paint a picture of the negotiations which is as comprehensive as possible, taking into account the Japanese, the British and Dominions, and the American positions. The Japanese proposal was negotiated over a period of two months and was ultimately defeated. What will become apparent during the course of the study is that the nature of the proposal changed substantially during the negotiations. Australia emerges as the winner who effectively managed to impose its own will on the overall perspective of the British Empire delegation, in order to reject the proposal. The American position remained ambiguous, though in the end it was President Wilson's unanimity decision which defeated the proposal.

Chapters 2 through 4 examine the Japanese motivations, each chapter dealing with one of the three explanatory factors of domestic politics, immigration and great power status. The second chapter analyses the domestic political origins of the proposal, which is an entirely new explanatory factor. It looks at the political origins of the proposal in the Hara government in late 1918 and how the proposal became part of Japan's peace policy. The most important revelation to be made is the inseparable connection made in domestic politics between the proposal and the League of Nations. An analysis of Japanese public opinion will be made, revealing that the Hara government's pro-League position ran against the prevailing view of the wider public which remained more pan-Asian and sceptical of the League. It will be suggested that Prime Minister Hara and his pro-Western supporters most likely needed to have a racial equality proposal in order make the acceptance of the League more palatable to a not insubstantial number who remained sceptical of the benefits which Japan would accrue in joining the League.

Chapter 3 deals with immigration, the predominant explanatory factor in the existing literature. It provides a detailed background to the history of anti-Japanese immigration policies in the Anglo-Saxon territories, and how this was perceived to be one of the major diplomatic problems for the Japanese Foreign Ministry. One of the main conclusions to be drawn from the chapter is that the racial equality proposal was perceived to have been about immigration precisely because of the bureaucratic interest of the Japanese Foreign Ministry. Most significantly, it will show how closely linked this explanatory category is to that of great power status as a concrete manifestation of Japan's unease with its international status.

Chapter 4 deals with the most important explanatory factor, that of great power status, in explaining the Japanese motivations. It develops the idea that the underlying intention behind the proposal was related to the much larger problem of Japan as an emerging non-white great power at the time. It will be argued that Japan encountered a number of serious challenges from the West in the period 1895–1919, contributing to Japan's underlying sense of insecurity as the only great power of Asian origin. This insecurity was often expressed in terms of Japan's isolation from the West, especially by the Anglo-Saxon powers. Moreover, there existed domestically a complex dialectical debate about Japan's identity, between those who saw it as essentially Asian and those who saw it as Western. This chapter suggests that the Japanese sought racial equality to be included as part of great power equality.

In Chapter 5, the British government's response is analysed. It is suggested that the two explanatory factors of immigration and domestic politics explain the British opposition. First, the British government had interpreted the proposal as implying immigration. This meant that the fate of the proposal was left in the hands of the British Dominions which had the control over issues relating to immigration. In this light, Australia had the vested interest of protecting the 'White Australia' policy which was perceived to have been threatened by the proposal. Australian Prime Minister Billy Hughes, partly through the force of his personality, had managed to impose his opposition on the British Empire delegation's official position. In probing further, it becomes clear that the domestic politics factor was at play, as Hughes was using his rejection of the racial equality proposal at Paris as an important plank of his election platform for the up and coming general elections in December 1919.

Chapter 6 analyses the American opposition. The three explanatory factors, immigration, domestic politics and the politics of bargaining at the peace conference, are examined. The first two factors worked only as background considerations and were not directly responsible for the ultimate decision made on the proposal by the American delegation at Paris. An analysis of the explanation based on the politics of bargaining reveals that there were two levels operating simultaneously within the delegation: one was the position held by the American peace commissioners, and the other was Wilson's personal position. The 'bargaining chip' theory was expounded by some of the American peace commissioners who took the view that the Japanese government had concocted the proposal as a political instrument to gain Shantung. The most important explanation, however, is that President Wilson used the proposal to appease the British in order to attain his own primary objective, the establishment of the League of Nations.

Finally, Chapter 7 offers conclusions of the study. It also attempts to make a retrospective analysis of how the rejection of the proposal could have affected Japanese politics and diplomacy in the interwar period. It is suggested that the implications of the rejection of the proposal for interwar Japan were twofold: as a contributing factor to the general sense of disillusionment towards the West in the 1920s, and as a test case used by the pan-Asianists and other apologists in the 1930s to show how Japan had been discriminated by the West. Lastly, some assessment will be made of the role which the racial equality proposal of 1919 played in the evolution of the principle of racial equality in the twentieth century. The significance of the proposal lies in what it reveals, both about Japan and about the nature of international society of 1919.

1 Negotiating racial equality at the peace conference

The purpose of this chapter is to 'set the scene' for the analysis of the racial equality proposal of 1919, by providing a narrative account of the negotiations at the Paris Peace Conference. As it makes no claim to be a general study, this chapter will focus exclusively on the negotiations for the racial equality proposal which took place in the League of Nations Commission.

The League of Nations Commission was established by the Preliminary Peace Conference at the plenary session of 25 January 1919 in order to draft the covenant of the League of Nations.[1] The racial equality negotiation covers the period from late January to late April 1919, when the Japanese government made two unsuccessful attempts in the League of Nations Commission to have a racial equality amendment accepted as an insertion into the covenant of the League. Broadly, the negotiation went through three phases: the first phase from late January to 13 February, when the first attempt to include racial equality as part of Article 21 failed; the second phase from 14 February to 11 April, when the proposal was defeated for the second time; and the final phase from 12 April to 28 April when the Japanese delegate made a final speech on the proposal in the plenary session of the conference. The account of the negotiations shows that it was a complex process which involved the reconciliation of many layers of conflicting perceptions, both externally between the three states and internally within each delegation. Moreover, it reveals that the 'racial equality' proposal evolved substantively in the course of two months from one redolent of 'immigration' to one that was truly abstract.

THE PROTAGONISTS

Before unravelling the diplomatic drama over the racial equality negotiations, let us briefly introduce the members and peace policies of the principal three delegations – the British Empire, the United States and Japan – which were at the heart of the racial equality controversy at the Paris Peace Conference.

The British Empire delegation was composed of five plenipotentiaries: David Lloyd George (Prime Minister), Arthur Balfour (Foreign Secretary), Andrew Bonar Law (Lord Privy Seal and Leader of the House of Commons), George Barnes (Minister without portfolio), and one representative in rotation from the British Dominions[2] and India whose representation was as follows: i) Canada: Robert Borden (Prime Minister), G.E. Foster (Minister of Finance), A.L. Sifton (Minister of Customs), C.J. Doherty (Minister of Justice); ii) Australia: William Morris Hughes (Prime Minister) and Joseph Cook (Minister of the Navy); iii) South Africa: Louis Botha (Prime Minister) and Jan Smuts (Minister for Defence); iv) New Zealand: William Massey (Prime Minister); v) India: Maharaja of Bikaner and Lord Sinha (Parliamentary Under-Secretary of State for India). The principal players in the racial equality negotiations were Foreign Secretary Balfour, Lord Robert Cecil and General Smuts (the latter two being appointed as British representatives of the League of Nations Commission), Australian Premier Billy Hughes and, to a limited extent, Canadian Premier Robert Borden. The British Dominions played a highly prominent part in the racial equality debate, which belied the otherwise more secondary positions they occupied within the delegation. On the whole, they remained marginal and uninterested in the wider spectrum of issues which concerned the British government at Paris.[3] Moreover, Prime Minister Lloyd George controlled much of the decision making.[4] He had a strong distrust of professional diplomats and preferred to consult his close circle of advisers and friends known as the 'Garden Suburb'.[5] The Foreign Office was only saved from obscurity because of Balfour, who managed to maintain a good personal channel of communications with the prime minister.[6]

In terms of war aims, Britain's initial objective on entering the war in August 1914 was the restoration of Belgian neutrality and this remained its core war aim for two and a half years.[7] This motivational objective incorporated other causes such as the protection of France against aggression, the destruction of 'Prussian' military domination, and the defence of the rights of small nations.[8] Apart from the core interest in maintaining the independence, integrity and unity of the British Empire, the British position at the peace conference was based on three things: first, to guarantee security for France; second, to settle territorial concessions; and third, to support the Wilsonian League of

Nations. The first two factors were intrinsically important for Britain, while the support for the League was a necessary concession to America's role in the war and in the peace.

In the light of the above, the Japanese proposal certainly was not a high priority for Britain. Basically, it would not have made much difference for Britain whether the Japanese proposal was adopted or not, as it was neither complementary nor contrary to core British interests. However, the interpretation of immigration attached to the proposal by the British government meant that the Dominions took over the negotiation to protect their vested interests. This became a considerable source of tension within the delegation.

The American Delegation to Negotiate Peace (the official title of the American delegation) was composed of five plenipotentiaries: President Woodrow Wilson, Colonel Edward House (special advisor to the president), Secretary of State Robert Lansing, General Tasker Bliss and Henry White (a Republican retired diplomat). President Wilson was by then so revered internationally that his arrival in war-torn Europe was hailed as the coming of the saviour. However, there was much controversy surrounding Wilson's unilateral decision to attend the peace conference because both Lansing and House believed that it would weaken his international stature as the prophet of peace.[9] Moreover, Wilson's autocratic method of decision making at Paris made the presence of the other peace commissioners redundant.[10] Hence the American delegation, though huge and well-manned, was internally very divided.

The United States' peace policy thus became the implementation of the Fourteen Points, first enunciated by Wilson in January 1918.[11] The two most important points made in the Fourteen Points were the implementation of the principle of self-determination in resolving territorial settlements in Europe, and the creation of a League of Nations which would ensure a just and equitable postwar international order. The strength of Wilson's moral position derived from the fact that the United States did not have vested interests in territorial possessions in the way that the other great powers had. The American role as victor was more as an arbiter of 'the conflicting interests of the different powers'.[12] In practical terms, the priority of the United States became the creation of the League of Nations, the embodiment of all the democratic ideals, which Wilson personally took over by being chairman of the League of Nations Commission with House as the other American representative.[13]

Finally, the Japanese plenipotentiaries to the conference consisted of Saionji Kimmochi, the delegation head, Makino Nobuaki as the *de facto* chief, Chinda Sutemi (ambassador in London), Matsui Keishirō (ambassador in Paris), and Ijūin Hikokichi (ambassador in Rome), with a grand total of sixty-four members. Saionji was the symbolic leader whose actual role at Paris was very limited due to ill health, but was nonetheless important as 'the Patrician Liberal' who strongly believed that Japan could not survive in isolation from the West.[14] Prime Minister Hara's selection of the plenipotentiaries reflected the pro-Western attitude of the new government, as most had some sort of connection with the Foreign Ministry.[15] Hara's views were strongly shared by Makino, who was effectively in charge of the delegation. Neither Hara nor Foreign Minister Uchida, who would have been the natural choice, felt it politically expedient to leave the newly elected government.[16] This undermined Japan's bargaining position at Paris, especially when lined up against the formidable 'Big Four' of Wilson, Clemenceau, Lloyd George and Orlando.[17]

As the Japanese peace policy at the Paris Conference will be discussed in detail in Chapter 2, it suffices here to say that it consisted of three demands. The first two demands, territorial in nature, were claims to the former German colonies and associated rights to the Shantung Peninsula in China and the Pacific islands north of the equator. The last demand, the central concern of this study, was the demand for a racial equality clause to be inserted into the covenant of the League of Nations.

A SURPRISING TURN OF EVENTS AT PARIS

The negotiations for the racial equality proposal were prompted almost accidentally by an exchange which took place between the Japanese plenipotentiaries and President Wilson on 22 January 1919. Wilson was taken aback that the Japanese offered only measured support for the League at the plenary session. Essentially, the Japanese government had not realised until then that the acceptance of President Wilson's Fourteen Points as a basis for armistice effectively meant the acceptance of the League of Nations.[18] Quite unexpectedly, the Japanese had to focus right from the beginning on the League of Nations, which meant activating the following contingency plan:

> Nevertheless, if a League of Nations is to be established, the Japanese Government cannot remain isolated outside the League and should there appear any tendency towards the establishment of a definite scheme [the League], the Delegates will so far as the circumstances allow make efforts to secure suitable guarantees

against the disadvantages to Japan which would arise as aforesaid out of racial prejudice.[19]

Accordingly, Baron Makino Nobuaki[20] and Viscount Chinda Sutemi set about 'translating' with much haste the above clause in the peace policy, which became known as the racial equality proposal.

First of all, Makino and Chinda regarded the United States as the most likely opponent of the Japanese proposal because of the unresolved problem of anti-Japanese immigration.[21] Despite their effort to see the Americans, it was not until the first meeting of the League of Nations Commission on 2 February that they were able to brief Colonel House, President Wilson's special advisor, about their 'general position regarding the abolition of racial discrimination'.[22] As the racial equality proposal was not Wilson's primary interest, Colonel House was entrusted with the negotiation. In negotiating with the Japanese, House's talent as conciliator and mediator[23] was put to good use. His non-abrasive, indirect approach favourably impressed Baron Makino and Viscount Chinda.[24] The Japanese delegates approached him because he was considered by the Japanese government to be 'pro-Japanese' in sentiment, as reported by Ambassador Ishii in July 1918.[25] House, accordingly, made all the right noises for the Japanese:

> I took occasion to tell them how much I deprecated race, religious, or other kinds of prejudices. It was not confined, however, to any one country or against any particular class of people; prejudice exists among the Western peoples against one another as well as against Eastern peoples. One can cite the contempt which so many Anglo-Saxons have for the Latins, and vice versa. This is one of the serious causes of international trouble, and should in some way be met.[26]

Encouraged by House's sympathetic attitude, Makino and Chinda submitted four different draft proposals to him between 5 and 12 February.[27] Having expressed interest in one of the proposals, House undertook to confer with Wilson who was consulted at least twice, on the 5th and 7th. Wilson subsequently agreed to present the preferred proposal[28] as his own amendment to the religious freedom article (Article 21). House noted that he had hoped to arrive at a formula which would not 'weaken the American or British Dominions' position and yet will satisfy the *amour-propre* of the Japanese'.[29] At this point in the negotiations, Wilson and House evidently perceived the Japanese proposal as a reasonable demand in line with the spirit of the covenant and not as a potential threat. Therefore, the first attempt by the Japanese to sound out the Americans had produced an unexpectedly encouraging response.

What is noteworthy about this stage in the negotiation was the extent to which House was involved in the day-to-day negotiation with the Japanese to come up with a satisfactory amendment. In the initial period, House was sympathetic to the Japanese proposal despite the fact that he perceived it essentially as one pertaining to the question of Japanese immigration.[30] Moreover, House must have suspected that the Japanese might raise the issue of immigration at the peace conference as he had instructed the Inquiry Commission, which was set up by him as a preparatory committee for the peace conference, to conduct a detailed study on Japanese immigration into the United States. The recommendations below made by the Inquiry Commission, perhaps not surprisingly, reflected closely House's general attitude towards the Japanese on this question:

> Although it is conceivable that Japan may not raise the question at the peace conference, yet it is likely that she will have something to say about it, and some assurance of fair treatment on this point would be of inestimable value in freeing the hands of the United States that it may the more effectively deal with the far bigger and more pressing problem of Japan in the Far East.[31]

Likewise, the Japanese considered Britain as the other potential stumbling block because of anti-Japanese immigration policies in the British Dominions, particularly in Australia and Canada. However, it seems that the Japanese did not first approach the British because they had expected Britain to support the proposal on the strength of the Anglo-Japanese Alliance. Moreover, they thought it beneficial to rely on the good offices of House, who had offered to discuss the amendment informally with the British.[32] It is highly likely at this point that the Japanese were expecting little or no resistance from Britain, especially as the more onerous task of persuading the Americans was achieved unexpectedly smoothly.

When House met the British Foreign Secretary, Arthur Balfour, on 10 February 1919, it is clear that Balfour understood House's main message to be that the racial equality proposal was primarily an immigration issue:

> Colonel House showed me a sheaf of papers, each one of which embodied an attempt to find a formula on the subject of Immigration

> which would satisfy the Japanese. In the absence of such a formula, the Japanese had intimated that they would find it difficult, or impossible to join the League of Nations.
>
> I observed that this was very much like an attempt at blackmail on the part of our Ally – to which Colonel House assented. But in whatever terms their action deserve to be described, it raised a problem which required solution. He then showed me his last formula, which began with a recitation (quoted from the American Constitution) of the eighteenth century doctrine, that 'all men were born equal'. Colonel House's view was that such a preamble, however little it squared with American practice, would appeal to American sentiment, and would make the rest of the formula more acceptable to American public opinion. He did not give me a copy of it, but, like all its predecessors, it seemed to me to suffer from the defect of indicating a sympathy on the part of the League of Nations with the principle of equal and unrestricted Immigration laws, which it was not the present intention of either the United States or the British Dominions to carry into practical effect. Speaking for myself, I did not believe that any of the English-speaking communities would tolerate a great Japanese flow of immigration; and if that were so, the insertion of any of the formula into the document establishing the League of Nations would have the triple disadvantage of exciting hopes in the Japanese public which could not be fulfilled; of exciting fears in the English-speaking population in new countries lest they should be fulfilled; and burdening the League of Nations with perpetual controversy incapable of satisfactory solution.[33]

Hence, it is evident from the above that House's initial approach to Balfour further confirmed the British perception that the Japanese proposal was the 'immigration' proposal which they had been anticipating.[34] The British Foreign Office sent a memorandum to Lord Robert Cecil on the same day outlining several points of objection to the proposal, one of which was that questions of immigration were problematic because they concerned not only the Japanese but immigration between the other Allied countries.[35]

Subsequently, it became clear that the British were far more sensitive to the opposition from the Dominions than had been previously assumed and had declared their formal opposition to the Japanese amendment. Accordingly, Makino and Chinda undertook to negotiate directly with Balfour and Cecil, instead of relying on House. Although personally sympathetic to Japan's position, Cecil maintained that questions such as religious freedom and racial equality, which were not directly related to the League, should not be included in the covenant.[36] It is worth pointing out that Cecil, at this early stage, indicated that such an important issue could not be decided on a simple majority.[37] Undoubtedly, he had to take into account the opposition of the Australian premier, Billy Hughes, who began the protracted battle against the proposal. In any case, the Japanese were taken aback by the British attitude which seemed to give primacy to the Dominion interest, at the expense of opposing their ally.[38]

THE FIRST ATTEMPT

Although Wilson had previously suggested that he would be interested in submitting the Japanese amendment as one of his own, both he and House were unable to arrive at a formula which was satisfactory to both Japan and Britain. Besides, he was now too preoccupied with wanting to complete a preliminary draft of the covenant before his departure to the United States on 14 February. Therefore, the Japanese decided to present the proposal independently to the League of Nations Commission on 13 February as an amendment to Article 21:

> The equality of nations being a basic principle of the League of Nations, the High Contracting Parties agree to accord as soon as possible to all alien nationals of states, members of the League, equal and just treatment in every respect making no distinction, either in law or in fact, on account of their race or nationality.

As Article 21 (the religious freedom article) was Wilson's favoured article, the Japanese considered it unlikely to be defeated. Nonetheless, the Japanese took precautions; the speech that Makino made on the occasion was deliberately low-key, in order not to antagonise those commission members who were sceptical of the Japanese proposal. Makino made remarks to soften the blow such as '[T]hat race discrimination still exists, in law and in fact, is undeniable, and it is enough here simply to state the fact of its existence', and 'an immediate realization of the ideal equality of treatment between peoples is not proposed', which played down the practical implications of the proposal.[39]

How was the amendment received by the other members of the commission? On the whole, the combined article of religious freedom and racial equality was too risky a formula for most members to support. The British Empire delegation under Cecil claimed that the subject matter had been discussed thoroughly, leading to serious problems for the British Dominions.[40] Despite the 'noble' nature of the proposal, he thought it advisable to postpone it to a later date. As for the Greeks, 'Mr Veniselos was of the opinion that questions of race and religion would certainly be dealt with in the future by the League of Nations, but that it would be better for the moment not to allude to them'.[41] Similarly, the French stated that since there was a correlation between race and religious questions, it would be better if both were eliminated.[42] Although the Chinese delegate, V.K. Wellington Koo, was 'naturally in full sympathy with the spirit of the proposed amendment', he expressed reservations pending instructions from his government.[43] On the other hand, Romania, Brazil and Czechoslovakia supported the proposal. However, the majority was in favour of Cecil's proposal to eliminate Article 21 altogether.

Wilson's personal commitment to racial equality was not significant, as he showed no qualms about dropping his religious freedom article when he realised that the opposition to the article, especially with the Japanese amendment attached, was too substantial.[44] His priority at this point was to have a complete draft covenant which he could take back to the United States on 15 February in order to convince his domestic public of the absolute importance of the League of Nations. In this period, there is hardly any record of how Wilson personally thought about the Japanese proposal.[45] Overall, it can be said that Wilson's interest in the proposal was marginal; it was one of those proposals which he could have supported if it did not impinge on his other interests. After this initial defeat, House was busily engaged in a damage limitation exercise with the Japanese, persuading them that it was not the Americans but the British who opposed the proposal.[46] Evidently, he was concerned about the negative publicity which the Americans were beginning to attract in Japan.

TOKYO'S VIEW

One of the problems which emerged in the first phase of the racial equality negotiation was the lack of input from Tokyo due to the problem experienced by the government in conducting diplomacy from a great distance. The government jealously guarded its power and wanted the plenipotentiaries to refer back all decisions to Tokyo, leaving little bargaining power at Paris. However, the pace set at Paris was too fast for Tokyo to respond effectively and efficiently. This was particularly true with the League of Nations, leading to the widening of a gulf between Tokyo's perception of the League and the associated issue of racial equality, and that of the plenipotentiaries based in Paris. This led Makino to make a request to the Diplomatic Advisory Council[47] on 3 February 1919 for more discretionary power, arguing that the credibility of the Japanese government on such urgent issues was being undermined by its inconvenient, circuitous decision-making process.[48] This resulted in a role reversal insofar as the question of the League was concerned, as the plenipotentiaries were obliged to make decisions on many detailed issues in the League of Nations Commission without first consulting Tokyo. Inevitably, some members of the Diplomatic Advisory Council resented this discretionary power exercised by Makino in Paris. Itō Miyoji[49] criticised Makino especially for being overzealous in supporting the League to the point of contradicting the government's peace policy, which adopted a more cautious attitude based on the domestic feeling of uncertainty about the organisation.[50] In fact, this criticism developed into a row in the council which forced Prime Minister Hara to defend Makino and take responsibility for his choice as one of the plenipotentiaries.[51] Thus, while the Diplomatic Advisory Council had no choice but to accept the decisions passed at Paris, there was much resentment in the council at being 'secondary' to the plenipotentiaries. Makino was subjected to harsh criticism of the decisions he took concerning the racial equality proposal, despite the absence of better alternatives proposed by the council.

Tokyo learned of the defeat of 13 February only on the 19th. However, the government immediately decided to pursue the resubmission of the proposal.[52] On 27 February, the Japanese government instructed the delegates as follows:

> The question of abolition of racial discrimination belongs to one of the important demands of the Imperial Government with regards to the League of Nations. Although it has been defeated once at the peace conference, it should not be abandoned because it would affect the future interests of the Empire. Hence, we must give careful consideration on how to accomplish our objective.[53]

On 4 March, the government instructed the delegates to negotiate with Balfour or with other suitable officials of the British delegation in order to stress the point that Japan was not demanding to have immediate changes in practical problems related to racial equality, but to have it accepted as an important principle of the League of Nations and world peace.[54] This was based on the realisation that the proposal was rejected because the British government had decided to take into account the position of the Dominions, which opposed it on practical grounds.

Meanwhile, as soon as the preliminary draft covenant was adopted in the League of Nations Commission, Wilson left for the United States on 15 February and did not return to Paris until 13 March. Generally speaking, Wilson's trip had heightened anxiety in Japan about the mounting American domestic opposition to the League of Nations, and in particular, the criticism which the racial equality proposal was attracting. In light of Tokyo's concern, Ambassador Ishii delivered an urgent note to Wilson before the latter's departure from the United States on 4 March, expressing Japan's willingness to compromise on the wording of the proposal to suit all parties concerned.[55] In retrospect, it appears that American domestic opposition to the racial equality proposal was fuelled by Ishii's speech given to the Japan Society in New York on 14 March which, while conspicuously dissociating immigration from racial equality, inadvertently had the opposite effect of strengthening the perceived connection between the two issues.[56] Moreover, the speech invited criticism in Japan because it was perceived by some that the racial equality proposal was intended precisely to have practical effects, such as facilitating immigration.[57] Gradually, as the Japanese realised that the United States could no longer support their proposal, a sense of crisis built up in the Diplomatic Advisory Council as Foreign Minister Uchida warned that any further effort to push the racial equality proposal might have the adverse effect of strengthening the American Senate's opposition to President Wilson.[58] This shows that the Japanese government was aware that its proposal was being adopted by the anti-League lobby in the United States as a weapon to discredit Wilson.

AUSTRALIA AS THE 'STUMBLING BLOCK'

As Tokyo was anxious to reach a compromise with the British Empire delegation, the second phase of the negotiations was characterised by an intensive interaction between the two delegations. It was Tokyo's policy to approach the British Empire delegation centrally by negotiating directly with the British government, which controlled the foreign policy of the Dominions.[59] This attitude underpinned the difficulty that Tokyo had in grasping that the British, once having interpreted the Japanese proposal as implying immigration, regarded it as a Dominion issue. As it became clear that the Australian premier, Billy Hughes, was the most persistent opponent of the Japanese proposal, Makino and Chinda saw him on 14 March in order to emphasise the importance of having the principle of racial equality accepted without any practical implications for immigration. The essence of Hughes's reply was that as the proposal touched upon a problem of immense practical importance, he could not ignore Australian public opinion, which was against it.[60] When Makino and Chinda requested further meetings with Hughes, he avoided seeing them on the pretext of illness.[61]

It is interesting that House's attitude changed in March when he began to focus more on the practical implications. He began to recognise that immigration did present an enormous obstacle, especially for the British Dominions as well as for the increasingly vociferous opposition from the American West Coast. By then, he had come to the conclusion that the adoption of racial equality in the way the Japanese had proposed was neither possible nor desirable. Thus, his energy was now focused on trying to dissuade the Japanese from pursuing what he now considered to be an unrealistic amendment.[62] By then, however, Makino and Chinda had reached a different conclusion, namely, that if the draft covenant were to be amended, Japan had no choice but to submit another proposal. In preparation, they requested further instructions from Tokyo on 20 March on the procedure to be taken, should their proposal be rejected for the second time.[63]

In the meantime, the Japanese made a dramatic change in the wording of their proposal. They presented Australian Attorney-General Robert Garran on the 22 March with a new proposal which read quite simply, 'By the endorsement of the principle of equality of all nationals of States members of the League.' This revised form was so remote from the amendment of 13 February that it was impossible to claim that the new proposal amounted to Japan's desire for unrestricted immigration. Nevertheless, for Hughes, it still conveyed the same message. In desperation, Makino and Chinda met Cecil on the 23rd to seek Britain's approval, only to be told that it was Australia's problem and that Britain was not in a position to give any definitive response.[64] Being in Paris, Makino and Chinda recognised the necessity of dealing directly with the Dominions, especially after seeing Cecil. However, Tokyo continued to disapprove of Makino and Chinda's decision to approach the Australians, by reinstating the instruction to negotiate directly with the British government, and to ask for American assistance, if necessary.[65] It seems that Tokyo was indignant at having to negotiate directly with Australia, which was only a junior member of the British Empire delegation.[66]

Initially, the Dominions as a whole opposed the Japanese proposal. However, after negotiating with the Japanese, Canada and South

Africa, they saw little reason in objecting to the proposal, and subsequently changed their position to accept a compromise formula.[67] The formula, which was no longer an article but an insertion into the preamble of the covenant, had been amended so many times that its wording could no longer possibly imply immigration. Nevertheless, Hughes alone remained stubbornly obstinate in his opposition. Now it was up to the Dominion premiers to convince Hughes to change his position in line with the other Dominions. The Canadian Prime Minister, Robert Borden, and Jan Smuts played an important mediating role towards the end of March, attempting to place pressure on Hughes to concur with the majority Dominion view, which was to accept the amended proposal.[68]

Borden arranged a meeting between the Dominion premiers, Cecil, Makino and Chinda on 25 March to see whether a compromise could be reached. At the meeting, the Dominion premiers objected to the word 'equality' because it applied not only to the Japanese but to the Chinese and the Indians, who were the main target of restrictive Dominion immigration policies. But the Japanese refused to delete the word because it was so central to the proposal. To break the deadlock, Borden suggested another wording of the proposal which read, 'By the endorsement of the principle of equality between nations and just treatment of nationals.'[69] This formula was agreed by all except Hughes who, after defending his position, stormed out of the room. Hughes's defiant behaviour was seen as a political statement made to his domestic audience in the run up to the general elections in Australia.[70]

The Japanese delegates tried to overcome this deadlock by appealing to Britain once again. On 26 March, they asked Smuts to talk to Lloyd George and ask him to bring his influence to bear on Hughes.[71] Because of Hughes's position as a Dominion premier, coupled with his difficult personality, Smuts argued that this approach would be counterproductive. On 31 March, Smuts passed on the news to the Japanese that Hughes might agree to a formula[72] in which immigration and naturalisation laws were mentioned as examples of domestic affairs not to be interfered with by foreign governments. Although Hughes came close to accepting one of the formulae on the condition that 'it did not confer any right to enter Australia . . . except as and to the extent that its government might determine', the Japanese by then had been pushed to their limits and rejected Hughes's solution.[73] Interestingly, the Japanese rejected it on the grounds that it was impossible to decide on such issues which needed to be discussed eventually in the League, especially in the light of Japan's immigration problems with the United States.[74] Despite Tokyo's decision to push for the acceptance of the principle *per se*, it shows that Makino and Chinda were not prepared to do so at any cost. Moreover, Makino replied that it was impossible to convince Japanese public opinion that Hughes's opposition alone could defeat the proposal which, the public felt, was unconditionally 'just'. Unusually blunt for Makino, he went on to state that he would not allow his nation's belief in the principle of equality to be treated as a 'trifle'.[75] Predictably, the rejection heightened Australia's conviction that the Japanese did have ulterior motives. Moreover, Smuts and Borden had to convince New Zealand, which tended to follow closely behind Australia, to agree to a compromise formula.[76]

As the struggle with the Dominions went on, the American stance continued to harden against the Japanese proposal. In his meetings with Makino and Chinda on 29 and 31 March, House disclosed that the United States would most likely have to support the British position due to the strength of the anti-Japanese lobby in the United States, especially on the West Coast.[77] Hughes's violent opposition seemed to have had a negative impact on the American position by agitating American public opinion.[78] House felt increasingly frustrated with Hughes's stubbornness on the one hand,[79] and with the dogged determination of the Japanese on the other. Tactically, the fact that the Japanese negotiated solely with House on the proposal eventually weakened their negotiating position. House's previously undisputed position as the eyes and ears of Wilson had diminished considerably by late March, due to a rift which had developed between the two during Wilson's absence from Paris. Makino and Chinda made no attempt to approach Wilson directly, possibly because the issue was not deemed to be important enough, and also because they did not have enough clout to negotiate directly with Wilson.

As Makino and Chinda fought on the front line in Paris, Tokyo began to despair over the seemingly endless obstacles faced by the proposal in Paris. On 30 March, Hara asked the Diplomatic Advisory Council to consider a possible course of action in case of the rejection of the proposal.[80] Personally, Hara believed that 'it was not a big enough problem to withdraw from the League of Nations'.[81] Although some members continued to argue about how 'just' the proposal was, the council unanimously concluded that the government should not, in any event, lose face over this issue. Hence, new instructions outlining various options were sent to the delegates on the same day.[82] The first option was to declare the specified passage[83] as an appendix to the League covenant, while, at the same time, to issue a statement declaring its acceptance as *prendre acte* of the conference. The second option was simply to accept the above declaration as an appendix to the covenant without obtaining a statement of fully-fledged support from member states. The last option was to register in writing the above declaration in the proceedings of the conference. The plenipotentiaries were to defer signing the covenant if none of the above options was possible. Back in Paris, the first two options were regarded as implausible as they demanded an insertion of the passage in the covenant. However, Makino and Chinda knew that they could avoid the ultimate embarrassment of deferring signature because the final option would be done as a matter of conference protocol.[84]

The efforts expended by all parties to persuade Hughes continued into early April.[85] On 3 April, Makino and Chinda met Lloyd George who apparently promised 'to do something' about Hughes.[86] Chinda followed this up with a letter to Lloyd George, asking him to exert his influence in order to postpone the last meeting of the League of Nations Commission and to take up the proposal with Wilson.[87] But Hughes remained adamant, and continued to register his opposition at every opportunity by threatening to make an inflammatory speech at the plenary session and to refrain from signing the covenant, should the Japanese proposal be inserted into it.[88] Hughes's determination was such that South African Premier Botha explained to Makino, 'strictly between ourselves, I think he is mad!'[89] During the period, Makino was able to depend on his friendship with Wickham Steed to prevent *The Times* from adopting an anti-Japanese tone.[90] By then, Cecil hardly took part in the negotiations.[91]

In the light of the intransigence of Hughes, the British Empire delegation as a whole had to adopt the united stance of opposing the proposal in the voting on 11 April. By then, there was a feeling also in the Japanese delegation that no other alternative existed but to submit the proposal in the League of Nations Commission and ignore Hughes's threat in the plenary session.

THE SECOND DEFEAT

At the fifteenth and the final meeting of the League of Nations Commission on 11 April, Japan presented a racial equality amendment in the form of an insertion to the preamble of the covenant which read:

> . . . by the endorsement of the principle of equality of nations and just treatment of their nationals . . .

In his speech, Makino emphasised the shift from demanding 'equality of races' to 'equality of nations':

> My amendment to the Preamble is simply to lay down a general principle as regards the relationship at least between the nationalities forming the League, just as it prescribes the rules of conduct to be observed between the Governments of the State Members. It is not intended that the amendment should encroach on the internal affairs of any nation. It simply sets forth an aim in the future international intercourse.[92]

By all accounts, Japan's case sounded reasonable and persuasive. Nevertheless, Cecil had to reject the Japanese amendment on the following grounds:

> The British Government realised the importance of the racial question, but its solution could not be attempted by the Commission without encroaching upon the sovereignty of States members of the League. One of two things must be true: either the points which the Japanese Delegation proposed to add to the Preamble were vague and ineffective, or else they were of practical significance. In the latter case, they opened the door to serious controversy and to interference in the domestic affairs of States members of the League.[93]

To this, Chinda retorted that the significance of the amendment lay not in the demand of race equality but of equality of nations; and if the amendment were rejected, Japanese public opinion would regard the League most unfavourably as it would be an indication that the equality of members of the League was not recognised.

Then Wilson as chairman opened the floor for discussion. Prime Minister Vittorio Orlando of Italy spoke in favour of the racial equality proposal:

> The equality of nations was a question which perhaps ought not to have been raised; but once having been raised, there was no other solution except that of adopting the amendment. Lord Robert Cecil had spoken of the practical reasons why its application would be difficult. Such an argument would carry weight if the Commission were considering the adoption of an Article in the Covenant which put the members of the League under a definite obligation. All that was now asked, however, was the insertion of a principle in the

> Preamble. If this principle were rejected, it would give rise to feelings which were hardly in harmony with the new organisation.[94]

Italy's support of racial equality appears to have been based on Orlando's personal position, generally supported by public opinion, that Italy should support a proposal which was in line with the sort of principles and ideals which the League was attempting to enshrine.[95] The French representative in the commission, Léon Bourgeois, agreed wholeheartedly with Orlando in support of the proposal. The French acceptance was based on two factors: first, 'it was impossible to vote for the rejection of an amendment which embodied an indisputable principle of justice'[96]; second, as part of the preamble outlining broad basic principles, states were not obliged to strict observance.[97]

Even the Chinese, who were confronting the Japanese over the Shantung question, expressed support as Wellington Koo stated:

> I should be very glad indeed to see the principle itself given recognition in the Covenant, and I hope that the Commission will not find serious difficulties in the way of its acceptance.[98]

It seems that China's position was complicated by two conflicting factors.[99] On the one hand, the Chinese naturally wanted racial equality because they were being racially discriminated against by foreigners including the Japanese. On the other hand, Koo did not want to antagonise the sensitivities of the British and Americans by appearing to be too enthusiastic because he needed their support for China's claim to Shantung.[100]

Greek Prime Minister Veniselos, who had previously opposed the religious freedom article in February, now supported the amendment because the nature of the issue had changed completely from the equality of races to that of nations.[101] Although the Japanese official sources did not give details of Czechoslovakia's support, Kramar stated that the amendment was in complete accordance with the spirit of the preamble especially with the phrase 'open, just and honourable relations'.[102] Only the Poles spoke against it on the technical grounds that it seemed impractical to incorporate a principle in the preamble which was not elaborated as an article, though Dmowski personally was entirely sympathetic to the Japanese proposal.[103]

President Wilson's speech is significant because this was the only occasion during the peace conference when he expressed publicly his thoughts on the racial equality issue. Although he did not speak directly against the proposal, it was a circuitous attempt to induce the

Japanese as well as the rest of the commission to shelve the issue for the time being, in order not to provoke any controversy when the League of Nations was just about to be created:

> The trouble is not with our discussions here, but with the discussions which would certainly be raised in the Plenary Council if the words suggested were introduced into this Covenant. My own interest, let me say, is to quiet discussion that raises national differences and racial prejudices. I would wish them, particularly at this juncture in the history of the relations of nations with one another, to be forced as much as possible into the background. . . . It is in my own mind for the purpose of quieting these prejudices, of letting them play no part in the discussions connected with the establishment of this League, that I am looking at this whole matter.[104]

He was anxious that this matter would not be raised at the plenary session on 28 April in order to prevent an open clash between the Japanese and Australians. However, the Japanese were not willing to retreat, especially after hearing the more than favourable general response to their proposal, and asked for a vote to be taken in order to ascertain how the commission stood on the issue. Due to the absence of Smuts and Hysman (Belgium), seventeen out of nineteen members of the commission voted. Those who voted for the amendment were Japan(2), France(2), Italy(2), Brazil(1), China(1), Greece(1), Serbia(1), and Czechoslovakia(1), totalling eleven. No negative vote was taken which meant that votes of the British Empire delegation, the United States, Portugal, Poland and Romania were not registered. It must be mentioned that the Japanese sources are not accurate on this point: they claim that Portugal voted for and Brazil voted against it.[105]

At this juncture, Wilson as chairman imposed a unanimity ruling which meant that the proposal was rejected in spite of the majority voting in its favour. Immediately, this decision was challenged by Makino and also by the French,[106] since majority voting was used to decide on the site of the League.[107] Wilson's justification was as follows:

> President Wilson admitted that a majority had so voted, but stated that decisions of the Commission were not valid unless unanimous . . . . In the present instance there was, certainly, a majority, but strong opposition had manifested itself against the amendment and under these circumstances the resolution could not be considered as adopted.[108]

By 'strong opposition', Wilson referred to the consistently declared position of the British Empire delegation. Hence, the most interesting aspect of this unanimity rule is that it allowed the United States to oppose the Japanese proposal without openly declaring its opposition, by relying on the strength of the highly publicised opposition of British Empire delegation. In the light of the situation, Makino left open the question of whether or not to raise the issue again at the plenary session by stating that Japan would attempt whenever possible to reinstate this 'just' demand.

Clearly, President Wilson played an instrumental role in defeating the Japanese amendment at the fifteenth meeting of the League of Nations Commission on 11 April 1919. This will be examined in detail in Chapter 6, but it is necessary to point out that the Americans were reluctant throughout the negotiation to affirm officially their opposition to the racial equality clause. Wilson managed somehow to maintain an ambiguous official position on 11 April, as testified by David Hunter Miller who recollected: 'The President spoke on the subject but did not speak directly against it, and as the negative vote was not taken the American delegation was not recorded.'[109] From the tone of speech made on the occasion, it is evident that his primary concern was to prevent a public row in the plenary session on 28 April over the issue.[110] Wilson perceived a great risk to the future of the League, should the racial equality issue become unmanageable by creating divisions in the plenary session. He tried to calm Japanese nerves by reiterating the importance of equality of nations in the League of Nations.[111] Essentially, what Wilson managed to do through unanimity voting was to place the onus of rejecting the proposal on Britain by insisting that 'At least one objection is insisted upon by one of the Governments concerned.'[112] Every member in the commission knew that it referred to the British Empire delegation. The British representative, Lord Cecil, was not impressed by Wilson's performance as he recalled, 'he [Wilson] did not show quite as much courage as I could have hoped in resisting the amendment'.[113]

As a final point concerning House, his record of the 11 April meeting, when the Japanese proposal was defeated, is worth analysing:

> The Japanese brought up their amendment to the Preamble. The President was for accepting it, but Cecil, under instructions from his Government, could not, and since I knew that Hughes would fight it and make an inflammatory speech in the Plenary Session, I urged the President to stay with the British, which he did, and in a speech made the argument I gave him.[114]

This diary entry is significant on two points. First, House states that Wilson was in support of the proposal even as late as 11 April. Second, House takes the credit for ultimately persuading Wilson to side with the British as he allegedly pushed a note at the crucial moment in the League of Nations Commission meeting which read, 'The trouble is that if this Commission should pass it would surely raise the race issue throughout the world.'[115] However, both of these points are somewhat contentious. For instance, no further evidence is available to suggest that Wilson was sympathetic to the racial equality proposal long after his brief initial interest in early February. On the contrary, Wilson had already sacrificed without much difficulty his preferred religious freedom article in the light of the opposition to Japan's insistence on including racial equality as part of it. We must also bear in mind that by April, House's ability to influence Wilson had diminished considerably as the relationship between him and the president had deteriorated irretrievably.[116] It seems highly unlikely under the circumstances that Wilson would have simply followed House's advice, against his own inclination, to oppose the proposal. Instead, if Wilson had decided not to support it, it was most likely because he had an alternative agenda in mind. Therefore, House's testimony should be treated with some caution as he seemed to be making an exaggerated claim in influencing Wilson on the crucial voting on 11 April.

The Japanese delegates reported back to Tokyo that domestic opposition in the British Empire and the United States had placed Wilson, House and especially Cecil in the extremely difficult position of having to reject an obviously reasonable proposal.[117] As the telegram reporting the proceeding was not despatched from Paris until 13 April, Tokyo did not hear of the news until the 15th. Consequently, the Diplomatic Advisory Council was finally informed of the unsuccessful result only on 21 April. The council strongly criticised the way in which the racial equality proposal was approached, first, for missing an earlier opportunity to raise the issue when the draft covenant was first submitted to the conference; secondly, for ignoring Japan's ally, Britain, and going directly to the United States to open negotiation; and thirdly, for substantially changing the substance of the proposal from equality of treatment eventually to just treatment.[118] Essentially, the plenipotentiaries were accused of deviating from the government's instructions by presenting an 'incomplete' proposal which did not have any practical implications, thereby effectively rendering the whole exercise meaningless.[119] The defeat of the racial equality proposal hardened the government's determination to 'win' the Shantung settlement, instructing the delegates to refuse signing the treaty, should the demand on Shantung not be accepted.

The most important observation to be made about this period is that the emphasis of the Japanese proposal had shifted from 'equality of race' to 'equality of nations'. The final amendment to the preamble – 'by the endorsement of the principle of equality of nations and just treatment of their nationals' – simply recognised the equality of nations and nothing more. In terms of the treatment of its nationals, it only referred to 'just' treatment and did not at all touch on 'equality' or 'non-discrimination'.[120] This shift reveals two things about the Japanese negotiating position. First of all, the ultimate success of the proposal became increasingly a matter of 'face' to Tokyo, as the unsuccessful tale of Makino and Chinda's negotiation with the Dominions began to embarrass the government back home. The shift in the meaning of the proposal occurred from 'race' to more generally 'equality' because the Diplomatic Advisory Council had emphasised the utmost importance of having the acceptance of the principle *per se* on 4 March.[121] This meant that the priority became one of finding an acceptable wording. Therefore, the council's criticism made of the negotiation on 21 April[122] could not be justified in the light of both their previous instructions and their lack of coherent strategy for the proposal. Secondly, the Japanese government showed itself to be entirely preoccupied with the Anglo-Saxon opposition, neglecting all the others. The fact that Makino and Chinda were swaying between the Americans and the British (and the Dominions) for encouragement and approval of their draft proposals implied that, for Japan, political acceptance of the proposal by the Anglo-Saxon powers was more important than the actual substance of their proposal. Otherwise, Japan could have made use of an opportunity for free international publicity by mobilising French and Italian support for the proposal, as well as that of the non-Western world, to champion its cause.

THE FINAL OPPORTUNITY

The final phase of the negotiations for racial equality covers the period from the defeat of the proposal on 11 April until 28 April when Makino made a final plea at the plenary conference. Tokyo did not send further instructions after the debacle on 11 April, but Makino and Chinda continued their effort to bring the proposal to an 'honourable' conclusion. British sources show that Smuts continued to negotiate with the Japanese in an effort to alleviate the risk of a heated confrontation, which Wilson was so anxious to avoid, between Japan and Australia in the plenary session.[123] Smuts tried to convince the Japanese not to reinstate the proposal at the plenary session on 28 April.[124] House also recorded visits made by Makino and Chinda on 15 and 26 April, although these meetings had not been reported back to Tokyo by the Japanese.[125] According to Smuts, the Japanese determination to persist with the negotiations stemmed from domestic public pressure:

> ...the public opinion in Japan was such that the Japanese Representatives could not leave the matter there, and they had proposed to move the amendment in the Plenary Session. It had been pointed out to them, however, that the amendment would be defeated there, and that such an open rebuff would have unfortunate effects; and they had finally agreed to confine themselves simply to a declaration reciting the history of the amendment and its failure, concluding that Japan, for her part, accepted the principle of equality of nationals, and would continue to urge its adoption in the future.[126]

There is no doubt that the Japanese government was under immense pressure domestically to succeed at the peace conference. The pressure was mounting, particularly as the two territorial settlements which the Japanese had taken for granted had not yet been satisfactorily resolved: the final verdict on the Shantung settlement was not made until 30 April, and the peace conference imposed the mandates system on the Pacific islands north of the equator instead of an outright annexation by Japan.

Towards the end of April, the level of tension was high among the great powers because of Italy's temporary withdrawal from the conference over the question of Fiume. In the light of the humiliation experienced over racial equality, it became crucial for the Japanese government to succeed in Shantung.[127] Balfour, who was appointed by the Council of Four to negotiate with the Japanese on Shantung, claimed that the Japanese were trying to put pressure on the council to reach a favourable conclusion on the Shantung settlement prior to the plenary session. His report to the council on the meeting with Makino and Chinda which took place on the 26 April was as follows:

> Makino came to see him [Balfour] again Sunday evening. With great delicacy but perfect clearness he had indicated that Japan wanted a decision on Japanese claims as a whole. He had pointed out that Japan was asked to agree to the League of Nations

> although she could not obtain recognition of her claims for equality of treatment. He had said that public opinion in Japan was much concerned on this question, that if Japan was to receive one check as regards Shantung, and another check as regards the League of Nations, the position would be very serious. Consequently, it was very important to obtain a decision on the question of Shantung before the Plenary Session to be held the same afternoon on the subject of the League of Nations. He understood that if Japan received what she wanted in regard to Shantung, her representatives at the Plenary Meeting would content themselves with a survey of the inequality of races and move some abstract resolution which would probably be rejected. Japan then would merely make a protest. If, however, she regarded herself as ill-treated over Shantung, he was unable to say what line the Japanese Delegates might take.[128]

Interestingly, Makino and Chinda's telegraph to the Foreign Ministry reporting the same meeting did not at all mention the sort of exchange which Balfour had mentioned. Instead, it reported in detail the clarifications made to Balfour on technical points concerning Japan's intentions in Shantung, as it became clear to the Japanese that Balfour had little understanding of the proposed settlement.[129] In any case, the fact that the Shantung negotiation ran parallel to the final phase of the racial equality negotiation led to a number of allegations that the Japanese government was using the rejection of the racial equality proposal as a means of obtaining Shantung.[130]

Moreover, Premier Hughes's continued intransigence on the issue meant that Cecil had to defend the British Empire's position, which was fast becoming a minority within the League of Nations Commission. Evidently, Cecil was deeply concerned about the negative impact of opposition to the proposal on Japan as well as on international opinion:

> If the amendment is moved by the Japanese and opposed only by the Australian member of the British Delegation, we shall be put in the somewhat difficult position of opposing our Japanese Allies on an issue on which the sentiment of the Conference will be overwhelmingly against us. Possibly Mr. Hughes might reconsider his attitude.[131]

The British government was unwilling to risk suppressing the Australian opposition. In the end, the British accepted that the racial equality proposal had to be sacrificed for the sake of imperial unity, especially as it was not considered as one of the more important issues at stake at Paris.

To everyone's relief, Makino made a 'peaceful' speech on racial equality at the plenary session on 28 April, which was recorded in the protocol as instructed by the Diplomatic Advisory Council. It seems that the Japanese did not whip up a storm on 28 April because this would have most certainly meant a loss of face in front of the international public, which in turn would have had an immensely negative impact on domestic public opinion. After the plenary session, Makino realised how problematic this issue had been for the British when he noted the look of relief on the face of Lloyd George, who came to congratulate him.[132] Evidently, the Japanese took the risk that the Council of Four would resolve the Shantung settlement in their favour without having first obtained the final ruling on the 28th, as the Shantung issue remained unresolved until 30 April. Luckily for them, Shantung was settled in Japan's favour.

How did Makino and Chinda justify the risk they took? A few days later, Tokyo learned from their plenipotentiaries that the racial equality amendment was not put to a vote at the plenary session because it was believed that the final amendment was too unsatisfactory in form as a result of countless changes and compromises.[133] Moreover, it was argued that some states would be induced to vote against their conscience in fear of endangering the friendship of Britain and the United States. Consequently, it was deemed expedient to simply clarify the position of the Japanese government and to have Makino's speech recorded in the protocol as originally instructed by Tokyo. Admittedly this report sounded more like a self-justification of the plenipotentiaries than the reality of what happened in the closing days of April, but Tokyo was happy to accept this version of events.

CONCLUSIONS

This chapter has shown the highly complex process of the negotiations between the three protagonists – Japan, the British Empire and the United States – which resulted in the defeat of the racial equality proposal in the League of Nations Commission. None of the delegations were, in any sense, united in terms of how they approached the proposal. In spite of the determination shown by Makino and Chinda, the lack of direction in their negotiating position revealed the lack of consensus within the government as to what the proposal was supposed to imply. Consequently, the proposal was susceptible to various forms of external pressure, mostly from the British Dominions, and underwent a substantive change in the period of just over two months. What sounded initially like an 'immigration' proposal ended up as an innocuous, abstract proposal of 'equality of states'.[134] The British government's decision to interpret the proposal as implying immigration meant that Australia was able to influence the official position adopted by the British Empire delegation. The tenacity with which Australian Premier Hughes opposed the proposal seems to underline the importance he attached to the interests it would affect. Although Colonel House played a central role in the negotiations at the beginning, ultimately it was President Wilson's decision to impose a unanimity rule which defeated the proposal in the commission. The peculiarity of the American position was that its opposition, though informally expressed to the Japanese, was never formally declared.

Needless to say, the account given in this chapter was mostly the official version of what happened within the context of the League of Nations Commission. It remains to be seen in the ensuing chapters what went on behind the scenes in each of the three countries in order to understand the true nature of this proposal.

2 Domestic politics and the League of Nations

Having now given a detailed account of the negotiations at the Paris Peace Conference, the rest of this study will be analytically structured. The purpose of this and the next two chapters is to attempt to explain why the Japanese government decided to submit the racial equality proposal. Each chapter treats independently three categories of explanations which were proposed in the introductory chapter as explanations for the Japanese motivations. This chapter begins by looking at the domestic reasons for the rise of the proposal. Chapter 3 then deals with the claim that the proposal was submitted in order to resolve Japanese immigration problems in the Anglo-Saxon territories. As a final section to explaining the Japanese motivations, Chapter 4 suggests that the explanatory category of great power status was the most significant in understanding the proposal from the Japanese perspective.

This chapter argues that domestic politics played a significant part in explaining the rise of the racial equality proposal in Japan. Indeed, one of the main weaknesses of previous studies on the subject is the tendency to neglect or give inadequate attention to domestic factors. The crux of the argument in this chapter is as follows. Prime Minister Hara,[1] who came into power in September 1918, was determined that Japan should adopt a pro-Western (*ōbei kyōchō*) foreign policy at the forthcoming peace conference. This was due to the fact that the previous wartime governments under Prime Ministers Okuma and Terauchi had followed expansionist policies, which had the effect of alienating Japan from the United States and Britain. In order to steer Japan back to the West, Hara was determined to support the creation of the League of Nations at the peace conference in spite of the not insignificant degree of scepticism expressed towards it domestically. Hence, domestic opinion divided into those who supported the League and those who opposed it, with the latter being more representative of national opinion (*kokuron*). In the light of the situation, it can be reasonably construed that the racial equality proposal had the role of appeasing these opponents by making Japan's acceptance of the League conditional on having a racial equality clause inserted into the covenant of the League.

The chapter is divided into two main parts. The first part explains the position of Prime Minister Hara who supported the League, then that of those who were either sceptical of or against it. The second part analyses public opinion in order to demonstrate the degree of scepticism towards the League which Hara had to face domestically, from pressure groups, the broadsheet newspapers and intellectuals. This shows the enormity of the task which Hara and his pro-Western supporters faced in convincing domestic opinion to accept his support for the League at Paris. The analysis will show that an intimate relationship was formed between the fate of the racial equality proposal and the support for the League of Nations domestically.

HARA'S SUPPORT FOR THE LEAGUE AND THE SCEPTICS

This section focuses on the importance of explaining the origin of the racial equality proposal within the context of domestic politics surrounding the Japanese government's decision to support the League of Nations at the peace conference. In the process, we shall look at why Prime Minister Hara considered it crucial for Japan to follow a more pro-Western policy at Paris by supporting the League. Moreover, we shall analyse the reasons why his critics within the government remained sceptical of his enthusiasm for the League. It is suggested that Hara and his pro-Western supporters had to convince the sceptics within the government to support the League, by implying that the support was conditional on having a racial equality proposal accepted by the peace conference.

The foreign policy-making machinery

The first step is to explain the foreign policy-making machinery which existed in Japan around the time of the Paris Peace Conference. There were three main bodies that influenced foreign policy: the Diplomatic Advisory Council (*rinji gaikō chōsa iinkai*), the Foreign Ministry and the *genrō* (elder statesmen). The prime minister exercised a considerable control over foreign policy, as is seen in the case of Hara. The military exerted influence indirectly through the Diplomatic Advisory Council and the *genrō*. Top-level consultations occurred frequently between the members of these bodies. During the Paris Peace Conference, the normal procedure for foreign policy making would be as follows. First, the Foreign Ministry would do the groundwork and submit a proposal to the Diplomatic Advisory Council for discussion and approval. At the same time, some members of the Diplomatic Advisory Council who had personal access to the *genrō* would consult them and seek their informal approval on the issue. Once the council had given its approval, the proposal would then be passed on to the cabinet which normally approved the council's decision as a matter of course. The purpose of this complex system was to encourage political unity in foreign policy. However, beneath the surface, there was much tension, especially between the Foreign Ministry and the Diplomatic Advisory Council.

The Diplomatic Advisory Council was established in June 1917 and acted as the highest foreign policy-making organ, directly under the auspices of the emperor, until it was dismantled in September 1922.[2] It was created as a means of unifying national opinion on foreign policy, and de-politicising foreign policy.[3] Due to its somewhat ambiguous constitutional status, the council attracted much criticism from the time of its inception.[4] Notwithstanding its problems, the council debated and made decisions on all foreign policy issues during the Paris Peace Conference. When Hara ascended to power in late September 1918, the council faced the challenging task of urgently formulating a peace policy. However, Hara was criticised for not convening the first meeting until mid-November 1918, and thereafter the council met sixteen times before the end of June 1919. It is highly significant that the council only met seven times from January to June 1919, when the heads of governments and the foreign ministers of the United States, Britain, France and Italy were negotiating their peace terms at Paris daily.[5] This can only indicate how psychologically remote the peace conference was for the Japanese government, and how preoccupied Hara was with domestic politics.

Within the Foreign Ministry, there were historically two factions vying for predominance. After the Bolshevik revolution in 1917, the Anglo-American faction began to have an upper hand over the Russian faction.[6] This was also reflected in the appointment of Shidehara Kijūrō as Vice Foreign Minister, who later became known for his own brand of diplomacy (Shidehara *gaikō*) which was perceived to be pro-Western, internationalist and based on economic cooperation with the British and Americans. Generally, the Foreign Ministry tended to be the most 'Western' of all government ministries, which reflected the elite, Western-educated background of the officials, but was not necessarily in tune with the rest of the nation. They took a *datsu-A* (escape Asia) view by seeking to protect Japan's interests, for instance in China, through cooperation with the Western great powers rather than confrontation.[7] With the departure of Gotō Shimpei, who belonged to the Russian faction, Hara's appointment of Uchida Yasuya[8] as foreign minister ensured the ascendancy of *ōbei kyōchō* (pro-Western, internationalist) diplomacy. Interestingly, the appointment of Uchida was seen as a disappointment by many who generally considered him to be mediocre.[9] Nevertheless, the choice of Uchida underlined Hara's need to have a Seiyūkai (the political party in power) sympathiser heading the ministry in order to control foreign policy.[10]

It must be emphasised at this point that there was much tension in the relationship between the two important foreign policy-making bodies, the Foreign Ministry and the Diplomatic Advisory Council. The establishment of the Diplomatic Advisory Council in 1917 as a superior body on foreign policy had effectively reduced the Foreign Ministry to an administrative organ, implementing the decisions made by the council. The Terauchi government especially tended to marginalise the Foreign Ministry, and its top officials were treated as mere junior officials. Although the creation of Diplomatic Advisory Council was supposed to strengthen Japanese foreign policy, the antagonistic relationship which it developed with the Foreign Ministry meant that, in practice, it had the contrary effect.[11] When the council was in session, Itō Miyoji often challenged the Foreign Ministry's pro-Western, internationalist view. Hara's role was that of a moderator who coaxed the anti-Foreign Ministry faction within the council to agree to a consensus which was closer to his personal position.

Then there were the *genrō* or elder statesmen, who had established themselves as an exclusive body on the basis of their proximity to the emperor and as guardians of Japanese politics.[12] Their extra-constitutional legitimacy derived from the fact that they were the leaders of the Meiji Restoration and came from the two most powerful feudal clans, Satsuma and Chōshū. Their major functions were as overseers of foreign policy[13] and, more importantly, as 'cabinet makers'.[14] Hence, they were very much part of the Meiji legacy and played a central role in providing political sanctity and legitimacy to the successive governments in the Meiji and Taishō periods. Gradually they outlived their usefulness, and disappeared in 1940 with the death of the last *genrō*, Saionji Kimmochi. At the time of the Paris Peace Conference, Yamagata Aritomo[15] as *genrō* wielded considerable power over Japanese politics. As a former general, Yamagata effectively acted as a spokesman for the military, which in turn controlled much of Japan's China policy. This explains why Hara was extremely careful to cultivate Yamagata's trust. It was difficult to govern effectively without sufficient approval from this powerful *genrō*. Although the *genrō* were technically excluded from foreign policy making with the establishment of the Diplomatic Advisory Council, their influence continued to be felt.

The degree of power exercised by the Diplomatic Advisory Council and the *genrō* in the foreign policy-making process meant that many issues became unnecessarily subjected to the political power struggle among the different policy-making bodies. Although Hara's rise to power in September 1918 indicated that the Foreign Ministry would regain its pre-eminence in foreign policy making, it continued to clash with the Diplomatic Advisory Council during the peace conference. Hence, Japan's peace policy needs to be understood in the light of the interplay of these institutions. It was up to Prime Minister Hara to get these influential bodies to agree on his preferred pro-Western approach.

Hara and his pro-Western foreign policy

It is necessary to explain Prime Minister Hara's view on foreign policy in order to understand why he came to regard Japan's support for the League of Nations as an integral part of his commitment to pursue a pro-Western foreign policy. Hara Kei, as leader of Seiyūkai, became prime minister after the dissolution of the Terauchi cabinet in September 1918. For the Japanese, Hara's rise to power symbolised a new era. As the first commoner to head the government, he was perceived to be the embodiment of the democratic spirit of the Taishō period, heralding the beginning of party politics (*seitō seiji*).[16] In reality, his government[17] was not necessarily progressive or democratic, but founded on a compromise between party and clan politicians which underlined his strongly realist approach to politics.[18]

In terms of foreign policy, Hara believed firmly in the need for Japan to cooperate with the West. His pro-Western attitude can be traced back to his career as a diplomat and, subsequently, as a political appointee working for the then Foreign Minister Mutsu Munemitsu in the 1890s. During the First World War, as head of Seiyūkai, he was highly critical of the aggressive initiatives especially the Twenty-One Demands of 1915 and the Siberian troop deployment, undertaken by the Okuma and Terauchi governments.[19] In his view, these policies alienated Japan from the Anglo-Saxon powers. Hara must have been especially sensitive to the essential need of Japan's to avoid international isolation, dating back to his first hand experience of dealing with the Triple Intervention of 1895 under Foreign Minister Mutsu. What was true then was still true in 1919, namely that Japan should avoid international isolation at all costs because it was not sufficiently strong to fend for itself against the combined forces of Western imperialist powers. In other words, Japan should never be prey to Western imperialism as this would end its national independence, the sustenance of which had been the national imperative of the Meiji leaders. This was why Japan had to work with, and not against, the Western great powers. What Hara advocated, then, was a foreign policy based on liberal internationalism which recognised the limits of Japan pursuing an independent policy.[20]

In practice, Hara's foreign policy entailed a number of conditions. First of all, Hara recognised the increasing importance of the United States and the necessity of improving Japan's relations with the country.[21] This was most clearly conveyed during the Siberian troop deployment crisis in 1918 when he stated that 'the future of Japan depends on the close relationship with the United States'.[22] It was crucial for Japan to maintain friendly relations with the United States, both as a means to further economic interests and to avoid military friction. Emphasis on economic diplomacy was based on the belief that a peaceful expansion of trade and investment was the best way of furthering the national interest.[23] Secondly, as part of Japan's effort to foster great power cooperation, his government took pains to reiterate the fundamental importance of the Anglo-Japanese Alliance as a 'cornerstone' of Japanese foreign policy.[24] The maintenance of the alliance was the easiest means of avoiding international isolation for Japan. Thirdly, Hara recognised the need to change Japan's China policy if Japan wanted to cooperate with the Western powers.[25] This implied non-interference in Chinese politics, support of a unified government in China, and participation in the Four Power Consortium.[26]

As a manifestation of his pro-Western attitude, it was logical that Hara should express his determination to support the League of Nations at the Paris Peace Conference. In fact, he never once deviated from this position throughout the peace conference, regardless of his critics.[27] He was supported by Makino Nobuaki, the acting chief plenipotentiary, who considered Japan's support for the League as the most important gesture Japan could make at Paris in terms of regaining it's damaged reputation among the Anglo-Saxon powers.[28] As is shown below, Hara's skill as an adept political negotiator was repeatedly put to the test during the domestic crisis over the League of Nations, and he had to fight hard to maintain this position in the Diplomatic Advisory Council. His need to maintain domestic consensus meant that it was often necessary to make compromises.[29] He had to manoeuvre carefully and skilfully among contending domestic elements to ensure that his preferred policies were supported by the government.

Preparations for the Paris Peace Conference

Hara's pro-Western attitude, which was in fundamental contradiction to the militaristic foreign policy favoured by his predecessor, Terauchi Masatake, meant that the Hara government had the unenviable task of urgently reformulating its peace terms as soon as it came into power in September 1918. However, in spite of his professed pro-Western attitude, his preoccupation with domestic politics left little time for foreign policy and his government suffered as a result of it.[30]

In contrast to the other great powers, all of which had invested considerable time and effort in preparations for peace, the Okuma and Terauchi governments immediately preceding Hara held a limited view of Japan's role in the war which was reflected in their attitude towards peace.[31] Basically, they tended to perceive the war as predominantly a European war, in which Japan's role was limited to confronting Germany in the East. Therefore, it was generally assumed that Japan had accomplished its fundamental objective for entering the war when it captured the German possessions in the Far East and the Pacific in 1914. With such a limited objective in mind, the Okuma government started preparations for peace in October 1914,[32] and established the Japan–Germany Peace Preparatory Committee (Nichidoku kōwa jumbi iinkai) in September 1915 under the Foreign Ministry to deliberate on armistice and peace terms.[33] The committee's agenda reflected the government's preoccupation with the desire to keep the East Asian settlement free of other great powers, in exchange for Japan's non-interference in the European settlement.[34] The problem was that the Japanese government continued to hold this view, which was based on assumptions dating back to 1914, as late as November 1917 when the Foreign Ministry, after having attended the Inter-Allied Conference in Paris, finally realised that the Western powers could not be kept out of the Far Eastern settlement. Since the government was premising its peace plan exclusively on the practical terms of a settlement in East Asia, it was thrown into confusion on discovering in late 1918 that the forthcoming peace was to be based on the Wilsonian

Fourteen Points of January 1918, which included not only the important principle of self-determination but also a promise to establish a new international order in the form of an association of nations.[35]

Soon after he came to power, Hara was strongly criticised for not paying enough attention to the peace conference.[36] In November 1918, he belatedly implemented measures to deal with the conference, just one month before the delegates were scheduled to leave for Paris. First he appointed two members of the Diplomatic Advisory Council, Makino Nobuaki and Itō Miyoji, to redraft a peace policy. Secondly, the Diplomatic Advisory Council established the Second Peace Preparatory Committee on 13 November 1918, with the aim of providing foreign policy guidelines, based on the Fourteen Points, to the Diplomatic Advisory Council and the peace delegation.[37] Thus, the revised peace policy comprised three major principles: (1) 'conditions of peace in which Japan alone has interest independently from the Allied and Associated Powers' which included the transfer of rights pertaining to the former German colonies of Tsingtao and the Pacific Islands north of the equator; (2) 'conditions of peace in which Japan has no direct interest' in which case Japan should be vigilant and try to contribute whenever possible; and (3) 'conditions of peace in which Japan has common interest with the allied and associated powers', for which the delegates are instructed to coordinate as much as possible with other allied powers.[38] In concrete terms, the first principle was the most important as it referred to the acquisition of rights to the Shantung peninsula and the Pacific Islands north of the equator. The third principle, a reference to the Wilsonian Fourteen Points, underlined Hara's pro-Western internationalist attitude which recognised the necessity of Japan cooperating with the Western great powers in creating a new international order.

There can be no doubt that the government suffered a setback in having to reformulate a peace strategy as late as November 1918, as a result of the combination of the limited perception of war aims by the previous wartime governments, and the lack of a well-deliberated peace policy on the part of the new government. In the short span of time available, the Foreign Ministry was unable to make a successful U-turn from its wartime policy and come up with a refreshingly new perspective on peace which resonated with the pro-Western attitude of the new prime minister, as well as encapsulating the spirit of the Wilsonian Fourteen Points. As a result, the only aspect of the revised peace policy which was remotely new was the support it expressed for the creation of the League of Nations. As we shall discover below,

Hara found it difficult to extract from the foreign policy-making machinery even this basic support for the League.

Therefore, Japan's participation at Paris was the first major challenge confronted by the new government, and it attracted much public criticism prior to and during the peace conference. It started off on shaky ground, as the government was first criticised for not having a well-prepared peace policy which would justify Japan's representation as one of five great powers at Paris.[39] Due to the delay in starting the domestic peace preparations, Hara was accused of relying too heavily on his 'wait and see' approach.[40] During the peace conference, the majority of criticism centred on the fact that the government was keeping the nation in the dark regarding the progress it was making at Paris. For instance, both Hara and Uchida refused to divulge the details of any of the issues discussed at the peace conference on the basis that any disclosure might jeopardise the negotiations in Paris.[41] Such criticisms belied the inefficient system of relaying information from Paris, which meant that the government very often was not privy to the latest information. Needless to say, the main opposition party, Kenseikai, made a political capital out of the inadequacies of Hara government, and its leader, Katō Kōmei, strongly criticised Hara's peace diplomacy as lacking in the dignity of a great power.[42] The general state of unpreparedness for the forthcoming peace conference did undermine the legitimacy of the new government in the eyes of the public.

Hara's pro-League politics and the sceptics

Having demonstrated the importance for Hara of supporting the League, we shall now turn to explaining why he faced substantial opposition domestically to his professed policy. Why were some in government so ambivalent or, more precisely, sceptical of the League of Nations? As has been suggested, the government was divided over its policy on the League. On the one hand, Prime Minister Hara and Makino supported the League because they recognised that Japan's support for the League, at least in principle, was a *sine qua non* of Japan's being part of the peace conference.[43] Hence, it was an important signal of Japan's willingness to cooperate with the West in order to prevent further international isolation of Japan. On the other hand, those who were sceptical of the League, including Itō Miyoji of Diplomatic Advisory Council, were suspicious of the idea of an international organisation, especially one led by the Anglo-Saxons. It is important to emphasise that Hara's pro-League position was not supported by everyone because a surprising number of influential government officials, including some at the Foreign Ministry, remained sceptical of the League. In the light of the circumstances, the consensus which Hara obtained from the foreign policy making machinery, especially the Diplomatic Advisory Council, to support his pro-League policy, was superficial.

Let us first examine the three factors which underlined scepticism of the League. First, the fact that there was little general information available, compounded by the lack of preparation by the Foreign Ministry on the League of Nations, meant that the majority in the government was desperately ignorant about the substantive aspects of the new organisation.[44] This was symptomatic of the general unpreparedness towards the peace conference, as a realistic assessment of the peace did not exist until Hara hastily instituted measures in November 1918. This failure to grasp the shift in Allied thinking on the basis for peace was a fundamental failure of Japanese diplomacy. It left Japan insensitive to the increasing importance given to the League of Nations by the Allied powers.[45] Although the Foreign Ministry had been aware of the Anglo-American interest in the League of Nations from early 1918,[46] the only information available before mid-1918 was a report compiled by the Bryce Commission and a short book by Marburg. This was later supplemented by a draft covenant brought back from Paris by an official who attended the Supreme War Council.[47] The inefficiency of the Second Peace Preparatory Committee, which was established precisely to rectify this problem, was staggering, as it continued to produce completely outdated and useless reports on the League two months after the League of Nations Commission had completed the preliminary draft covenant.[48] Basically, the Foreign Ministry did not take the League of Nations seriously until it was almost too late. It was not until mid-October 1918 that Ambassador Chinda in London informed Foreign Minister Uchida that the League of Nations might become an important issue at the peace conference, and that he would ask the British to pass on the relevant information to Japan.[49] It is also noteworthy that even as late as 14 December 1918, Makino, on his voyage to Paris, felt the need to emphasise the importance of the League as an issue at the peace conference.[50] Clearly, the lack of general preparedness in Japan regarding the League only increased apprehension and anxiety towards the new organisation.

Secondly, there was the view generally expressed in the Foreign Ministry that the League of Nations would most likely infringe Japanese sovereignty. Vice Foreign Minister Shidehara's view that the

League of Nations would pose a serious problem if it meant Japan's losing control of its own destiny to an international body, was representative of the ministry.[51] Even Makino, who became the chief spokesman in favour of the League of Nations within the Diplomatic Advisory Council, was personally apprehensive about the idea of relinquishing state sovereignty to an international organisation.[52] Moreover, he was concerned that Japan's independence would be restricted if it were to act always in concert with other states, and to have to carry out obligations externally.[53] Obviously, this general apprehension reflected Japan's confusion about the power the League would have. For many in Japan, it was not an easy task to restrict sovereignty voluntarily in favour of a collective body in which Anglo-American domination appeared to be the only certainty.

Thirdly, it cannot be denied that the suspicion of the ultimate purpose of the League was connected to the general suspicion in which the Anglo-Saxon powers were held. The sudden prominence of the League of Nations on the peace agenda of the Allied powers in 1918 was perceived as being indicative of the Anglo-Saxon powers' vested interest in furthering their own world dominance. In those who did not ascribe to the *ōbei kyōchō* view, suspicion of Britain and the United States ran deep. They believed that Japan had been unfairly treated by these powers, as seen in the case of the anti-Japanese immigration legislation and the 'unfriendly' attitude shown towards Japan during the First World War. This sort of conspiracy view was strongly argued by Itō Miyoji in the Diplomatic Advisory Council, who saw the League as simply another form of political alliance for maintaining a *status quo* to the advantage of the West.[54] There was much doubt as to whether the League would be a truly fair organisation, benefitting both the weak and the powerful.[55] There was also the view that the whole idea of the League seemed too hypothetical and unrealistic to be workable, especially as Wilson, who was its principal advocate, had not yet announced any concrete plan.[56] Although these were valid criticisms, they did not emerge from a well-informed, well-deliberated position. As a result, they revealed the intuitively suspicious attitude held towards the United States and Britain.

In the light of the above, the consensus to support the League, which Hara had extracted from the Diplomatic Advisory Council, was a fragile one. The question of the League of Nations was first raised in a draft memorandum entitled, 'Proposals for comments on Wilson's Fourteen Points',[57] on 13 November 1918 by Foreign Minister Uchida in the council. Under the relevant section on the League, the government recommended taking appropriate measures concerning possible 'racial prejudice' in the new organisation. However, some members of the Diplomatic Advisory Council were not convinced by Uchida's document and continued to be sceptical of the League, bringing the council to a standstill over this issue on 8 December.[58] Because of the urgency of the situation, Hara was forced to conclude at the 8 December meeting that Japan's participation as one of great powers obligated it not only to support the League in order to avoid international suspicion, but also to agree to it in principle, should it become a major issue at the conference.[59] The final push given in the Diplomatic Advisory Council to support the League owed much to Makino's determination. In the end, the government appended a supplementary document entitled, 'The Government's view on President Wilson's Fourteen Points', which contained Japan's policy towards the League of Nations as below:

> This is one of the most important questions. The Japanese Government is in favour of the ultimate aim of the League: but, in view of the racial prejudices which have not yet entirely been banished from among the nations, there is a danger, depending upon the nature of the measures taken to secure the objects of the League, that its establishment will in practice produce results gravely detrimental to Japan.
>
> Further, the question of the relations between the nations joining the League and those not joining it, and their respective treatment, must of necessity be one of the greatest difficulty.
>
> It is accordingly thought desirable to aim at the postponement of any discussion of concrete proposals for the League, and to confine the proceedings to the settlement of a draft of the general desire, leaving the working out in practice of the scheme as an outstanding problem for the nations, to be considered until a future appropriate occasion when the draft of a practicable scheme can be submitted to examination and debate.
>
> Nevertheless, if a League of Nations is to be established, the Japanese Government cannot remain isolated outside the League and should there appear any tendency towards the establishment of a definite scheme, the Delegates will so far as the circumstances allow make efforts to secure suitable guarantees against the disadvantages to Japan which would arise as aforesaid out of racial prejudice.[60]

The above passage reveals a highly ambivalent attitude towards the League, and acts as a reminder of how weak the consensus obtained by Hara really was. In a sense, the document is a masterful piece of compromise, designed to placate all sides. Although it acknowledges that the League was an important question, it states explicitly that the government was only 'in favour of the ultimate aim of the League', and *not* in favour of its establishment at Paris. In fact, three of the four paragraphs are used to elaborate why it was best not to pursue the League any further at this stage. Only at the very end does the document concede that the League may be created, and if so, then the Japanese delegates should 'make efforts to secure suitable guarantees against the disadvantages to Japan which would arise as aforesaid out of racial prejudice'. It was this last passage which became the basis for the racial equality proposal.

Ultimately, the Council compromised on the position that the government would support the League only if absolutely necessary, in which case it would take measures to prevent 'racial prejudice' against the Japanese. Otherwise, the plenipotentiaries should try to postpone the drafting or creation of the League until a later date. In practice, the compromise decision was ruthlessly undermined especially by Itō Miyoji. He repeatedly accused Makino of not abiding by the government's instructions, by giving the false impression at Paris that the Japanese government was more supportive of the League than it actually had agreed to be.[61] Itō's attitude reflected a fundamental uneasiness with Makino's liberal internationalist approach. Nevertheless, Hara got what he wanted, which was for Japan to support the establishment of the League at the peace conference, as a means of paying lip service to international cooperation with the great powers.

Contrary to the general perception that the Japanese held a uniform position on the racial equality proposal, the Japanese government was divided internally over the issue of the League of Nations. Evidently, domestic political considerations played a key part in influencing the peace policy preferred by Prime Minister Hara and his pro-Western supporters. From this perspective, it is reasonable to suggest that the racial equality proposal can be seen as a means of appeasing the sceptics who did not share Hara's conviction that Japan needed to court the Anglo-Saxon powers at the Paris Peace Conference in order to avoid international isolation of Japan.

PUBLIC OPINION AND THE RACIAL EQUALITY PROPOSAL

In this section, we shall look at how public opinion regarded the racial equality proposal. Since public opinion as an analytical category is too broad and all-encompassing, this study deals specifically with three of its sectors, namely, pressure groups, the broadsheet newspapers and the intellectuals. The racial equality proposal became a *cause célèbre* for the Japanese public because of its symbolic importance as a concrete manifestation of all of Japan's fears and expectations of the new government and international order. The intense public interest in the issue dominated the domestic debate from November 1918 until May 1919. The views expressed by some sectors of public opinion, such as pressure groups and the broadsheets, reflected more closely the view of the League sceptics in the government who remained fundamentally suspicious of the West than that of Hara and his pro-Western enthusiasts, who considered Japan's support for the League as a crucial component of peace diplomacy. Hara's perspective was closely identified with the liberal intellectuals. This section illustrates further the domestic politics explanation, that the Hara government needed to placate public opinion which remained sceptical of the League, but which at the same time placed unrealistic expectations on the government to succeed at Paris.

The pressure groups

Hara's pro-League policy was put to another test when a number of pressure groups emerged in Japan in January and February 1919. Ostensibly, these shared the objective of supporting the government's peace policy, but in reality, they appeared to have had an underlying agenda of exerting high-profile pressure on the government. Members were drawn from the principal political parties including Seiyūkai, the armed forces, journalists and various public associations. On the whole, they tended to be critical of Hara's pro-Western perspective, and their ultimate objective was not so much to have the racial equality proposal accepted, but to put pressure on his *ōbei kyōchō* policy. These groups focused their 'support' on the racial equality proposal largely because of its symbolic value of standing up to the West. The very emergence of these pressure groups underlines the importance of the League and the racial equality proposal to national opinion (*kokuron*).

One of the largest of these pressure groups was the League to Abolish Racial Discrimination (*Jinshuteki sabetsu teppai kisei taikai*), which started off as a public movement among some military and public officials to emphasise the importance of racial equality to Japan's peace policy in late January 1919. It held its first mass public meeting in Tokyo on 5 February with representatives from the three political parties – Seiyūkai, Kenseikai and Kokumintō – as well as members of the House of Peers and twenty-four other public associations, totalling some three hundred participants.[62] One of its key organisers was Tōyama Mitsuru, the leader of the ultra right-wing Genyōsha (Dark Ocean Association). On 5 February, the League cabled a declaration to President Georges Clemenceau that 'The Japanese nation expects of the Peace Conference the final abolition of all racial discrimination and disqualification.'[63] Events then took an ominous turn when, on 14 March, they decided that if the government failed to secure racial equality, a new organisation should be created to mobilise public opinion to overthrow the government.[64] The second mass meeting was held on 23 March and attended by two hundred people representing now some thirty-seven public associations, who debated whether or not Japan should withdraw from the League of Nations if it refused to accept such a fundamental principle as racial equality. They concluded that 'The Japanese nation opposes a League of Nations not based on the abolition of racial discrimination.'[65] This resolution was personally delivered to Foreign Minister Uchida on 24 March.[66] A month later, on 24 April, two hundred people assembled to declare that 'The Japanese nation refuses to join a League of Nations which does not acknowledge the abolition of racial discrimination.'[67] Representatives visited Hara and Uchida on 1 May to insist that the government should persist in pursuing racial equality since Italy's withdrawal from the conference would create a more favourable environment for Japan.[68] From the frequency of the telegrams reporting the activities of the association to Paris, it is obvious that the government felt much pressure from this group and was particularly concerned about the negative effect this association would have on the peace policy.[69] Moreover, the fact that the association incorporated some members of Seiyūkai is indicative of the dissatisfaction felt by some in the ruling party of Hara's policy to support the League. What is noteworthy about this particular association was that it tended to be pan-Asian in its orientation.[70] This meant that it was, in fact, taking a stance against the Hara government's pro-Western peace policy by identifying the racial equality proposal as being sympathetic to its own pan-Asian inclination.

Although the above association was the most 'threatening' to the government, there were others which also attempted to influence it. For instance, the government received a memorandum from the League for People's Diplomacy (Kokumin gaikō dōmeikai) on 6 December 1918, demanding an abolition of all racially prejudiced politics in the British and American territories against the Japanese and Chinese.[71] Probably the most respectable of these associations was the Association for Publicists of Peace Issues (*Kōwa mondai yūshikai*) which included many members from the House of Peers and the Diet. It held a mass meeting on 24 March 1919 attended by some two hundred people and debated many aspects of the government's peace policy.[72] On racial equality, they argued that there was no reason why any country should reject such an important principle of international justice, but also criticised the government for wanting to separate the principle of racial equality from its practical aspect of immigration. They drew up a resolution expressing their support for the following: the abolition of racial discrimination, acquisition of the right to Shantung and the German islands in the Pacific, preservation of Japan's sphere of influence in China, and establishment of Japan's position of pre-eminence in East Asia. Moreover, they opposed the abolition of conscription, and international labour laws which might be unsuitable for Japan's national circumstances. This resolution was delivered to the prime minister on 1 April.[73]

The Japan–America Association (Nichiboshikai) was composed of people who had at some point lived in the United States. It attracted four hundred participants to a meeting on 22 March, specifically to debate the racial equality proposal.[74] Guest speakers included Okuma Shigenobu (former prime minister), representatives from the American Peace Association and the Christian Youth Association, and the editor of *The Japan Advertiser*, an influential English language daily in Japan. There was a discussion of the problem of racial discrimination and how the discriminatory treatment of the Japanese could be improved in the United States.

What these pressure groups demonstrated was the extent to which the Hara government had to live up to expectations placed upon it by a group of opinion leaders who tended to hold perspectives which did not mirror those of the pro-Western clique in the government. It is highly significant that many of the key participants tended to be pan-Asianists, who believed that Japan's future lay with Asia and not with the West.[75] Moreover, the pan-Asianists included the military officials who were evidently frustrated with the inclination of General Tanaka Giichi, the Army Minister, to be cooperative with Hara's pro-Western policy at the peace conference, including a cautious support for the League.[76] The Foreign Ministry was preoccupied with these pressure groups, mostly due to the concern that the activities of these groups would jeopardise the sensitive negotiations at Paris.[77] When Makino and Chinda often referred to the need to satisfy public opinion as the reason for persisting in the negotiations, it was these groups that they meant. This is illustrated by the case below, when Chinda informed

Colonel House of Japan's decision to submit the amendment on 13 February:

> Viscount Chinda called again to say he could get nothing definite from the British and that he intended to present a resolution himself which would be more drastic than the one the President agreed to accept. His idea is that while it will not be adopted, it will be an explanation to his people in Japan.[78]

There is no doubt that these pressure groups managed to exert considerable pressure on the government which was still new, yet to be tested by the public, and moreover, professed to be pro-Western, an attitude which was perceived to be not entirely representative of the national opinion as a whole.

The broadsheets

Racial equality dominated the national editorials of the leading newspapers, conveying a strong sense of public interest and excitement. In general, the broadsheets supported strongly the government's proposal for racial equality. Racial equality appealed to the nationalistic instinct of the general public because it reflected the public's shared experience of the past and seemed more immediately relevant than the strategic territorial demands in Shantung and the Pacific islands.[79] However, despite their support for racial equality, they were generally sceptical of the League of Nations which reflected their suspicion of the West.[80] Thus, the strength of broadsheet interest in the racial equality proposal no doubt put a fair amount of pressure on Hara and his supporters, whose declared support for the League did not gain majority public support. The study of the broadsheets[81] presented here is based mainly on the three leading newspapers of the period – *Tokyo nichi nichi shimbun*, *Asahi shimbun* and *Yomiuri shimbun*, predecessors of today's three big daily newspapers.[82] It must be borne in mind that the press coverage was not evenly balanced because only *Tokyo nichi nichi shimbun* had its foreign correspondent in Paris, whereas the other two had to rely on external agencies such as the Associated Press and Kokusai Tsūshin, which was a semi-official Japanese press organ set up in Paris to cover the peace conference. Our analysis of the broadsheets is based on three themes: first, the relationship between the League of Nations and the racial equality proposal; second, the role of Premier Hughes and President Wilson; and third, the failure of the proposal.

First, however, it is worth noting that the broadsheets seemed to have had initially a clearer vision than the government of Japan's need to demand racial equality within the framework of the League of Nations. For instance, *Kokumin shimbun* published an article entitled 'The League and Racial Discrimination – One Impediment to Permanent Peace', on 3 November 1918:

> For Japan the most important question in connection with President Wilson's League of Nations is the mode of dealing with the racial discrimination idea. The object of the League's formation will not be fully realised, it would seem, so long as Japanese and other coloured races are differentially treated in white communities . . . . The main objects of Mr. Wilson's League are the perpetuation and the freedom and equalization of the races of the world.[83]

Press coverage shows that by November 1918, the press had started treating the racial issue as a potential time bomb.[84] By early December 1918, the three major broadsheets – *Tokyo nichi nichi shimbun, Yomiuri shimbun* and *Asahi shimbun* – had launched an all-out offensive on the racial equality issue demanding that the government propose a solution at the conference. In the light of how inefficient the Hara government had been over preparations for the peace conference, it is intriguing that the broadsheets were so well-briefed on this subject. For our purposes, however, it will be suffice to say that there was much early speculative interest in the broadsheets about the League of Nations, and how the League might deal with issues of race and racial discrimination.

The first theme in the analysis is the general tendency in the broadsheets to express scepticism towards the League of Nations, which reflected the scepticism expressed within the Hara government as mentioned above.[85] The predominant reason expressed for this was the apprehension that the League was essentially an Anglo-Saxon scheme. Although the League was supposedly created with the worthy objectives of promoting international justice and world peace, which appeared to some to be too utopian and unrealistic in any case,[86] there lingered the fear that it was an attempt by the British and Americans to institutionalise their superiority.[87] This kind of negative sentiment was hardly surprising, as it reflected the general distrust with which the Japanese regarded the West in the period and, in particular, the Anglo-Saxons. This distrust was mostly based on the deterioration of Japan's relationship with these countries during the war, but also on the belief that the Japanese had been unfairly treated on the basis of race by the West.[88] Understandably, the Japanese public was sceptical about the sincerity of the worldwide Wilsonian initiative to perpetuate justice, when it was the United States which was instituting discriminatory measures against Japanese immigrants.[89] To make matters worse, Britain seemingly condoned the behaviour of Australia, which was unquestionably being unreasonable in opposing the racial equality proposal. One alarmist scenario had depicted the League as a Christian conspiracy to produce a two-tiered world, where the Christian countries occupied the upper level and the non-Christian coloured countries occupied the lower.[90] Incidentally, the seeming determination in the broadsheets to view the West as a threat is reminiscent of the 'Yellow Peril' argument popularised in the West earlier in the century. It is noteworthy that the general characterisations made by the Japanese of the Anglo-Saxons were 'unfair' and 'selfish'.[91] Not surprisingly, the very same qualities were attributed to the Japanese by the Americans and British during the First World War.

It is striking that the broadsheets maintained the dual position of being on the one hand sceptical of the League, while on the other hand, supportive of the racial equality proposal. This seemingly paradoxical position was tenable because the racial equality proposal was perceived to be more important than the creation of the League of Nations.[92] More often than not, the discussion of the League of Nations was subordinated to that of the racial equality proposal; or more precisely, the League of Nations tended to be discussed mainly within the context of the racial equality debate. This means that the racial equality proposal was given greater weighting as an issue than was the League of Nations. Because the broadsheets generally believed that racial equality was an uncompromisingly 'just' demand, the acceptance or non-acceptance of the proposal was considered as the principal determining factor in judging the credibility of the League as an organisation worthy of promoting international justice.[93] Consequently, in the eyes of the public, the legitimacy of the League was inextricably linked to the fate of the racial equality proposal. Moreover, it was argued that Japan had a moral duty as the non-white great power to demand racial equality for the sake of greater international justice.[94] In the broadsheets, it can be said that the racial equality issue became central to Japan's understanding of the League of Nations, and as a result, little effort was made to consider the League on its own merit.

Second, public opinion was insistent upon finding scapegoats for the difficulties which the racial equality proposal was having in the negotiation. *Tokyo nichi nichi shimbun*, with its own Paris special correspondent, was convinced that Australian Premier Billy Hughes was the chief obstacle to the success of the proposal. The initial reason for singling out Hughes can be traced back to the interview he gave to the *New York Herald* in January 1919, when he revealed that Australia feared the possibility of a Japanese southward invasion. This interview greatly offended the sensibilities of the Japanese by its lack of diplomatic tactfulness and because it explicitly accused Japan of harbouring dishonourable intentions.[95] While Australia felt threatened by the prospect of Japanese 'invasion' southward in the Pacific, the Japanese felt equally threatened by Australia's determination to institute the 'White Australia' policy in the mandates in the Pacific.[96] Nevertheless, what really puzzled the Japanese public was the general disposition of the peace conference to favour Hughes's argument which was so blatantly 'racist' as far as the Japanese were concerned.[97] This resulted in an exaggerated perception of Hughes's ability to influence the great powers. There was much speculation before the 11 April meeting in the League of Nations Commission that Hughes would again block the Japanese proposal.[98] In the end, when the proposal was defeated for the second time, Makino blamed Hughes for fomenting a new crisis in Japanese–Australian relations.[99] However, *Chūgai shōgyō shimpō* gave a surprisingly accurate version of the events, arguing that Hughes was affected by the domestic political situation in Australia, and that his opposition did have a material effect on the British and American positions.[100]

As far as the perception of President Wilson was concerned, the Japanese considered him to be hypocritical. Although the public did not generally have much faith in the League of Nations, Wilson was initially perceived with some respect as an advocate of universal principles of justice. Therefore, the Japanese had expected Wilson to support fully racial equality as a principle in line with international justice. When the news arrived that Wilson was forced to reconsider his position on the racial equality clause in the light of the mounting opposition in the United States against Japanese immigration, the Japanese felt deeply betrayed.[101] Moreover, the broadsheets argued that his hypocrisy went further in demanding an insertion of the Monroe Doctrine, which was a peculiarly American foreign policy doctrine in the covenant, while at the same time rejecting racial equality, which was so evidently more fundamental to peace.[102] In fact, one article criticised the Japanese delegates for not demanding an explanation directly from Wilson for this unashamed contradiction.[103] What aggravated the whole situation was the disclosure that Wilson had used his position as chairman to impose unanimity voting in order to defeat the proposal.[104] It doubtless confirmed the underlying suspicion that the Anglo-Saxons were egoistic, pursuing only their own self-interest.[105] Clearly, the public perception of Wilson's contribution to the demise of the proposal was qualitatively different from that of Hughes. One editorial aptly summarised the prevailing feeling: 'The world had great expectations of Wilson but he has proven to be self-interested and we are getting tired of it all.'[106]

Third, how did the broadsheets come to terms with the failure of the proposal which, after all, was responsible for sustaining public interest in the peace conference throughout the entire duration? Interestingly, this event occasioned a wave of criticism and deep self-reflection. The tendency to link the fate of the racial equality proposal with the League of Nations meant that the failure of the proposal cast serious doubt on the future of the League as a viable international organisation. This manifested itself in two ways. First, it was argued that Japan should not join the League if it would not accept racial equality.[107] This view was spearheaded on 6 April 1919 by Okuma Shigenobu, a populist former prime minister who had contributed frequently to racial discourse (*jinshuron*) in the past two decades.[108] His public standing and popularity gave much credence to this perspective, which was taken up by the right-wing press. Second, the Anglo-Saxons' role in defeating the proposal was seen as a testimony to their self-interest in wanting to create the League.[109] One editorial denounced the Anglo-Saxons for their high-handed approach which single-handedly crushed the ideals of the League of Nations.[110]

Denouncing the Anglo-Saxons and the League of Nations, however, had the effect of heightening the sense of international isolation. There were many introspective reflections on why Japan was internationally isolated. First, the Japanese felt isolated from their ally, Britain. They felt betrayed by Britain, which had supported Australia at their expense over the racial equality proposal. Moreover, this betrayal implied that the British had a more detached attitude towards the Anglo-Japanese Alliance than did the Japanese.[111] *Tokyo nichi nichi* gave the following reasons for the cooling off of the relationship between the two long-standing allies: Japan benefited the most out of the war and was not very helpful towards its allies; there was a widespread perception that Japan was increasingly pro-German and militaristic; Japan's expansionist policy in China; and the existence of an intense commercial rivalry between Britain and Japan during the war.[112]

Moreover, the Japanese generally felt disliked by the other powers, especially the United States and China. For instance, *Asahi* cautioned that Japan was perceived by some as the 'Germany of the East' because of its militaristic and expansionist policies. Since it appeared that this anti-Japanese propaganda were being disseminated by the Chinese, *Asahi* argued that what Japan had to do was to foster genuine friendship with China and also to stop engaging in activities which could be so misconstrued.[113] It only made matters worse when reports such as the one claiming that the United States disliked Japan more than Germany appeared.[114] Particularly striking was the publication of an interview with Senator Phelan of California, the foremost political agitator of the anti-Japanese movement in the United States, when he detailed the reasons why the Americans disliked the Japanese.[115] In the light of the general sentiment, one right-wing paper argued that Japan should give up its attempts to be identified with the West and accept isolation because, no matter what Japan did, it would be isolated internationally.[116]

The exacerbated sense of isolation did not stem from the racial equality issue alone, as there was an earlier snub when Japan was excluded from the Council of Four in late March. This incident led to comments that the Japanese delegates were increasingly isolated from the Western great powers.[117] The official explanation provided by Makino that the Big Four was formed to discuss purely European matters was rejected because it was obvious that the group would have considerable power over the general postwar settlement and that Japan would not be able to have much effect on these decisions.[118] In the face of mounting public discontent over the generally unfavourable disposition of the Anglo-Saxons towards Japan, Ogawa Heikichi, a prominent member of the ruling political party, concluded that although Japan's international position seemed certain on the surface, in reality not everyone was favourable to Japan, which needed to work hard in order to maintain its position.[119] This underlines the extreme sensitivity of public opinion on the question of great power status which, in turn, revealed how fragile Japan's great power status really was.

The broadsheets were harshly critical of the government's diplomatic failure over the racial equality issue. The Hara government was accused of 'weak diplomacy' (*nanjaku gaikō*) as attested by their inability to win over the opponents of this obviously 'just' demand.[120] It was suggested that the Foreign Ministry should be thoroughly scrutinised to rectify its ineptitude.[121] Moreover, *Yomiuri* had been criticising the government since mid-March for submitting the proposal when so many other more important problems were at stake.[122] Its view was that Japan should not compromise its position as a great power over this issue.[123] Later on, the same editorial stated that

Japan should not be embarrassed about the defeat of the proposal because it was submitted for the sake not of self-interest but of universal justice. Basically, Japan's failure to obtain racial equality simply implied that its national power was not commensurate with obtaining such a high ideal.[124]

In summary, racial equality became a focus of broadsheet journalism during the Paris Peace Conference. The racial equality proposal became a disproportionately important issue for the public because its fate was directly linked to the equity or inequity of the League of Nations, and by extension, of the Anglo-Saxon powers. The broadsheets' sentiment reflected a more nationalistic and Japan-centric perspective, which contrasted with Hara's pro-Western internationalist perspective. Because the broadsheets had a tendency to view the League of Nations as being secondary to the racial equality proposal, the League could only be important and relevant to them if the proposal was accepted.

The intellectuals

An examination of the position of the intellectuals offers a more profound insight into the racial equality debate in Japan. In this section, we shall focus on five intellectuals who made important contributions to this debate. Ishibashi Tanzan and Yoshino Sakuzō represent the liberal, pro-Western perspective, while Nakano Seigō and Konoe Fumimaro represent the pan-Asian perspective. An exception to both perspectives is the controversial thinker, Fukuda Tokuzō, who did not fit neatly into any of the two categories and yet whose public prominence disconcerted not a few, including the British. On the whole, the intellectuals tended to perceive the racial equality proposal as an issue of principle rather than of policy, and Hara's position came closest to that of the liberal intellectuals.

Let us begin with the intellectuals who advocated greater cooperation with the West, thus, closest to Hara's pro-Western policy. Ishibashi Tanzan (1884–1973) belonged to a small influential group of progressive liberals who were highly critical of the hypocrisy of mainstream liberals because the latter generally endorsed the somewhat contradictory position of supporting liberal democracy domestically on the one hand while condoning imperialism abroad on the other.[125] Ishibashi was one of the few people in Japan to recognise the importance of the League of Nations as he introduced two proposals for a peace league in October 1915.[126] During the Paris Peace Conference, Ishibashi enthusiastically supported the creation of a league of nations as a 'democratic international government' with three main tasks: first, as a legislative body making legislation on problems arising internationally; second, as an administrative body with a secretariat; and third, as a judicial body with a system analogous to domestic judiciary.[127]

Nevertheless, Ishibashi strongly criticised the government's attempt to achieve racial equality.[128] Ideally, he supported a demand for racial equality. In reality, however, he could not tolerate the hypocritical attitude of the government, which unashamedly demanded racial equality while practising blatant racial discrimination domestically and internationally. Japan discriminated against Chinese workers by prohibiting their employment by Japanese employers. Taiwanese and Koreans were also often targets of unnecessary discrimination, both in terms of trade and property rights.[129]The government even discriminated between its own citizens, by preventing the institution of universal suffrage.[130] In other words, how could the government have any credibility when it was discriminating against everyone including its own people? Although Ishibashi did not make a direct connection between racial equality and immigration, he regarded anti-Japanese immigration policy, particularly in the United States, as an emotive issue which could not be eradicated by simple legislation.[131] Ishibashi was impatient over the Hara government's hypocritical, half-hearted attempt at racial equality which so clearly belied reality.

How different was the position of Yoshino Sakuzō (1878–1933), a flagship liberal, who led the Taishō democracy movement?[132] Yoshino's thinking was in line with popular liberalism whose version of democracy (*minponshugi*) supported the popular ideal of 'constitutionalism inside, and imperialism outside'.[133] Yoshino's essentially pro-Western view of the importance of cooperation with Britain and the United States coincided with that of Ishibashi, as evidenced by the former's support of the Anglo-Japanese Alliance as a basis of peace in East Asia. Wilson's Fourteen Points had a profound impact on Yoshino, who immediately adopted Wilsonism as his political and philosophical mantle, giving particular emphasis to the importance of self-determination as a general political principle.[134] In January 1919, Yoshino enthusiastically declared that Japan should support the prevailing world trend for greater international justice by consolidating democracy internally and establishing equality externally.[135] Hence, Yoshino was an enthusiastic proponent of international cooperation and, thus, of the League of Nations.[136]

On the racial equality question, Yoshino perceived an inherent problem in making the proposal credible internationally. Admittedly, he considered the timing of the proposal to be appropriate as a reaction to the discriminatory treatment which the Japanese had been receiving in Australia and the United States.[137] However, he cautioned that a proposal of universal principle must be separated from a proposal that appealed to self-interest. As such, the Japanese proposal would be regarded as emanating from the standpoint of a victim of discrimination and would not gain significant support at Paris. Thus, he challenged the pressure groups, such as the League to Abolish Racial Discrimination, to answer the question of whether they were demanding an absolute principle or a relative principle of racial equality. He impatiently demanded that these groups stop discriminating against the Koreans, if they really wanted racial equality. Moreover, he drew attention to the fact that even if the racial equality proposal were adopted, it would still not resolve the anti-Japanese movement in the United States, because the root cause of the immigration problem did not lay in racial discrimination but in other factors as well.[138] All in all, Yoshino, though fundamentally supportive of racial equality as a principle, was critical of the proposal because it lacked sincerity and credibility coming from a government and activists who blatantly practised discrimination against fellow Asians.

Of the *ajia shugi* (pan-Asian) proponents, both Nakano Seigō and Konoe Fumimaro attended the Paris Peace Conference, Nakano as a journalist and Konoe as personal assistant to Chief Plenipotentiary Saionji. Nakano Seigō (1886–1943) was an influential political activist who, though he became an acknowledged ultra right-winger in the 1930s, was democratic, pan-Asian and nationalist during the period under study. He was strongly influenced by pan-Asian thinking through Genyōsha, an ultra-nationalist and pan-Asian organisation, and his intellectual mentor, Ukita Kazutami. During this period, Nakano's political thinking had four characteristics: first, it was imperialistic in stressing the absolute importance of protecting Japan's interest particularly in East Asia; second, it was pan-Asian in promoting an alliance between Japan and China and, on a wider level, an Asian alliance to fight against Western powers;[139] third, his opposition to the Anglo-Japanese Alliance[140] led him to promote a Russo–Japanese alliance as a means of countering the former; fourth, he was critical of the militarist diplomacy, which revealed his strongly anti-clan, anti-military and anti-bureaucratic sentiment.[141] On the question of race, Nakano wrote that peace and justice seemed applicable only to relationships between the great white powers and consequently, it was Japan's mission to prevent the coloured race from being excluded from the world.[142]

Nakano was deeply disappointed by and highly critical of the way in which the Hara government conducted diplomacy at Paris.[143] From the start, the Japanese delegates had the wrong attitude, which was to be grateful to the Western great powers for bestowing Japan with great power status at the conference.[144] Moreover, he was irritated by the government's blindness to an implicit coalition between Britain and the United States, where Britain had tacitly agreed to support American claims in the Far East despite the Anglo-Japanese Alliance.[145] Nakano abandoned the peace conference in early February 1919 to pour his energy into raising national consciousness, because the low standard of political awareness in Japan was partly responsible for the 'pathetic performance' of the government.[146]

How did Nakano perceive the government's effort concerning racial equality? Fundamentally, Nakano supported the idea of promoting racial equality at the peace conference because of its universal significance, guaranteed to win support from China, India and all other oppressed nations in the world.[147] His view was that immigration represented only a small fraction of this much larger and important issue. However, what Nakano criticised was the tactics of the Hara government in presenting this worthwhile proposal in a manner which lacked the conviction, preparation and energy necessary to give momentum to issues of this kind.[148] He claimed that the global importance of racial equality would have made it extremely difficult for Britain and the United States to sustain any opposition. As it was, the Japanese delegates were content to sit back after having gained initial sympathy from Colonel House and to trust the alliance to bring the British around to agreeing to it. Nakano criticised the inability of the delegation to perceive that the United States was not going to agree to such a proposal and was only letting Britain do the dirty work of opposing Japan on this issue since the Americans were already confronting Japan on Shantung and the Pacific islands.[149] On the whole, Nakano's distrust of an Anglo-American 'coalition' extended to his perception of the racial equality proposal as being a victim of this conspiracy. Moreover, he condemned the inadequacy of Japanese diplomacy, which exposed Japan's lack of political maturity as a nation.

As a key political figure in Japanese politics in the late 1930s, Konoe Fumimaro's (1891–1945) perspective on the League and the racial equality proposal deserves some scrutiny. He wrote possibly his most influential piece, '*Eibei hon'i no heiwashugi o haisu*' (Abolish the Anglo-American Based Peace), which appeared in an influential pan-Asian journal, *Nihon oyobi nihonjin* in December 1918, immediately before his departure to attend the Paris Peace Conference as one of Saionji's attendants. In the article, he severely criticised those Japanese who blindly espoused the Anglo-American notion of peace as being the only legitimately humanitarian and democratic one.[150] According to him, peace as defined by the Anglo-Americans implied the maintenance of a *status quo* based on their national interests and consequently, was a far cry from justice and humanity. The League of Nations was simply a manifestation of Anglo-American interests in a disguised form. Konoe urged the Japanese nation to become more Japan-centric, which entailed the recognition of the rightful existence of Japan and its mission to fight against any force that might impinge on this sovereign right. According to one analysis, Konoe believed that Japan should change the existing international system which favoured only the Anglo-Saxon powers.[151] This belief was based on his espousal of the theory of the right of national existence (*kokumin seizonken*) which considered the principle of equal opportunity of states as the true manifestation of international justice.

One of the major arguments made by Konoe in this article was the demand for racial equality.[152] Although he cited Japan's history of frustrated attempts to overcome numerous restrictions placed on the Japanese and other peoples of the yellow race by Australians and Canadians, his demand for the abolition of racial discrimination ultimately was not based on the economic argument but on a universal moralistic argument of 'justice and humanity'.[153] Konoe's claim for racial equality was pan-Asian insofar as he had identified it with the anti-West attitude,[154] but he fell short of calling for a racial alliance with Asia in order to counter Western racism. In the end, Konoe's argument on racial equality, though couched in terms of 'justice' and 'humanity', ended up as a specific claim to suit Japan's particular national circumstances.[155] At the peace conference, he continued to believe that great powers were self-interested, as was best evidenced in the failure of the racial equality proposal, a just demand, and the concomitant success of the Monroe Doctrine, which was so clearly antithetical to the League of Nations.[156] However, his views of Wilson were modified to acknowledge the significance of the Wilsonian principle of self-determination as one of the central tenets of the peace conference. Moreover, Konoe showed a deeper understanding of the anti-Japanese problems in the United States as he realised that racial prejudice was not something which could be eradicated overnight and required a long-term strategy.[157]

Fukuda Tokuzō (1874–1930) was a controversial radical thinker who,.along with Yoshino Sakuzō, was one of the leaders of the Taishō democratic movement.[158] As a champion of social reform, he was most noted for his virulent opposition to Anglo-American capitalism. He was critical of Britain, whose economic expansionism continued to oppress the world purely to satisfy selfish national interest.[159] He accused Britain of adopting a double standard in its diplomacy, which purported to protect and foster trade, but in reality was simply protecting British capitalists.[160] However, his argument faltered in the eyes of some when he justified the rise of German militarism as the only possible counter-force to British capitalism because German militarism was a smaller evil in comparison.[161] In fact, his readiness to identify with Germany had made him seem inappropriately too pro-German, which made him many public enemies.[162]

It is not surprising that Fukuda was highly critical of the League of Nations which, he was convinced, was an Anglo-American scheme.[163] Characteristically, he denounced the League as an organisation designed to further British capitalistic expansion.[164] Fukuda contended that unless the British and Americans renounced their capitalistic expansionism, the League would have little use as an organ to prevent future wars. He was certainly not sympathetic to Wilson, as he believed that only the outcome of the peace conference could justify Wilson's advocacy of liberal democracy.[165] Interestingly, he perceived the two great causes of war to be economic greed and racial hatred. Fukuda argued that one of the best uses of the League would be to control the eruption of war as a result of racial oppression. Moreover, he stressed the importance of demanding racial equality and religious freedom to test Wilsonian idealism because he distrusted Wilson's eloquent pronouncements. He believed that it was fundamentally important to eliminate these discriminations, as the existence of religious discrimination, for instance, meant that only Christians were treated as humans.[166] Thus he argued that Japan, as representative of the coloured race, should make efforts to bring racial equality to fruition. It appears that Fukuda was supportive of racial equality as long as it stayed within the confines of his anti-capitalistic perspective. However, the defeat of the racial equality clause in the League of Nations Commission at the Peace Conference crushed what little sympathy he felt for the League, as it strengthened his conviction that the League of Nations was an imperialist organ which ignored the seemingly legitimate claim for racial equality of the only non-white great power.

As a concluding remark on the intellectuals' contribution to the racial equality debate, it may be noted that all considered racial equality as an issue of fundamental importance.[167] However, beyond this lowest common denominator, there was not much agreement between the *ōbei kyōchō* liberals and *ajia shugi* thinkers. Ishibashi and Yoshino supported the League of Nations as a new international order, based on cooperation with the West, whereas Nakano, Konoe and even Fukuda regarded the League with suspicion, especially in light of the fact that it was predominantly Wilsonian in its origin and, therefore, Anglo-Saxon domination in disguise. Although Ishibashi and Yoshino differed considerably on the general points concerning the government's foreign policy, they concurred in their criticism of the government's hypocrisy in demanding racial equality on the one hand, while practising racial discrimination on the other. In fact, their view on the principle of racial equality was refreshingly progressive by contemporary international standards. Nakano attacked the government from another angle, criticising the failure of diplomacy in the racial equality negotiation. Konoe saw hypocrisy in the American position which rejected racial equality while demanding the Monroe Doctrine. Fukuda considered racial equality a litmus test of the sincerity of Wilsonian idealism. Broadly speaking, Prime Minister Hara's support for the League of Nations was closer to the position of the liberal intellectuals,[168] and in opposition to the *ajia shugi* thinkers whose position was more representative of the national opinion (*kokuron*) as evidenced in the broadsheets and pressure groups.

CONCLUSIONS

This chapter has suggested that domestic political considerations played an important role in explaining the emergence and the subsequent prominence of the racial equality proposal in the domestic debate surrounding the Japanese government's decision to support the League of Nations at Paris. It has been shown that Prime Minister Hara was determined to adopt a pro-Western line in foreign policy, due to the deterioration of Japan's relations with Britain and the United States during the First World War. This manifested itself in his support for the League at the peace conference. However, the problem was that his view tended to represent the minority and was not representative of the majority of the nation which took a more nationalistic and uncompromising attitude towards the Anglo-Saxon powers. What the unexpectedly widespread opposition to the pro-League policy revealed was the depth of pan-Asian attitude which permeated the Japanese society. This meant that Hara had to convince sceptics at all levels in order to have his pro-League policy accepted. The sceptics were everywhere: in the government, in pressure groups, in public opinion as evidenced through the broadsheets, and among the intellectuals. It is particularly noteworthy that the general public and pan-Asian intellectuals concurred in their strongly suspicious attitude towards the League of Nations and Wilsonian idealism.

Having seen the pervasiveness of scepticism towards the League, it is not difficult to understand the need felt by Hara and his supporters to justify domestically the decision to support it. It can be plausibly construed that the racial equality demand, by imposing a condition on Japan's acceptance of the League, had the effect of appeasing the sceptics, both in the government and among the public, who might otherwise have resented the idea of Japan's succumbing unconditionally to international (or more precisely, Anglo-Saxon) pressure to join the League. In this sense, this study shares the view that the proposal had a symbolic role as Japan's response or challenge to an Anglo-Saxon dominated League of Nations.[169] Therefore, it seems reasonable to conclude from the evidence that the Hara government's pro-League policy temporarily acquired legitimacy behind the façade of the proposal. Because the proposal was acceptable to all Japanese, it played an important domestic political role in justifying the government's support for the League.

3 Immigration and the 'diplomacy of saving face'

This chapter attempts to reassess critically the explanatory category of immigration to see whether the unassailable importance given to the argument in the existing literature – that the racial equality proposal was intended to solve problems related to anti-Japanese immigration practices in the Anglo-Saxon territories – withstands critical scrutiny. The chapter is divided into two parts. First, an historical background to the problem of Japanese immigration in the Anglo-Saxon territories is given, depicting the long-standing Japanese sensitivities towards the problem and the measures implemented by the Japanese Foreign Ministry to counter it. The second part examines the perspective of the Foreign Ministry, which needed urgently to resolve this problem. Essentially, the Foreign Ministry was most concerned about the negative implications which anti-Japanese immigration policies would have on Japan's status as a great power. Therefore, it tended to perceive the significance of the problem as being entirely symbolic, in wanting to 'save face'.[1] Consequently, the actual draft proposals submitted at the peace conference did, indeed, have an 'immigration' slant precisely because of the input from the Foreign Ministry officials at Paris, revealing the extent of their bureaucratic imperative to resolve the problem relating to Japanese immigration.

HISTORICAL BACKGROUND TO JAPANESE IMMIGRATION

The problem of anti-Japanese sentiment in the Anglo-Saxon territories started in the 1890s and became a regular feature of domestic political life in these territories. There were two problematic destinations for Japanese immigrants. The first was the British Dominions, including Australia, Canada, South Africa and New Zealand, all of which practised some sort of discriminatory measures to limit Japanese and other Asian immigrants entering and settling in their territories. The second area was the United States, especially on the West Coast in California. Historically, the Japanese government had been concerned about minimising potential damage to Japan's prestige which would arise out of discriminatory treatments given to its nationals in foreign territories. To a large extent, the Japanese government had been effective in containing the seemingly endless series of problems associated with anti-Japanese immigration policies through voluntary diplomatic initiatives, as is shown below. Nevertheless, such efforts made by the Foreign Ministry were seriously jeopardised by frequent outbursts of anti-Japanese sentiment in these territories threatening to undo the goodwill maintained precariously by an enormous diplomatic effort.

Why was immigration so problematic for the Japanese government? The central problem lay in the dual nature of immigration as a policy area. On the one hand, it remained essentially a domestic issue from the perspective of the Anglo-Saxon territories accepting the immigrants. On the other hand, it was solely a diplomatic issue from the perspective of Japan, which was sending the immigrants. The Japanese did everything possible to close this gap by appealing to the British and American governments to tighten their grip over immigration within their respective domestic polities. Although the Japanese government had reasonable success in containing the problems through their own measures, it was unable to convince London and Washington to reciprocate with extending similar levels of control over the immigration policies practised in their Dominions and provinces. Hence, the Japanese continued to be unsuccessful in the diplomacy of immigration in spite of the enormous effort invested in resolving the issue because the federal governments could do little and, moreover, had little desire to intervene in provincial and Dominion politics. Let us illustrate the problematic nature of Japanese immigration into the British Dominions and the United States respectively, from an historical perspective.

Japanese immigration to the British Dominions

As far as the British Dominions were concerned, the British government attempted successfully to circumvent the problem of Japanese immigration in the Dominion territories by having a strict demarcation between immigration as a Dominion issue, and foreign policy as a British imperial issue. This meant that, in practice, the Japanese government had to deal with the Dominions individually on a bilateral basis in order to reach any agreement on issues relating to immigration. Nonetheless, though it is true that all Dominions practised discriminatory immigration policies of one sort or another, the perceived risk coming from Japanese immigrants differed considerably among them. This meant that the most effective way of countering anti-Japanese measures for the Japanese government was to deal with the Dominions individually.

The Dominions developed and sustained discriminatory immigration policies largely because of the perception of economic and racial threats posed by non-white immigrants. The perceived economic threat posed by these non-white immigrants, such as lowering the standard of living and increasing competition through unfair practices, was tangible since it referred to the socio-economic indicators which were perceived to be threatened by these immigrants, who could disrupt the *status quo* created by the white society. The racial threat was less tangible, and often went hand in hand with economic threat, but sometimes took a distinct tone. It was a double-edged sword: on the one hand, there was the racial superiority complex of the whites; on the other hand, this racial arrogance was paradoxical and fragile because it was inseparable from the fear of the non-white race contaminating the white settler societies by racial miscegenation. It is important not to underestimate the perceived threat. Even with the 'white' immigration policy firmly entrenched, the Australian Prime Minister Billy Hughes stated:

> We have lifted up on our topmost minaret the badge of white Australia, but we are, as it were, a drop in a coloured ocean ringed around with a thousand million of the coloured races. How are we to be saved?[2]

It was precisely the racial connotation of statements and sentiments such as the one above which humiliated the Japanese Foreign Ministry. Therefore, in spite of the fact that Japan was recognised by Britain as one of the great powers, in the treatment of its immigrants by the Dominions, it generally fared not much better than China or India.

The Canadian immigration policies can be characterised in three ways. First, they were based on a quota system which tended to be racially discriminatory against non-white immigrants. For instance, the Immigration Act of 1910 denied entry 'of immigrants belonging to any race deemed unsuited to the climate or requirements of Canada'.[3] Second, the problem of non-white immigration was a regional one, concentrated in the Pacific province of British Columbia, where the provincial legislature prohibited the discriminated category of immigrants from voting in provincial elections, and subjected them to occupational discrimination in areas such as fishing and the public service sector.[4] However, the regional nature of the problem meant that Ottawa was not necessarily understanding or sympathetic of the plight of the province in wanting to restrict Asian immigration. Third, the Canadians practised selective discrimination against their immigrants, which meant that the Chinese and Indians fared worse in reality than did the Japanese, mainly because of the diplomatic efforts expended by the Japanese government as well as Canada's consideration towards Japan as a great power.

Historically, Japanese immigration to Canada started in 1884[5], and peaked in 1908 when 7,985 Japanese entered the country.[6] The Japanese government managed to establish a successful *modus operandi* with the Canadian government where, it had agreed to restrict voluntarily the number of its immigrants to Canada through the Lemieux Agreement of 1908, which was subsequently enforced by Canada's Immigration Act of 1910.[7] As a result, the Japanese population was 17,700 in 1924 (out of which 16,000 lived in British Columbia) as opposed to 60,000 Chinese, and the cumulative annual figure for all categories of Japanese immigrants entering the country averaged around 600.[8] This measure of voluntary restriction of Japanese immigrants to Canada by limiting the number of passports issued became the preferred method for the Japanese government, as will be seen below. It also helped that the Canadians did not feel much threat from Japan, despite having a sizeably larger Japanese immigrant community than any other Dominion, because Canada felt geographically secure with the United States and Britain on two sides.[9] Partly as a result of the successful operation of this agreement, and partly as a sign of goodwill shown towards Britain's ally, the Canadian government generally respected the Japanese government's desire not to be named explicitly in any discriminatory immigration policy which would discredit Japan's international status.[10]

Among the Dominions, Australia represented possibly the most difficult case for the Japanese Foreign Ministry, which had to deal with the damaging diplomatic implications of anti-Japanese sentiment in the country. As the effects of the 'White Australia' policy in the context of the Australian opposition to the racial equality proposal of 1919 will be discussed later in Chapter 5, it will suffice to allude generally here to the measures taken by the Japanese government in the light of the discriminatory measures taken by the Australian government. Australia had a long history of anti-Oriental sentiment dating back to 1855, when the State of Victoria implemented restrictive immigration measures to curtail mainly Chinese coolie and Indian indentured labourers.[11] Japanese immigration did not become a problem until 1894, in Queensland in the pearl shell fisheries. This problem, when it surfaced, was swiftly resolved by the Japanese government, which had agreed to control the immigrant population in the region.[12] It was the 'White Australia' policy of 1901 (Immigration Restriction Act) which made both Australia and the white immigration policy universally notorious.[13] This was modelled on the 'Natal formula' which served the implicit objective of excluding Asian immigrants without directly referring to their racial origins through the use of language tests on incoming immigrants.[14] This method originated in South Africa in 1897 to circumvent the British imperial sensitivity expressed over racially-based immigration policies which would offend Japan, in particular.[15]

Similarly, the Japanese government attempted to curtail the flow of Japanese into Australia by employing the preferred method of voluntary restriction of its immigrants through the Passport Agreement of 1904. Therefore, Australia had no increase in Japanese nationals, many of whom were temporary resident pearlers (special exemption gained in 1902 at Thursday Island and Broome to employ cheap Japanese pearlers), who averaged 416 per annum between 1902 and 1922, and passport holders, who averaged 44 per annum from 1904 to 1920.[16] The actual number of Japanese residents in 1911 was 3,489, less than the 1901 figure of 3,554.[17] The non-European origins of residents in Australia in 1911 were 0.82 per cent Asian, 0.11 per cent African, and 0.08 per cent Polynesian.[18] In practical terms, Australia's treatment of the Japanese, though legally harsh, was 'deferential'.[19] Contrary to Premier Barton, who did not much care about the effects of the 'White Australia' policy towards Japan, his successor, Alfred Deakin, took a more conciliatory approach towards the Japanese.[20] Although the immigration policy remained intransigent towards the Japanese, based on the assumption that the Japanese should not permanently reside in Australia, Deakin at least attempted to avoid open confrontation with Japan over the immigration question. Continuous diplomatic efforts expended by the Foreign Ministry were not entirely in vain as, in the case of Canada, Australians tended to treat Japanese immigrants better than other non-white immigrants, largely due to Japan's status as a great power.[21] However, the problem lay not so much in the legal implications of the 'White Australia' policy as in its political implications which, as is described below, remained a highly controversial issue in Japan's relations with Australia.

Comparatively speaking, the problems of anti-Japanese immigration practices in South Africa and New Zealand were marginal. For example, the problem of anti-Japanese immigration was not a practical issue in South Africa because for most Japanese, South Africa remained a distant land just as much as Japan remained a distant land for South Africans.[22] Instead, the problem for South Africa lay in Indian immigration, which was strictly controlled by several immigration bills passed in 1902, 1903, 1904 and 1906, designed to restrict Asian immigration.[23] It seems that the only reason for the lack of a conflicting relationship between Japan and South Africa on account of immigration was the near non-existence of Japanese immigrants wanting to settle there. Even then, according to the Governor-General of South Africa, the entry of Japanese immigrants was very tightly controlled by the South African government:

> I understand that about two or three years ago the Department of the Interior agreed with the Japanese Consul at Cape Town to allow the conditional entry of Japanese immigrants to the Union on temporary permit, provided that such immigrants were able to comply with the provisions of the Immigration Laws respecting the educational test and money deposits. These temporary permits were for specific periods and were in each case granted on the recommendation of the Japanese Consul.[24]

By September 1918, only eight permits had been issued to Japanese immigrants allowing temporary entry.[25] In fact, it was commented by one Japanese newspaper that the restrictions imposed on Japanese immigrants were so severe that only officials were allowed to enter.[26] However, the geographical distance between the two helped to alleviate any potentially damaging implications of such a policy in South Africa.

New Zealand had a 'White New Zealand' policy which was targeted against mainly Chinese immigrants.[27] Although there was an initial fear that the Chinese population would increase uncontrollably after the first influx of Chinese coolie labourers in 1866, the threat no longer existed after the early 1880s due to a series of immigration restriction acts designed to limit Chinese immigrants.[28] Nonetheless, the level of anti-Chinese sentiment in the country remained constantly very high. In practice, none of this affected the Japanese government as the number of Japanese settlers in New Zealand was negligible.[29] However, the Foreign Office in London remained concerned, especially about the high level of anti-Oriental sentiment, lest New Zealand should interfere with the already delicate diplomacy with Japan by naming the latter in their numerous immigration restriction acts.[30]

Whatever threat the New Zealanders felt from the Japanese, it was a perceived threat only.

Generally speaking then, the Japanese had been successful in implementing voluntary restrictions to control the number of Japanese immigrants entering the British Dominions up until 1919. In the light of the low number of Japanese immigrants actually residing in the Dominions, it seems that the threat from Japanese was largely imaginary rather than real. Moreover, the Dominions tended to respect Japanese sensibilities in not wishing to be named as the targeted group of immigrants for the former's anti-Oriental immigration measures, ironically through the use of the 'Natal' formula.[31] This was in line with the British imperial concern that the Dominions should not practise racially-based immigration policies, for fear of offending Japan. Therefore, it can be said that the Japanese Foreign Ministry had managed to find a *modus operandi* with the Dominions which did provide a modicum of stability in British–Japanese relations. What diplomacy could not resolve, however, was the eradication of anti-Japanese sentiment at the grass-root level. The Japanese knew that it provided only a temporary respite to the problem which required a permanent solution.

Japanese immigration into the United States

Historically, Japanese–American relations had been marred by occasional confrontations over the question of Japanese immigrants entering the United States, especially in California. For Japan, immigration problems with the United States posed a much greater diplomatic 'headache' than with the Dominions collectively, because of the political strength of the anti-Japanese lobby in California. In the pre-1919 period, the most notable diplomatic incident was the 1913 Californian Alien Land Law, which had seriously jeopardised the bilateral relationship. It can be said that immigration acted as a serious impediment to improving bilateral relations.

The earliest record of Japanese immigration into the United States goes back to 1868, when 148 labourers went to work on sugar plantations in Hawaii.[32] This expedition encountered many problems, which led the Japanese government to refuse all further requests for contract labourers until 1885. The Japanese Foreign Minister Inoue signed a convention in January 1886 with R.W. Irwin, an American national appointed as consul-general for Japan in Hawaii, which sent 30,000 Japanese into Hawaii between 1885 and 1894. With the Hawaiian revolution in 1893, the controlled immigration system set up by Inoue and

Irwin collapsed, resulting in a flood of Japanese immigrants who mostly settled on the West Coast in California. The route of Japanese immigrant workers into the United States was thus established and the Japanese immigration problem became largely a Californian issue.

Before elaborating on the rise of the anti-Japanese movement in California, let us put the so-called 'Japanese problem' into perspective. According to the United States census, the Japanese population in the country was as in Table 3.1.[33] It is important to bear these numbers in mind in order to appreciate fully the exaggerated nature of the anti-Japanese movement relative to the population in question and its destructive impact on US–Japanese relations in the early part of the century.

Historically speaking, the American West Coast had a strong anti-Oriental attitude, dating back to at least the 1882 Chinese Exclusion Act. It appears that the subsequent initial anti-Japanese movement was simply a continuation of the anti-Chinese movement.[34] The movement's beginnings can be seen in the late 1890s, culminating in the first reported anti-Japanese meeting in April 1900 in Seattle, and followed by another in May 1900 in San Francisco.[35] As in the case of the British Dominions, Japan's victory in the Russo–Japanese War precipitated the revival of the idea of the 'Yellow Peril'. From the end of March 1905, the *San Francisco Chronicle* ran a year-long anti-Japanese campaign which, as it was the most influential West Coast newspaper, doubtless had a great impact in turning popular opinion against the Japanese.[36] In May 1905, the Asian Exclusion League was formed, initially as an extension of San Francisco labour unions.[37] These domestic movements made diplomatic relations very sensitive. For example, President Roosevelt was obliged to make a distinction between the Japanese and the Chinese in order not to offend the sensibilities of Japan, whose rising global status could no longer be ignored.[38] The Japanese government responded to the anti-Japanese movement by agreeing in 1907 to voluntarily restrict Japanese labourers by stopping the issue of passports, which turned out to be

Table 3.1 Japanese population in the United States, 1900–1920

Year	*in the US*	*in the Pacific Coast*	*in California*
1900	24,326 (0.03%)	18,269 (0.7%)	10,151 (0.6%)
1910	72,157 (0.08%)	57,703 (1.4%)	41,356 (1.7%)
1920	111,010 (0.1%)	94,490 (1.7%)	71,952 (2.1%)

an effective mechanism for keeping the number of immigrants into the United States to a fairly low and steady level for many years.[39]

Undoubtedly, the most controversial development in the history of anti-Japanese movement in the United States before 1919 was the Californian Alien Land Law of 1913, which left a deep scar on Japanese–American relations for many decades to come. The crux of the problem was that it was specifically targeted against Japanese immigrants, limiting leases of agricultural land to maximum terms of three years and barring further land purchases by Japanese aliens. The justification given by Washington was that the law was based purely on economic and not political or racial reasons.[40] In one of many official protests from the Japanese government, Ambassador Chinda wrote to Secretary of State Bryan:

> The provisions of law, under which it is held that Japanese people are not eligible to American citizenship, are mortifying to the Government and people of Japan, since the racial distinction inferable from those provisions is hurtful to their just national susceptibility.[41]

Not only did the Japanese argue that the legislation contravened the 1911 commercial and navigation treaty, but they objected emphatically to discrimination only against the Japanese, its not being applicable to other immigrants.[42] Under pressure from the Japanese government,[43] President Woodrow Wilson appealed to the Governor of California, Hiram Johnson, not to embarrass the federal government in its relations with Japan.[44] However, Wilson's plea fell on deaf ears, leaving the situation to deteriorate substantially to the point where Wilson and the cabinet discussed mobilisation of the fleet in the Pacific against Japan.[45] This underlined the seriousness with which the Japanese perceived the immigration problem, to the extent that it was considered to be a justifiable *casus belli*.

During the height of the tension, Wilson spelt out his thoughts on why the legislation offended the Japanese so much:

> It arises out of the implication in that we do not want to have intimate association in our life with the Japanese, which is but an implication – a suggestion – of feeling on our part that they are not on the same plane with us. That, of course, is something that diplomacy itself cannot handle. It is a fundamental, subtle, delicate and yet radical thing. It touches a man's pride; he cannot tell you just where you touched it, but you have touched the sorest spot in him.[46]

What Wilson was suggesting is that the Japanese perceived the problem as one of symbolic inferiority of their nationals. It should be mentioned that Wilson dared not publicly criticise the Japanese government for not giving the same rights to Americans in Japan, as he was apprehensive that this would only excite jingoistic elements in Japan and worsen the situation.[47]

Primarily, as in the case of the British Dominions, the reasons for the anti-Japanese movement were twofold – economic and racial. Officially, the Japanese immigrants were 'aliens ineligible for citizenship' for economic reasons. Theodore Roosevelt claimed that Oriental labourers were a threat to the American labour class because of cheap, competitive labour.[48] In fact, this was a classic 'catch-22' situation in which the earlier Japanese immigrants were discriminated against for lowering the standard of living of white American workers, while later immigrants, who attempted to aspire to better social status, were equally condemned for their 'Protestant ethic' which challenged white businesses and professions.[49] In vain, Wilson tried to convince Chinda that the 1913 law was passed in California because of the 'industrial ascendancy' of Japan and 'The Californians . . . never meant to humiliate the Japanese from a racial standpoint'.[50]

Notwithstanding the economic justifications, it could not be denied that there was a strong racial undertone in the anti-Japanese legislation. Racialist arguments were frequently regurgitated by many politicians such as the California Democratic leader, Senator James Duval Phelan:[51]

> The fundamental objection to the coming of these people is their non-assimilability. They cannot become a part of our composite Nation. They remain foreign. Where there has been intermarriage, the issue is degenerate and the vices of both strains are exaggerated in the offspring. We do not believe that they can, by any stretch of imagination, become a part of the American people, and, that ultimately, the same race question, which arose in the South – will arise, a possibility, which certainly should be avoided.[52]

By 'non-assimilability', Phelan was referring to racial and, concomitantly, social non-assimilability which arose from a perception that the Japanese were such a distinct racial group that no amount of acculturation could ever mask their foreignness.[53] However, 'non-assimilability' was refuted by the Inquiry Commission,[54] which explicitly pointed out that the argument that the Japanese were non-assimilable overlooked their remarkable ability to adopt and adapt to the Western civilisation in a short period.[55] Thus there was an inherent contradiction in the argument of exclusionists who, on the one hand, objected to Japanese settlement because of fear that 'a Jap was a Jap', and on the other hand, were alarmed by the rate of Americanization of Japanese immigrants, especially of the second generation.[56]

Although the anti-Japanese movement eased slightly during the First World War due to Japanese participation in the Allied war effort, it nonetheless remained high on the bilateral diplomatic agenda. In 1917, President Woodrow Wilson was reminded by his special advisor, Colonel House, that the Japanese ambassador had considered the treatment of its nationals in the United States as a major problem in Japanese–American relations.[57] About a year later, in July 1918, Ambassador Ishii Kikujirō intimated to Colonel House that Japan needed an outlet for its population to expand, to which the latter had readily expressed an agreement.[58] Although the Japanese government continued to show determination to improve the status of Japanese immigrants, there was still no apparent solution in sight by the end of the war.

As in the case of the British Dominions, the perceived threat from Japanese immigration in the United States was generally more symbolic than real, though more real than it was in the Dominions. It is clear that the Japanese Foreign Ministry had always been vigilant in taking immediate measures to alleviate practical problems encountered by the rise in the number of Japanese immigrants. As a result, Japanese immigration remained tightly controlled, and stayed well within the officially acceptable figures. Nevertheless, this did not prevent the rise of anti-Japanese sentiment in many of these places. The Japanese government felt continuously under pressure from the seemingly endless series of immigration restriction bills enacted everywhere in the British Dominions as well as in the United States. Possibly it was more successful in quelling the anti-Japanese sentiment in the former than in the latter, because the political lobby against Japanese immigration was much stronger in the latter.

IMMIGRATION AS 'DIPLOMACY OF SAVING FACE'

Having explained the historical importance of immigration for the Japanese Foreign Ministry, we must now ask why immigration was such an important diplomatic issue for the Foreign Ministry. It appears that the Foreign Ministry gave priority to resolving the 'immigration' issue for two reasons. First, it was concerned about the negative implications which anti-Japanese immigration practices would have symbolically on Japan's status as a great power. Second, evidence suggests that the majority of senior officials at the ministry felt it was urgent that a satisfactory solution be found to the problem of immigration, hence making this a bureaucratic priority. Thus, it is argued here that the Foreign Ministry officials expressed their vested bureaucratic interest in resolving the problem of immigration when they drafted the racial equality proposal at the Paris Peace Conference.

Japan's international reputation as a great power

It has been suggested that the Foreign Ministry considered the importance of resolving the problem of Japanese immigration as being largely symbolic. It seems that the primary concern of the ministry had been one of maintaining the international reputation of Japan. The concern that lower-class immigrants such as coolie labourers, not to mention pimps and prostitutes, would damage Japan's national prestige, can be witnessed in the report sent to Tokyo in 1888 by an official that '. . . the shameless activities of . . . undesirable Japanese will no doubt impair Japan's national honour and dignity'.[59] As a reflection of their diplomatic efforts, the Japanese government implicitly expected their immigrant nationals to be accorded the sort of treatment in foreign territories which was commensurate with the international prestige of Japan as a great power. In reality, the treatment of Japanese immigrants was considerably worse than that of many other European immigrants from other countries which, in the eyes of the Japanese, were less important than Japan in terms of international status.

What the Japanese government feared most was the symbolic implication of being singled out as the 'undesirable' immigrant nation. Hence, the perceived value attached to the issue of immigration by the Japanese Foreign Ministry was not practical in terms of wanting to improve the treatment of its nationals *per se*. In other words, the Ministry was primarily concerned with the implications that discriminatory treatments of its citizens by foreign governments would have on the status of Japan as a great power. According to one acute observer, 'It was entirely a matter of prestige', and: 'The Japanese had always cared less about the fact of exclusion than about the symbol of discrimination, the label of an inferior people'.[60] It must be borne in mind that Japan, as a rising non-white great power, was extremely sensitive about its newly-acquired international status. In 1915, Foreign Minister Katō remarked on the 1913 immigration crisis:

> What we regard very unpleasant about the Californian question . . .

> is the discrimination made against our people in distinction from some other nations. We would not mind disabilities if they were equally applicable to all nations. We are not vain enough to consider ourselves at the very forefront of enlightenment; we know that we still have much to learn from the West. But . . . we thought ourselves ahead of any other Asiatic people and as good as some of the European nations.[61]

Surprisingly, this attitude towards the issue of Japanese immigration had hardly changed since 1897, when one of the Japanese diplomats expressed a remarkably similar sentiment:

> The point which caused a painful feeling in Japan was not that the operation of the prohibition would be such as to exclude a certain number of Japanese from immigration to Australia but that Japan should be spoken of in formal documents, such as Colonial Acts, as if the Japanese were on the same level of morality and civilisation as Chinese and other less advanced populations of Asia.[62]

Evidently, the Japanese considered themselves more civilised than the other less advanced peoples against whom immigration restriction acts were normally applied. Therefore, the fact that the Japanese were being discriminated against was a loss of face not only to the West, but also to Asia, especially the humiliation of being lumped together with the Chinese and Indians when the Japanese were trying to stake out their position of leadership in Asia (*tōa no meishu*).

As Japan's fortunes rose as a great power, it became glaringly evident that there was an inherent contradiction in the treatment of Japan as a first-class nation (*ittō koku*) and of the Japanese as second-class citizens in the Anglo-Saxon territories. The Foreign Ministry was concerned because the discriminatory treatment of Japanese immigrants highlighted the gap which existed in the paradoxical reality of Japan's dual position internationally. That is, the reality of Japan as a great power did not at all tally with the reality of Japanese immigrants as targets of discrimination in some countries. This discrepancy was particularly painful for Japan. In this sense, the Foreign Ministry was particularly sensitive about anti-immigration legislation because it concerned the national pride of Japan.[63] All in all, the problem of anti-Japanese immigration legislation was a source of constant consternation for the Foreign Ministry, which was solely responsible for bringing about a satisfactory face-saving solution.

The bureaucratic priority of the Foreign Ministry

In the light of the above, the satisfactory long-term solution to the Japanese immigration problems in the Anglo-Saxon territories had, by 1919, become an important bureaucratic priority of the Foreign Ministry. There is ample contemporary evidence in support of this position. For instance, Makino Nobuaki, the chief negotiator on the racial equality proposal (whose views will be explored in greater detail in the following section), identified this issue as the most pressing priority for the ministry.[64] Vice Foreign Minister Shidehara attested that the 'race problem' was the root cause of anti-Japanese problems in the United States, and that the ministry had been trying to bring about a satisfactory solution to the problem whenever opportunities arose.[65] In fact, Shidehara went so far as to say that the government had intended 'to do something' about it at the peace conference. Ambassador Ishii in Washington believed that discriminatory treatment in immigration was one source of international conflict, and that the immigration problem was simply another form of racial problem.[66] Finally, Foreign Minister Uchida purportedly ascribed to the view that racial equality surfaced as a means of resolving the immigration problem, which he claimed, worsened after the Russo–Japanese War.[67] Consequently, the combined evidence from Shidehara, Ishii, Uchida and Makino underlines the Foreign Ministry's deeply rooted perception of the anti-Japanese immigration policies in the United States and the British Dominions as a major diplomatic problem for Japan.

In a more speculative realm, it is possible to conceive of many circumstantial considerations which could have affected the perceptions held by these senior officials, inducing them to arrive at this consensus over the immigration issue. One of the most obvious considerations is the bureaucratic prestige of the Foreign Ministry itself. The senior officials must have been embarrassed by their inability to resolve this problem, despite the persistent efforts made by them throughout the period 1910–20. Surely, it cannot be too harsh to suggest that the pride and competence of the ministry was at stake over the issue? As is shown below, their inability to have the racial equality proposal accepted at the peace conference did contribute to undermining their bureaucratic credibility.

Another obvious consideration is the vested interest of the Foreign Ministry in giving wholehearted support to the pro-Western foreign policy orientation of Prime Minister Hara. In 1917, under the last Terauchi government, the Japanese Foreign Ministry had been temporarily usurped of its position of primacy in foreign policy making by the establishment of the Diplomatic Advisory Council. In September 1918, the emergence of Prime Minister Hara signified a favourable change for the Foreign Ministry as Hara was a known supporter of pro-Western, internationalist foreign policy. Thus, the Paris Peace Conference provided the ideal occasion for 'the second coming' of the Foreign Ministry, and for it to reclaim its lost ground. Ironically, this renewed emphasis on a pro-Western attitude must have placed increased pressure on the ministry to succeed on the immigration front, because its inability to do so could undermine the very policy of international cooperation which it was trying to support. Bearing in mind that the pro-Western attitude tended to be in the minority in the rest of the nation, which remained instinctively pan-Asian, political opponents would be only too happy to claim that even the staunchly 'pro-Western' and 'internationalist' Foreign Ministry could not convince the Anglo-Saxon states to drop the offensive discriminatory practices. Hence, the cost of not resolving this issue satisfactorily was high, as the pan-Asianists and other opponents to the government's pro-Western policy would willingly accuse the ministry of weak-kneed diplomacy (*nanjaku gaikō*).[68]

Thus there was much at stake in terms of multiple 'faces' which Japan needed to save: one being the bureaucratic reputation of the Foreign Ministry domestically, another being Japan's image as a 'Western' great power, and yet another being Japan's image as leader of Asia. The so-called immigration problem was symbolically important because it signified the fact that Japan had not truly attained the great power status it purported to have had. The Foreign Ministry acutely felt the need to rectify this inconsistency. Therefore, it is fair to suggest that the Foreign Ministry did have a vested interest in making positive initiatives 'to do something' about this issue at the Paris Peace Conference.

The Foreign Ministry's agenda at Paris

Having established that Japanese immigration into the Anglo-Saxon territories had been one of the longest standing diplomatic problems for the Foreign Ministry, it appears that the ministry seized the opportunity to resolve the issue in the form of a racial equality proposal at the Paris Peace Conference. This crucial link between the bureaucratic interests of the ministry and the situation surrounding the drafting of the proposal in the League of Nations Commission at Paris has not been adequately explored hitherto. In doing this, it becomes evident that the racial equality proposal can be understood to have implied immigration principally because of the wording of the proposal, which embodied the bureaucratic interest of the Foreign Ministry.

Let us examine closely the moment of the birth of the racial equality proposal at Paris. As has been explained in Chapter 1, its beginnings at the peace conference can be traced back to an incident between the Japanese plenipotentiaries and President Wilson on 22 January 1919, which exposed how completely out of touch the Japanese government had been about the whole question of the League of Nations.[69] Until then, the Japanese government had incorrectly worked on the assumption that there was still the choice of not creating the League at the peace conference. This surprise revelation at Paris implied that the general position taken by the Diplomatic Advisory Council hitherto on this issue was obsolete and irrelevant.[70] As has already been noted above, the Hara government's original directive issued to the peace conference delegation in December 1918 did not at all specify the wording of the so-called racial equality proposal, let alone that it should resolve immigration problems. Instead, Makino and Chinda had to base their draft proposal on the only relevant part of the peace policy which read:

> Nevertheless, if a League of Nations is to be established, the Japanese Government cannot remain isolated outside the League and should there appear any tendency towards the establishment of a definite scheme [the League], the Delegates will so far as the circumstances allow make efforts to secure suitable guarantees against the disadvantages to Japan which would arise as aforesaid out of racial prejudice.

In the absence of detailed guidelines from Tokyo, it was inevitable that the wording of the racial equality proposal reflected the particular perspective of those who had an immediate input in drafting it in Paris.

In the light of the importance which the Foreign Ministry had given to resolving problems of Japanese immigration, it is not too difficult to understand how the unexplained enormous leap was made by Makino and Chinda from the above instruction, which was vague and unspecific, to the first proposal submitted to the League of Nations Commission at the peace conference on 13 February 1919:

> The equality of nations being a basic principle of the League of Nations, the High Contracting Parties agree to accord as soon as possible to all alien nationals of states, members of the League,

> equal and just treatment in every respect making no distinction, either in law or in fact, on account of their race or nationality.

It is curious that this metamorphosis has never been questioned before. The proposal cited above, to all intents and purposes, does sound like a proposal intended to effect a better treatment of Japanese immigrants in the member countries of the League. The most important point to be made here is that the above proposal reflected the immigration issue precisely because that was the desired intention of those who drafted it. This shows that both Colonel House and Foreign Secretary Arthur Balfour were under no illusion when the latter commented that the proposal was 'a formula on the subject of Immigration which would satisfy the Japanese', because that was, in fact, the underlying intention by Makino and Chinda when the subject was first broached at the peace conference.[71]

It was demonstrated above that, for historical reasons, the linkage between the racial equality proposal and immigration was strongly perceived by the Foreign Ministry. As Makino himself argued, one of the long-standing unresolved issues in Japanese diplomacy was the anti-Japanese immigration legislation enacted in the United States and the British Dominions.[72] Both Makino and Chinda, who were the principal negotiators of the racial equality proposal, had painful personal experiences of the row over the Californian Alien Land Law in 1913, Makino as foreign minister and Chinda as ambassador to Washington.[73] In retrospect, Makino must have had immigration in mind at the 2 December 1918 meeting of the Diplomatic Advisory Council, when he voiced concern that the race problem should be raised at the peace conference in order to force the Americans to reassess the problem of racial discrimination.[74] The problem was that he only implicitly referred to immigration through the use of the term 'race problem' which, of course, was not necessarily synonymous with immigration to everyone present. In any case, as the chief architect of the proposal at the peace conference, his perspective on the issue had important implications. There is enough evidence to suggest that, for Makino, the racial equality proposal, as it was initially drafted and negotiated, was meant to have the implicit objective of redressing the long-standing problem of anti-Japanese immigration policy in the United States.[75] Again, as stated above, Makino's perspective was widely supported in the Foreign Ministry by Uchida, Shidehara and Ishii. Therefore, it is fair to say that neither Makino nor the Foreign Ministry were driven by altruism to fight for universal racial equality or universal abolition of racial discrimination. Instead, they saw the government's racial equality demand as an opportunity to resolve the discriminatory treatment of Japanese immigrants in the Anglo-Saxon countries.[76] This is why the first two drafts of the proposal,[77] which were shown to the Americans on 4 February 1919, can be interpreted as suggesting immigration as the main issue.

In fact, the entire negotiations over the racial equality proposal at Paris can be understood from the perspective of Makino and Chinda, whose determination to resolve this problem reinforced the tenacity of their negotiating position. This explains why the Japanese first broached the subject with the Americans, who were considered to be the biggest stumbling block because of the problems of Japanese immigration in the United States.[78] This explains also the painstaking repeated attempts made by them to negotiate with the British Dominions, especially Australian Premier Hughes, who doubtless was equally determined not to let the Japanese get their way. In fact, the determination of Makino and Chinda to have their preferred formula accepted was such that they rejected the overture made by Hughes on 31 March 1919 to accept a formula which made a specific exemption of immigration.[79] By then, Tokyo deemed it crucial as a matter of 'saving face' to have some form of racial equality proposal accepted by the peace conference, rather than what the Foreign Ministry wanted which was to have a proposal which would resolve the specific problem of immigration.[80] In the end, the position of Makino and Chinda became untenable because of the increasing pressure placed on them both from the Anglo-Saxon powers and from Tokyo to make the proposal into a more universal, abstract one, thereby pushing it farther away from the original intention of resolving immigration problems. This division of view demonstrates that it was the bureaucratic vested interest of the Foreign Ministry which determined its initial preferred wording of the proposal, reflecting the immigration issue.

It is important to emphasise that this perspective, which equated racial equality with immigration, was not the official line taken by the government as a whole. Generally speaking, there was the problem of the lack of a clearly-defined notion within the Japanese government as to what the racial equality proposal entailed. Because of the great haste in which the Hara government had to formulate a comprehensive peace policy, the original instruction on the racial equality demand was never fully developed into a coherent strategy. Although it has been suggested that Makino and Chinda had an implicit agenda of resolving the anti-Japanese immigration problem, Tokyo never officially endorsed the idea, which implied that the proposal could only be negotiated implicitly as an immigration proposal. This was attested to by Foreign Minister Uchida, who made a mysterious remark that although the proposal was not officially linked to immigration, immigration was nevertheless discussed in the racial equality negotiations with the British and the Americans.[81] The fundamental problem of lack of consensus within the government, especially in the beginning, as to the precise meaning of the proposal, and the absence of strategy in attaining the objective at the conference made the Japanese negotiating position generally ineffective. In fact, Tokyo did not have any further input into the racial equality proposal after 8 December 1918 until 19 February 1919, when the report that the amendment was defeated on 13 February reached Tokyo.[82] Significantly, there was no discussion in the Diplomatic Advisory Council concerning the precise nature of the demand during the crucial formative period of late January and early February 1919, nor was there any record of a discussion of the proposal from the perspective of immigration in the council. Although it has been suggested that the lack of input made by the government in Tokyo was indicative of its indifference towards the proposal,[83] it seems that this had also to do with inefficiency in conducting diplomacy from a distance, as well as the general lack of preparedness on the issue of the League of Nations.

Needless to say, the emphasis on immigration in the original draft by Makino and Chinda was highly significant, as it left an indelible perception in the British Dominions and the United States that the Japanese proposal was genuinely about immigration. Hence, the explanation that the racial equality proposal was intended to resolve Japanese problems concerning the immigration issue is valid as far as Makino and the Foreign Ministry were concerned. Interestingly, the Foreign Ministry began to dissociate publicly the racial equality proposal from immigration halfway through the negotiations at Paris, when it became clear that its identification with immigration by the Anglo-Americans would result in the failure of the proposal. The most noteworthy attempt was made by Ambassador Ishii in his keynote speech to the Japan Society in New York, which was intended to dispel any fear that the Japanese were proposing a 'free immigration' proposal by stating categorically that the racial equality proposal had nothing to do with immigration. Sadly, this effort produced exactly the opposite effect of linking more closely the two separate issues of racial equality and immigration.[84]

The failure of the Japanese delegates to secure the racial equality proposal was attributed to the bureaucratic ineptitude of the Foreign Ministry, especially as the delegation was composed predominantly of Foreign Ministry officials.[85] During the peace conference, the Japanese plenipotentiaries were placed under enormous pressure to succeed on the racial equality proposal, as was pointed out in the previous chapter. The leader of the opposition stated to the meeting of the Kenseikai that 'it will be a serious diplomatic blunder' for the Foreign Ministry not to succeed in this demand.[86] Because of the fact that the plenipotentiaries were all intimately connected with the Foreign Ministry, the failure became a matter of ministerial reputation. Rumours circulated that there was to be 'a severe shake-up' of the Foreign Ministry as a consequence.[87] In retrospect, the criticism made by Nakano Seigō, who attended the peace conference as a journalist, was the most devastating; he expressed the opinion that it was a national crime to send a diligent old person like Makino, who was 'out of touch with the reality of national opinion', with so-called confidential documents consisting of bits of old newspaper clippings, to fight for Japan's national interests.[88] Nakano makes a valid point that the government and the Foreign Ministry were 'out of touch with the reality of national opinion' because, as was noted in the previous chapter, the pro-Western policy of the Hara government was not necessarily representative of national opinion.

As a summary, it can be said that the draft proposal submitted by Makino and Chinda did have the unmistakable influence of the immigration issue because the proposal reflected the bureaucratic priority felt by the Foreign Ministry to resolve this problem at the peace conference. However, it was shown that the conviction held by Makino and Chinda was representative of the minority of pro-Western liberals who included the Foreign Ministry officials and a group of supporters surrounding Prime Minister Hara. This meant that Tokyo lacked consensus on how to proceed with the negotiation of the proposal, which debilitated the bargaining power of Makino and Chinda in Paris.

CONCLUSIONS

This chapter has argued that although the 'immigration' explanation was important in understanding the motivations of the Japanese, this perspective was most strongly advocated by the bureaucratic interests of the Foreign Ministry. This distinction between the Foreign Ministry's view and those of other groups and individuals needs to be emphasised, as the bureaucratic priorities of the ministry did not necessarily reflect the views held in other parts of the government, nor public opinion. Essentially, the Foreign Ministry believed that it was an urgent priority to find a satisfactory solution to the discriminatory treatment of Japanese immigrants into the Anglo-Saxon territories. It was urgent because the discriminatory treatment of these immigrants was perceived by the ministry, as well as by the nation, to symbolise the inferior position of the Japanese with regard to the Western great powers. In other words, it denigrated the status of Japan from being one of the five great powers of the world, attending the Paris Peace Conference of 1919, to a third-rate 'coloured' nation. Hence its importance to Japan was almost entirely symbolic. In this sense, the proposal can be explained as essentially a 'diplomacy of saving face', or *memmoku gaikō*, for Japan as a great power. Therefore, the explanatory category of immigration, as a practical manifestation of Japan's insecurities of being a non-white great power, is very closely related to the explanatory category of great power status, to which we shall turn in the next chapter.

4 Japan's status as a great power

In this final chapter explaining Japanese motivations, we shall examine the applicability of the explanatory category of great power status. The argument put forward is as follows. As the only non-white great power of the time, Japan had insecurities regarding its status *vis-à-vis* the other great powers, which were all Western in origin. Although the source of this insecurity may not be immediately obvious, it derived largely from the cumulative result of Japan's historical experience of foreign relations with the Western powers since the late nineteenth century. Hence, in spite of the fact that the Western powers generally acknowledged Japan as one of the great powers, Japan felt that it was not treated equally by the other powers. The Japanese perceived that the difference between them and the Western great powers lay in the intangible aspect of their national characteristics, namely in their racial and cultural origins. In the light of this, the Japanese were especially sensitive about their status, not only in terms of how they perceived themselves but also of how others perceived them. Therefore, Japan sought to demand recognition of the racial equality of the Japanese to the other Western great powers. In doing so, they effectively challenged the *status quo* by making an important implicit claim that great power status should also explicitly include the racial equality of great powers.

In order to prove this argument, it is necessary to analyse Japan's historical experience as the only non-Western great power in the period leading up to 1919. The first part of this chapter examines Japan's rise to great power status and its associated challenges in the period preceding the First World War. In order to understand the domestic dimensions of Japan's great power status, the development of two main perspectives – *ajia shugi* (pan-Asian) and *datsu-A ron* (escape Asia) – in foreign policy debates, used extensively to explain or justify Japan's policy in East Asia, are addressed. Japan was historically sensitive about the racial aspect of its international identity, as can be seen in the prominence of *jinshuron* (racial discourse) in foreign policy debates.

The second part of the chapter consists of an analysis of Japan's policy in the First World War. It suggests that Japan became increasingly isolated, as a result of a number of wartime policies which antagonised both Britain and the United States. Moreover, the very wording of the Japanese government's directive on the peace policy in 1918 indicates that Japan had intended from the beginning to secure racial equality for itself *vis-à-vis* the Western great powers. Hence, the explanatory category of universal principle is not applicable to understanding the Japanese motivations, because Japan had never intended to demand the universal racial equality of all peoples. As the purpose of this chapter is to explain why the question of great power status was fundamental to understanding the proposal, only the relevant aspects of the main historical events will be discussed.

The definition of 'great power'

To many observers, Japan in 1919 seemed secure of its great power status, having ascended as one of the five great powers at the Paris Peace Conference. At Paris, Japan was ranked the fifth great power behind the United States, Britain, France and Italy.[1] It seems appropriate at this juncture, before going into the analysis, to provide a working definition of the term 'great power' as it is used in this work.

The most useful definition for our purposes is to be found in the work of Martin Wight and Hedley Bull on international society.[2] They attribute to great powers four characteristics which distinguish them from other powers. One of the foremost of these is military strength.[3] Martin Wight advocates the view that '[t]he self-revelation of a great power is completed by war',[4] and similarly, Hedley Bull claims that 'the members of this club are all in the front rank in terms of military strength'.[5] Historically, military power has been a prevalent factor due to its explicit nature, that is, it is one of the few components of a state which exists almost exclusively for external purposes. Hence, it becomes the most easily recognisable factor for other states. Secondly, great powers were described as having 'general interests'.[6] Incidentally, this characteristic was also used by the Paris Peace Conference in distinguishing great powers from lesser powers as 'powers with general interests' and 'powers with particular interests'.[7] Strictly speaking, it would have been more accurate to define Japan as a regional great power because its interests were geographically and strategically confined to East Asia, as opposed to the Western great powers whose interests were global; however, the term 'regional great power' did not exist at the time. The third criterion is recognition by others of having the status of great power.[8] Essentially, one cannot be a self-proclaimed great power since this means having a special status which can only be granted by others of the same standing, and thus invariably leads to the question of membership of a particular grouping within the society. Fourthly, there was the self-imposed role as a manager of the international system, deriving from a shared sense of responsibility and a need for cooperation among great powers to maintain order in the system.[9] This condition stresses the 'commonality of interests' among the great powers.

These were the criteria applied by the Western great powers to Japan, and to which Japan duly complied in order to become a great power. On the surface, Japan had diligently fulfilled the criteria in order to gain this much-coveted status. However, one must not forget that these criteria were originally set by and set for European powers, and had never been tested on great powers of non-Western origin. Therefore, it seems fair to say that Japan's acquired status as a great power was one which was essentially Western in its characteristic, and hence can plausibly be insufficient when applied to a non-Western state. In fact, the definition was predominantly based on the concept of power, and of the power hierarchy in international society. It assumed a basic notion of equality among the great powers which allowed them to operate as an elite group within international society. However, it did assume that all shared the common heritage of 'Western' civilisation in terms of cultural, religious and philosophical traditions, until Japan joined the ranks. It was not entirely unreasonable then that Japan should feel, once having attained that status, that something was lacking in its essential characteristics. To Japan's great frustration, great power equality based on the political and military criteria did not sufficiently guarantee absolute equality. More specifically, from Japan's perspective, the existing great power definition lacked the most fundamentally important aspect of the equality of great power status, that of racial equality. It can be stated that what Japan sought through the racial equality proposal was to obtain the equality of Japan to the other great powers on the basis of race, which was not explicit in the definition as it stood. In this sense the proposal was a highly significant one, although this may not have been immediately evident at the time; Japan, a new insider, was attempting to impose a new criterion, racial equality, on the hitherto Western-centric definition of great power.

JAPAN'S RISE AS THE NON-WHITE GREAT POWER BEFORE 1914

This section attempts to argue that Japan's rise to great power status in the period before the First World War was not without its share of internal and external contradictions. First, it explains briefly the contemporary debate on foreign relations which attempted to identify Japan as either a pro-Western (*datsu-A ron, ōbei kyōchō shugi*) or pan-Asian (*ajia shugi*) nation. This shows the problematic nature of Japan's identity as it was projected internationally. Second, we look at another distinctive aspect of the contemporary debate – the racial discourse (*jinshuron*) – which reveals the importance of racial identity in Japanese thinking. Lastly, we attempt to demonstrate through historical examples that Japan's status was periodically challenged by the Western great powers in the pre-1914 period.

The East–West debate in foreign policy

However consensual Japan might have appeared to the outside world, it was riven internally with contradictory intellectual forces, especially in the debate on Japan's foreign relations and, by extension, the question of its international status. It is necessary to introduce, albeit briefly, the two main perspectives which existed in the period in foreign policy debates. In the early days of post-Restoration Japan, there developed a tendency domestically to justify or to explain foreign policy in terms of one of two competing perspectives, namely *ajia shugi* (pan-Asian) and *datsu-A ron* (escape-Asia). Basically, *ajia shugi* saw Japan's place as being in Asia, and *datsu-A ron* saw it as being in the West. There were many subtle variations of both *ajia shugi* and *datsu-A ron*.[10]

Commonly, *ajia shugi* and *datsu-A ron* were used to explain the changing pattern of Japan's foreign policy debates which evolved so as to adjust to the changing political situation in East Asia. For instance, the development of the two perspectives can be lineally explained as follows.[11] In the early days of Meiji, *nisshin teikeiron* (Sino-Japanese coalition) flourished. Japan sought to align with China because it was perceived that their shared cultural background and a long bilateral, historical association made China the most natural ally of Japan, to protect jointly their national independence from the West. However, as China failed to modernise rapidly, Japan began to lose confidence in the former as its equal partner. A shift in attitudes then occurred, from one of mutual respect to one more critical of China's incapacity to fight against Western imperialism. Japan sought increasingly to reform China in order to help it become more modernised and Westernised like Japan, because this was perceived by the Japanese to be the only conceivable way of countering the Western threat. This is known as *shinkoku kaizōron* (reform China) or *ajia kaizōron* (reform Asia). Both *nisshin teikeiron* (Sino-Japanese coalition) and *shinkoku kaizōron* attempted to find a framework for cooperation with China against the West, albeit with different emphases. Nonetheless, *shinkoku kaizōron* was abandoned eventually when it was perceived that Japan was being disadvantaged by its association with backward countries like China and Korea, because the Western great powers would be likely to confuse Japan with them. It became imperative for Japan to escape from Asia (*datsu-A ron*) and join the West because it was already there in spirit, having modernised and Westernised. The 'escape-Asia' perspective has been attributed especially to a pre-eminent Meiji thinker, Fukuzawa Yukichi[12], who formalised the idea in his ground-breaking article, '*Datsu-A ron*' published in 1885.[13] This linear interpretation of the evolution of foreign policy debates points towards Japan's inevitable graduation from an Asian to a Western nation.

However, it has been said that too much reliance on the *ajia shugi* versus *datsu-A ron* axis as an explanation of Japanese foreign policy is problematic for a number of reasons. According to Banno Junji, it is historically inaccurate to take these two dominant perspectives on foreign policy at face value as schools of thought because they were essentially 'expressions' (*hyōgen*) of the 'understanding' (*ninshiki*) of 'reality' (*genjitsu*) held by those who were engaged in foreign policy debates.[14] Therefore, *ajia shugi* and *datsu-A ron* were not necessarily concrete reflections of the reality to which they referred. In analysing how some of the prominent Meiji thinkers and politicians used these two expressions, Banno concludes that they were used to explain the same policy or situation at different times depending on the degree of perceived tension in the Sino-Japanese relationship.[15] Fukuzawa Yukichi, mentioned in the preceding paragraph, provides an interesting example. Banno states that although it is generally understood that Fukuzawa used his famous '*Datsu-A ron*' (escape Asia) article in 1885 to promote a new direction in Japan's East Asia policy, due to Japan's disillusionment with the weakness of China, in reality it was a well-camouflaged justification of why Japan gave up temporarily its interest in Korea, having witnessed the impressive strength of Chinese forces which had successfully quashed the pro-Japanese uprising in Korea in 1884.[16] This challenges the established understanding that *datsu-A ron* was synonymous with *tairiku shinshutsuron* (continental expansion),[17] at least as far as Fukuzawa's precise usage of the term was concerned. Banno argues that in this particular instance, *datsu-A ron* actually indicated a heightened sense of apprehension about China and a corresponding decline in the desire to expand on the continent. The most important message in Banno's work is that *ajia shugi* and *datsu-A ron* should not be treated as schools of thought or ideology, because this would lead to misunderstanding and misrepresenting history. Basically, these two expressions catered to the need, felt by the Meiji leaders, to find justifications for Japan's newly found continental expansionist tendency, which the indigenous value system (*nihonteki kachikan*) had failed to provide.[18] Therefore, Fukuzawa and others sought to justify them either as a reaction against Western imperialism (*ajia shugi*) or as a positive response to Western imperialism (*datsu-A ron*) in East Asia.

There was a gradual shift in the thinking of those in the public (*minkan*) who continued to support the *ajia shugi* (pan-Asian) type of policy towards China after Japanese victory in the Sino–Japanese War of 1895. It has been suggested that the rise of a more nationalistic *ajia shugi* reflected public dissatisfaction with the government's overly pragmatic, and pro-Western, approach to foreign policy.[19] The supporters of *ajia shugi* increasingly demanded a more moralistic, sentimental basis for justifying the government's imperialist diplomacy, which would have an appeal on grounds other than the pursuit of national interests. There was a rise in the number of ultra-nationalist groups such as Genyōsha (Dark Ocean Association) and Kokuryūkai (Amur River Association) which demanded that Japan act as 'leader of Asia' (*iōa no meishu*). Konoe Atsumaro,[20] one of the influential figures in the pan-Asian movement who pushed for *shinkoku kaizōron* (reform China) through his Tōa dōbunkai (East Asia Common Culture Association), advocated the 'preservation of China' (*shina hozen*) from the Western powers. However, this slogan was a convenient cloak for hiding an increasingly more imperialistic ambition of controlling Manchuria, especially after the Russians occupied it in 1900.[21] In 1898, Konoe called for solidarity of the same race (*dōjinshu dōmeiron*) between the Japanese and Chinese to fight against the white race, on the grounds that East Asia would ultimately become a theatre for rivalry between the white and yellow races.[22] These right-wing supporters of *ajia shugi* attempted to justify Japan's continental expansion into Korea and Manchuria as its prerogative as 'leader of Asia'. Clearly, this shift in pan-Asianism reflected the changing balance of power in East Asia after 1895, as revealed by both Japan's victory over China in 1895 and the increasing threat from Russia.

The existence of these two competing intellectual and political currents indicates the complexity of dealing with the whole question of Japan's identity as it was projected internationally. As the perception of self-identity was obviously closely linked to the perception of its international status, the dilemma arose as to whether Japan should consider itself as a Western or an Asian great power. Even though the Japanese government might have played the 'Western' card internationally, it seems that there was no clear domestic mandate to underscore that position. In other words, there existed in the pre-1919 period a sizeable group within Japan which was in opposition to the general *datsu-A* (escape Asia) tendency of the government, and in favour of a more pan-Asian policy.

The rise of *jinshuron* in foreign policy debates

The rise of *jinshuron* (racial discourse) in mainstream Japanese foreign policy debates is an important and highly relevant aspect of this period. As will be seen, one of the fundamental reasons for the public uproar over the fate of the racial equality proposal at the Paris Peace Conference was precisely because it hit a raw nerve of a nation which was extraordinarily sensitive to issues related to race or, more precisely, the Japanese race. In order to understand *jinshuron*, it is necessary to distinguish between two types of arguments – *jinshuron* and *bummeiron* (discourse on civilisation) – which are sometimes conflated.[23]

It is commonly known that Japan's sensitivity to race could be traced back to the Sino–Japanese War, when Kaiser Wilhelm II first coined the phrase, the 'Yellow Peril'.[24] Evidently, the newly emergent imperialist Japan was perceived to be a threat to Western imperialism because Japan was culturally and religiously incompatible with the Western great powers.[25] In this sense, the Yellow Peril concept was both racial and cultural in connotation. For the Japanese, the concept had highlighted the 'foreign-ness' of Japan, culturally and religiously but most of all racially. This left a bitter after-taste, inflicting 'permanent damage', according to one Japanese diplomat, on the Japanese nation.[26] Henceforth, *kōkaron* (the Yellow Peril debate) as one variant of *jinshuron* gained regular usage in foreign policy debates. Although there had always been, to some extent, a racial element present in foreign policy debates, *jinshuron* became a high profile issue after 1895. It has been mentioned previously that Konoe Atsumaro advocated 'solidarity of the same race' (*dōjinshu dōmeiron*) in 1898 because of the prospect of racial rivalry between the white and yellow races.[27] Such a view, expressed also by Yamagata in 1899, was clearly a reflection of how menacing the white Russian threat had appeared to the Japanese in light of the Russian occupation of Dairen and Port Arthur.

Otherwise, in foreign policy debates, there was much concern over the rising world trend towards racial confrontation. Takahashi Sakue, a well-known international lawyer and member of the House of Peers, expressed such fears and recommended that Japan should coalesce with the Eastern race (i.e. the Chinese) in order to face this threat.[28] This was an alarmist response to the government's pro-Western attitude. It spelled out the dangers of the government's policy of joining the West against Japan's natural racial alliance with China, in that it effectively went against the growing world trend of confrontation between the Western and Eastern races. Solidarity with China was important because it was impossible for Japan to fight this racial conflict alone. Not only *kōkaron*, but also other ideas such as *jinshu sensō* (racial war) and *jinshu kyōsō* (racial rivalry) stayed henceforth in the public consciousness, and were used in mainstream public debates by the ultra-nationalistic wing of pan-Asian thinkers and groups, and also by mainstream politicians. The extent of public interest in *jinshuron* can be witnessed in a prominent pan-Asian intellectual journal, *Taiyō*, which dedicated a special issue to 'The Clash of the Yellow and White Peoples' in February 1908.

On the other hand, *jinshuron* is often confused with and conflated with *bummeiron* (discourse on civilisation). Commonly, *jinshuron* is regarded as an *ajia shugi* (pan-Asian) type of argument, whereas *bummeiron* represents a *datsu-A ron* (escape Asia) point of view. As we have seen, *jinshuron* emphasises the racial aspect of Japanese identity in opposition to the 'whiteness' of the West. *Bummeiron* argues the distinctness of the Japanese race on the basis not of race, but of civilisation and culture. Confusion sometimes arises because *bummeiron* supporters used racial issues to explain why Japanese civilisation was different from and superior to the rest of Asia, and how it effectively belonged to the West. Okuma Shigenobu[29] participated in the *jinshuron* debate by presenting a *bummeiron* argument in January 1904, when he spoke on the 'Yellow Peril' at his *alma mater*, Waseda University.[30] His point was that the 'Yellow Peril' was a result of 'national' (*minzokuteki*) misunderstandings, leading to increased tension based on jealousy and rivalry felt towards Japan by the Western states.[31] Okuma published a short volume in 1919 where he argued that racial antagonism was really a conflict of civilisations, and that Japan had shown through the years that it was a civilised nation (*bummei kokka*) worthy of belonging to the ranks of the Western civilised nations.[32] An interesting example of the confusion over *bummeiron* can be seen in the response of the non-Western world to Japan's victory over Russia in 1905. The war had important psychological implications for nationalist movements in Asia because the Japanese victory was a symbolic annihilation of the myth of the invincibility of white men.[33] This was ironic because while the colonised peoples saw the victory as an advancement of eastern civilisation, the Japanese themselves tended to perceive of their victory as a proof of their achieving the 'civilised' status of the West.[34] Hence, for the Japanese who supported the '*datsu-A nyūō*' (escape Asia, enter Europe) view, the war was a war of the two civilisations in which Japan had demonstrated its capacity to belong to Western civilisation by becoming a civilised nation (*bummei kokka*).[35] All in all, the prevalence of the *jinshuron* in domestic political debates underlines how important the idea of race was in contemporary Japanese thinking.[36]

Western challenges to Japan's great power status

It is commonly perceived that Japan's rise to great power status was a smooth and relatively unproblematic process. However, such a perception tends to represent predominantly the Western-centred definition, which assessed Japan's 'progress' according to the sort of criteria applied to Western great powers as defined above. Moreover, many Japanese tended to collude with this view because it presented the image of Japan as a 'super' nation, which had managed to accomplish the difficult process of modernisation as well as becoming a great power in a matter of the few decades since 1868. Needless to say, it seems equally important to cast a critical eye on the process because of the underlying tensions which often remained unexplained behind the façade of success. If one takes a closer look at the period between the Sino–Japanese War of 1895 and the First World War – the period of consolidation of Japan's international status – it is possible to discern at least three serious challenges posed by the West to Japan's newly acquired great power status. These challenges appeared in the form of the Triple Intervention of 1895, 'the Yellow Peril' as seen in the light of Japanese victory over Russia in 1905, and the Californian Alien Land Law of 1913.[37] In examining these challenges, it becomes evident that Japan's status was regularly 'tested' by the West, which invariably had the effect of undermining Japan's sense of confidence and security as a great power.

Let us begin with the Sino–Japanese War of 1895 and the subsequent Triple Intervention of 23 April 1895, which was arguably the first serious political and military challenge to Meiji Japan mounted by the West. Without a doubt, the Sino–Japanese War of 1895 was an epoch-making event in East Asia; it formally reversed the traditional balance of power which had existed between Japan and China, whereby Japan became the undisputed 'leader' of East Asia – the title hitherto traditionally conferred on China. This implied that the Western powers could no longer operate in the East Asian arena, especially with regard to the future of China, without taking Japan's interest into consideration. In terms of Japan's gains from the war, China acknowledged the 'independence' of Korea which meant that Japan now had *de facto* informal control over Korea.[38] This was obviously a great source of satisfaction for the Japanese, whose expansionist desire for Korea was finally realised, while at the same time it removed a long-standing source of tension in the Sino–Japanese relationship. The acquisition of Formosa was another factor which strengthened Japan's position relative to China. Japan was also promised the Liaotung Peninsula, but this failed to materialise due to the Triple Intervention of Russia, Germany and France in the immediate aftermath of the war.

The greatest impact of the Triple Intervention on Japan was undoubtedly psychological. The war had strengthened Japan's position *vis-à-vis* China in a number of ways, but it had also exposed Japan's isolated position internationally. Japan was publicly humiliated by being robbed of one of the fruits of victory in the face of a joint threat by the three European powers. This amounted to a complete 'loss of face' to China and Korea. According to the then Foreign Minister Mutsu, Japan failed to obtain assistance from Britain and the United States during the crisis because of its political isolation from the great powers in East Asia.[39] One could argue that Japan should have taken some appropriate diplomatic measure to prevent the intervention, especially as one Japanese official indicated that Japan did have some notion of the possibility of Russian, French and German action against Japan prior to the event.[40] However, this was all submerged under the anger over the perception that Japan had become the victim of 'bullying' by the West. Because the war was highly popular domestically and a source of jingoism and patriotism, the impact of the Triple Intervention was devastating.[41] As the nation expressed outrage at the Western behaviour, anti-foreign sentiment reached such a height that it could only be quelled by a special decree from the Meiji Emperor, declaring that 'under these circumstances we do not consider that the honour and dignity of the empire will be compromised by resorting to magnanimous measures and by taking into consideration the general situation of affairs'.[42]

Japan learned two painful lessons from this experience. First, it needed to build up its military rapidly in order to strengthen its standing among the Western great powers.[43] Second, it should never again be isolated internationally from other great powers.[44] Japan learned that it should not operate unilaterally in international relations, especially when its objectives threatened, or were perceived to threaten, the interests of other great powers. Henceforth, the government consciously tried to 'cooperate with the West' (*ōbei kyōchō*) and operate within the Western great power framework; that is, Western imperialism. It seemed at the time that this was the only alternative available, since Japan had symbolically turned its back on Asia by imposing the Treaty of Shimonoseki, a Western-style 'unequal' treaty, on China as well as having previously imposed a similar unequal treaty on Korea (the Treaty of Kangwha in 1876). The symbolic act against China was to be repeated when Japan, as one of the Western great powers, played a major part in quashing the Boxer Rebellion in 1900. In this sense, the Sino–Japanese War had symbolised Japan's 'escape' from Asia.

Seen in this light, the Anglo-Japanese Alliance of 1902 was one positive indirect outcome of the Triple Intervention. After the Sino–Japanese War, the Russian threat loomed increasingly large in East Asia.[45] The only way for Japan to counter this threat effectively was to form an alliance with another Western power as a counterbalance. Hence, Britain became the object of Japan's policy of 'cooperation with the West' (*ōbei kyōchō*), and the Anglo-Japanese Alliance was signed in 1902.[46] Its aim was to maintain the *status quo* in the Far East and to preserve the territorial integrity of China and Korea.[47] There was euphoria in Japan over the signing, because it not only relieved the 'inferiority complex' which the Japanese had been harbouring since the Triple Intervention but it also enhanced Japan's international prestige.[48] For Britain, the alliance was a pragmatic arrangement whereby ' . . . the burden of *Pax Britannica* . . . could be shared with another power'.[49] Japan, feeling secure in the thought that the alliance would protect it from international isolation, clashed with Russia in 1904–5.

In spite of the popular perception of the Russo–Japanese War of 1905 as a watershed in Japanese history, it produced unexpectedly negative consequences for Japan. First, there was intense anxiety within Japan that the victory would lead to a resurgence of the 'Yellow Peril' in the West. This led the government to take the exceptional preemptive action of sending two special public relations envoys to the United States and Europe respectively, from February 1904 to October 1905. Their objective was to disseminate Japan's side of the story by emphasising the self-defensive nature of the war, and denying the rise of 'the Yellow Peril' and any religious interpretation of the war as one of Christians versus heathens.[50] In other words, its mission was to prevent the alienation of Japan as a non-Christian nation from the white Christian West.[51] Such intense concern over the 'Yellow Peril' underlined Japan's deep sense of insecurity that if the West turned against Japan, it would be left isolated from both the West and East.[52]

Secondly, it is necessary to elaborate on the claim that the victory did not ease the sense of international isolation. The victory had established Japan's status as great power in East Asia, according to the Western definition of the term, by demonstrating militarily its capacity to confront and defeat a traditional European power, Russia.[53] The war had managed to secure for Japan its long held territorial ambitions of controlling Korea and the southern part of Manchuria. Needless to say, the victory had a qualitative impact in changing both Japan's self-perception and the Western powers' perception of Japan as a great power. Most significantly, Japan was now perceived as a credible threat to Western imperial interests in East Asia and the Pacific. There was also the feeling on the part of Japan that it had begun to be diplomatically isolated.[54] What was worrying was that this sense of insecurity was developing despite the fact that Japan was fully following a *datsu-A*, *ōbei kyōchō* (cooperation with the West) path in foreign policy.

There were a number of external reasons for Japan's uneasiness about its international position. First of all, Japan's position in East Asia had become generally more complicated due to the involvement of more powers in its security arrangements. For instance, the defeat of Russia was only a temporary respite: there was now pressure on Japan to protect the Liaotung Peninsula from both Russia and China, especially as the Chinese began to insist on claiming back the territory.[55] In order to safeguard its sphere of interest, the Japanese government negotiated the Russo–Japanese and Franco–Japanese agreements in 1907. Second, there emerged the problem of Japan's China policy, which became a source of increased tension in Japan's relations with the West, especially the United States. Essentially, Japan's imperialistic ambitions in China became increasingly more difficult for the Western powers to contain after the 1911 republican revolution in China, which created a temporary power vacuum on the continent.[56] For example, Yamagata Aritomo, who had shown a *datsu-A* inclination in his pronouncements after 1905, became increasingly pan-Asian in his views after the 1911 revolution, coinciding with the change in national outlook which increasingly demanded that Japan obtain Manchuria.[57]

This period was marked by the increasing prominence of *jinshuron* (racial discourse) as a feature of Japan's identity, and its relationship with the more chauvinistic version of *ajia shugi* (pan-Asian) perspective in foreign policy debates. In any case, the apparent success of Japan in the Russo–Japanese War was not without its problems, as Japan became marked as a real threat in the eyes of the Western great powers.

The case of the Californian Alien Land Law of 1913 has already been discussed in some detail in the previous chapter. It is sufficient here to state that it was one of the most serious challenges posed by the West to Japan in terms of undermining Japan's international status at the basic level of race. Although the problem of anti-Japanese sentiment in the Anglo-Saxon territories was widely prevalent,[58] this particular legislation of 1913 remains unique in that it inflicted inordinate humiliation on the Japanese government because it was, specifically targeted against Japanese immigrants. By 1913 Japan was to all intents and purposes, a great power. By focusing on the undesirability of Japanese immigrants, the Californian Alien Land Law, in spite of positing the economic argument that the Japanese immigrants posed an economic threat to the American way of life, had managed openly to segregate the Japanese on the basis of race.

As previously mentioned, the Japanese were most concerned about the symbolic implication of being discriminated, as 'inferior people'.[59] Makino Nobuaki, the chief Japanese negotiator on the racial equality proposal in 1919, said of the 1913 Californian Alien Land Law that it was particularly painful because it involved the physical characteristics of the Japanese people.[60] Basically, the Japanese government was humiliated because it was unable to convince the Americans that the Japanese were not a race inferior to white Americans. This failure was especially painful as the Japanese considered themselves to be a civilised nation belonging to the West. The Japanese immigration problem symbolised the fact that Japan's status as great power could not eradicate the Anglo-Saxon view of Japanese as undesirable immigrants.[61] It highlighted the gap between the way Japan saw itself and the way in which the West saw it. Domestically, it produced some bitter reactions, as some public figures such as Nakano Seigō saw the whole problem as originating from the feeling in the Anglo-Saxon territories that the Japanese were being 'cheeky' in achieving this 'Western' status despite having 'yellow faces' and belonging to an inferior race.[62] In any case, the psychological impact of the national humiliation experienced at the hands of the Americans over this incident was to have a lasting impact on Japanese thinking. It made the Japanese doubly aware of the seemingly unbridgeable racial gap between themselves and the other great powers.

What can be said generally about Japanese foreign policy from the early Meiji period to the outbreak of the First World War is that while the government was pursuing faithfully a pragmatic foreign policy based on imperialist ambitions of continental expansion, there was a reaction against the government's strongly *datsu-A* (escape Asia) bias in favour of a more *ajia shugi* (pan-Asian) orientated approach, which emphasised the importance of the traditional relationship with China. This was reflected in the *datsu-A ron* versus *ajia shugi* debate. Although Japan's position in East Asia was gradually being established through the Sino–Japanese and Russo–Japanese Wars, and the Anglo–Japanese Alliance of 1902, Japan always remained wary of being politically isolated from the Western powers. One of the side effects of this innate fear of international isolation was the popularisation of *jinshuron* (racial discourse) in foreign policy debates. *Jinshuron* was a defensive measure in which the Japanese attempted to find a niche based on racial affinity with China, in a world which was perceived to be becoming increasingly racially antagonistic towards Japan. In this context, the issue of race as expressed through the *jinshuron* debate became an important aspect of Japan's national identity. Moreover, it remains significant that the challenges which Japan had to confront from the West in the pre-1914 period, had ingrained in Japan the sense that its status among the great powers was not at all secure.

THE IMPACT OF THE FIRST WORLD WAR

This section continues the analysis of the explanatory category of great power status by looking at Japan's experience during the First World War. It is argued that Japan's sense of insecurity increased as a result of the deterioration of its relations with Britain and the United States. For Japan, participation in the First World War was 'the grace of Heaven',[63] because it allowed for an expansion of Japanese control in East Asia, stimulated the domestic economy and bolstered national confidence.[64] Not surprisingly, Japan's participation and its ambitious continental policy in China during the war were viewed with much suspicion by Britain and the United States. To illustrate the growing sense of alienation from the Anglo-Saxon West, we will examine briefly Britain's perceptions of Japan, Japan's China policy and the Siberian troop deployment issue of 1918. Lastly, we will discuss the impact that this sense of insecurity had on *jinshuron* (racial discourse) during the First World War.

Britain's changing perception of Japan as an alliance partner

Without a doubt, Britain was the most important Western great power for Japan from the signing of the Anglo–Japanese Alliance in 1902 until its termination in 1923. It was this alliance which saved Japan from international isolation throughout the difficult period of consolidation as a great power. Apart from the technical benefits, the alliance provided a regular official channel of communication with Japan, a country still barely known by the West. In this sense, the alliance was an important means of understanding Japan, and similarly for Japan, it was a means of understanding Britain and the West in general. Hence, whatever problems existed between the two countries, it was this alliance that bound them together and that bound Japan closer to the politics of Western imperialism in East Asia. It was generally true that the deterioration of the relationship with Britain was a considerable source of concern for Japan.

Why did the relationship deteriorate substantially during the First World War? There are many reasons for this. One of Britain's first problems with Japan was the way in which the latter had grabbed the opportunity to enter the war. Japan declared war on Germany on 23 August 1914 on the basis of its obligations under its alliance with Britain.[65] It sent troops to Shantung, capturing Tsingtao by November, and followed this by the capture of the German colonies in the Pacific, north of the equator.[66] The problem was that Japan delivered an ultimatum to Germany without first consulting Britain, even though this was done in response to Britain's request for Japanese protection of British vessels in the Pacific.[67] Needless to say, the swiftness of the actions and the readiness of the Japanese government to take advantage of the situation in East Asia made Britain suspicious of Japan.[68]

Another issue which caused ill will was Japan's alleged reluctance to assist the European war effort. Japan's limited conception of war aims meant that Japanese military assistance did not extend readily beyond East Asia and, when it did, it came on the basis of a *quid pro quo* which the British resented.[69] The British requests for naval assistance in the Mediterranean and the Baltic Sea in September and November 1914, and for military assistance on the Western Front, were all refused. However, Britain succeeded in obtaining Japanese naval assistance in February 1916 in the Indian Ocean and the Straits of Malacca, in exchange for adding Australia and New Zealand to the 1911 Treaty of Commerce and Navigation and removing restrictions on Japanese doctors practising in the Straits Settlements; and in January 1917 for enlarged general naval cooperation, in exchange for British support for

Japan's claims to Shantung and the Pacific islands north of the equator, which was confirmed eventually in the secret agreement of 1917.[70] Notwithstanding the view that Japan made a sizeable contribution to the war effort and was unfairly criticised,[71] there seems to have existed the view among contemporaries that Japan gained more than it gave in the war. Paradoxically, the Japanese felt that their assistance was not being fully appreciated by the British.[72]

Not surprisingly, the British Foreign Office did not have friendly sentiments towards Japan. First of all, the fact that both the British ambassador to Tokyo, Sir Conyngham Greene, and his counterpart in Peking, Sir John Jordan, were unsympathetic to the Japanese implied that much of the information and diplomatic analysis coming in from these postings tended to project Japan in an unfavourable light. There are many examples of Greene's critical comments about the Japanese, of which the following, written in 1915, is an example:

> The Japanese are, however, ambitious, conceited, and to use Baron Kato's own epithet, arrogant. They are bent on making themselves the masters on this side of the Pacific, and they have their eyes fixed on the *post bellum* settlement.[73]

The most devastating proof of the deep-rooted distrust of Japan in the Foreign Office can be seen in the description of the Japanese in its *Paris Peace Conference Handbook on Japan*:

> The pride of the race in its achievements is, like its loyalty and patriotism, exaggerated. The astonishing progress the country has made in the last fifty years, and the victories gained over China and Russia, have to some extent turned the heads of the Japanese, and made them think themselves superior to Western nations, and look down with contempt upon other peoples of the East. They do not perceive their own lack of creative talent; they are apt to forget that in this second borrowing from abroad the things taken from the West were material rather than moral, which was not, to the same extent, the case in the first instance, when China was the model; and they are inclined to overlook the enormous advantage which Japan possessed in the adoption of reforms which were based on Western models. At no cost to herself, without expenditure of time or thought, labour or money, she plucked the fruit of generations of toil in Europe and America. She levied toll on all the world. Profiting at once by the improvements made in the course of centuries in every field of human energy, she began her career of

> constructive progress at the point which other countries had then reached, and continued her advance in line with them. Such considerations do not occur to the Japanese mind.[74]

It was fortunate for Japan, in spite of the generally negative feeling towards Japan in the Foreign Office, that the successive Foreign Secretaries of the period, namely Lord Grey and Arthur Balfour, recognised the importance of maintaining the alliance.[75] Balfour famously stated that a paper alliance was crucially important where there was no natural alliance, and that he 'never imagined that the Alliance rested on anything beyond narrow self-interest'.[76]

While the Japanese were feeling alienated from Britain, the British were also sensing that the Japanese were losing confidence in the former's ability to persevere to victory. This was aggravated by Japan's willingness to keep the option open for a possible rapprochement with Germany, especially during the Terauchi cabinet.[77] Moreover, the incident over the Zimmermann telegram only helped to deepen the sense that Japan was not acting as a loyal ally.[78] Accordingly, Balfour was reputedly concerned enough about the deterioration of Anglo–Japanese relations in 1917 that he was seriously considering the possibility of a defensive treaty with the United States, in which Britain would come to the rescue of the US if it were attacked by Japan but would remain neutral if the United States were to attack Japan.[79] In a sense, the British War Cabinet's decision to send Prince Arthur of Connaught on a goodwill mission to Japan in 1918 was a desperate attempt to dispel increasing anti-British sentiment in Japan.[80]

Conflicting policies towards China

Generally speaking, the American perception of Japan was negatively influenced by the conflicting policies each country adopted towards China. The primacy of China in American Far Eastern policy clashed with Japan's China policy. Historically, China had always been Japan's principal preoccupation in foreign policy. However, the United States had carved out for itself a different role in China, part of which was to act as China's moral tutor by encouraging its fledgling democratic nationalist movement and shielding it from the grabbing hands of the other great powers.[81] Evidently, the Americans considered a new democratic nationalist China as a more compatible future partner for them in the Pacific than Japan. They were generally critical of Japan's interventionist policy, for instance, the supposed prevention of China from entering the war until August 1917 in order to protect Japan's captured rights in Shantung.[82] Notwithstanding the difficulty in assessing the balance of the American position, between moralistic aspirations in foreign policy such as defending China and more practical vested interests in areas like trade,[83] there was an unmistakable underlying tone of morality in the American policy in China.[84] This contrasted with an overtly expansionist policy pursued by Japan. Thus, there was a fundamental incompatibility in their respective China policies which exacerbated their mutual distrust.

The notification of the Twenty-One Demands on 18 January 1915 was the most controversial example of Japan's imperialist ambitions in China.[85] It included the notorious Group Five of Demands, which was designed to bring China halfway under Japan's control by stipulating the appointment of influential Japanese as political, financial and military advisers to the Chinese government. In fact, the Demands were so overtly imperialistic that Yamagata did not agree to the final form until after the controversial Group Five was deleted.[86] Interestingly, the public was, on the whole, very supportive of the Demands. Even the leading liberal intellectual Yoshino Sakuzō considered that 'it was necessary for Japan's survival' because the 'preservation of China' (*shina hozen*) was essential to Japan's national independence.[87] Indeed, only a very small minority strongly condemned the government's manoeuvre as being opportunistic.[88]

On the whole, both the Americans and the British responded negatively to the Twenty-One Demands. Although neither power took any direct action against the Japanese over this issue, there seems little doubt that their sense of distrust of Japan had hardened as a result. The Americans strongly condemned the Demands because they were a blatant attempt by the Japanese not only to control China but, indirectly, to quash Chinese nationalism. Not only did this turn the tide of Chinese nationalism into an anti-Japanese movement, but the devastating long-term foreign policy implication was to make an enemy out of the United States.[89] Interestingly, in spite of the moral indignation which the Americans expressed at the effrontery of the Japanese government over the Demands, the American government stopped short of taking any punitive measures against the Japanese.[90] It seems that the failure of the United States to respond with anything other than verbal condemnation revealed a division within the administration on how to handle Japan, as well as the realisation that Japan should be treated with caution and could not be punished at whim.[91] This shows that although the underlying American sentiment could be broadly categorised as anti-Japanese, the reality of the American perception of Japan was not so simplistic. In reality, the Americans were concerned about the deterioration of the relationship, as they remained wary of what Japan might do if the United States supported China and whether there was a risk of endangering Japanese–American relations.[92] This led the United States to sign the Ishii–Lansing Agreement of November 1917 which, however innocuous, had the effect of placating domestic opinion in the respective countries.[93]

Although the British had acted with more restraint than the Americans, they had been snubbed nevertheless by Foreign Minister Katō who failed to consult them before the Demands were imposed.[94] The Japanese insisted that they had made the claims based on the conversation which took place between Katō who was then the Japanese ambassador in London, and Foreign Secretary Grey on 9 August 1914, when Grey reportedly said that Britain would not object to Japan's continued possession of the captured territories after the war, should Japan declare war on Germany.[95] The incident had the effect that Britain lost confidence in its ally, Japan, whose action was often compared to that of Germany in invading Belgium, and in Katō, who had hitherto been the personification of Anglo–Japanese friendship.[96] Most of all, the British residents in China vented their anger towards Japan through the English-language press such as the *Tientsin Times* and *North China Herald*. In contrast, *The Times* in London was surprisingly circumspect, withholding publication of the Twenty-One Demands when they became available from a Chinese source, and more generally, withholding anti-Japanese articles during the war.[97]

The intensity of opposition from Britain and the United States did concern many in the Japanese government, including Yamagata who supported a Russo–Japanese agreement as an additional check against the United States in China.[98] Having recognised the mistake made in the Twenty-One Demands, the Japanese government had to rectify the immense damage the incident had inflicted on Japan's international reputation. It is important to stress here that the British were placed in the increasingly difficult position of having to balance Japan on the one hand and the United States on the other, especially as American–Japanese relations deteriorated substantially after the Twenty-One Demands.[99]

The problem of Siberian troop deployment

The sense of distrust felt by the United States towards Japan was most clearly manifested in the Siberian troop deployment. In January 1918 the British government, on behalf of the Allied forces, asked the

Japanese government to send troops to Vladivostok to protect armaments. The debate over Japanese involvement in the Siberian troop deployment placed Britain in a difficult position. The British government, not wanting to alienate the United States, whose perceived importance for Britain's future was increasing every day, had to show restraint despite its natural inclination to support Japanese intervention, and had tried to strike a balance between Japan and the United States.[100] In January 1918, Balfour expressed concern to Lord Milner about the American distrust of Japan in asking for Japanese troop assistance in Siberia:

> In your letter, you seem to assume that the main obstacle to giving Japan a free hand is British suspicion; but I think that you will find that the U.S.A. are much more suspicious than we are. When I was in America, I found that the State Department took a profoundly gloomy view of Japanese policy. I did what I could to combat suspicions which seemed to me, on the evidence, somewhat excessive; and the subsequent Japanese mission may have done more. Nevertheless, I think that you will find that Washington (which must clearly be consulted before Japan is invited by the Allies to take solitary action) would be very hostile to the scheme . . . .[101]

The basic position of the Americans was to oppose repeatedly the French and British requests for Japanese troops to be deployed in Siberia, on the basis that Japanese forces might permanently occupy Siberia.[102] Officially, the Americans were opposed for two reasons: first, the Russians might misunderstand Allied intentions in sending Japanese troops, and consequently, this might push them towards Germany;[103] and second, this deployment would arouse strong opposition in the United States because of the strength of anti-Japanese sentiment.[104] The first reason does not seem convincing because it was clear from the British and French that military expediency overshadowed whatever political sensibilities the Russians might have had. It seems that the crux of the American opposition lay in the second reason which meant unofficially, according to House, that:

> The race question in particular will be sharply emphasised and attempts made to show that we are using a yellow race to destroy a white one. This may result in the American Press and public getting out of hand and adopting an attitude which will be resented in Japan and cause serious friction between the two peoples.[105]

In fact, even the British were taken aback by the American distrust of the 'yellow race'. As Sir William Wiseman, who knew House intimately, wrote in March 1918:

> The American hatred of all yellow races is thinly, if at all, disguised; the very thought of the yellows being brought in to redress the balance of the whites is repugnant to them, especially when it may involve the consequent loss of commercial advantages in the new and lucrative market of East Russia.[106]

Thus the American government was principally concerned about the effects of Japanese troop deployment on American domestic opinion, which was unsympathetic towards Japan at this point. What the Siberian troop issue demonstrated was the depth of distrust felt by the Americans towards the Japanese, which derived not only from military–strategic reasons but also from the underlying racial tension.

In Japan, this incident[107] had the effect of dividing the Terauchi cabinet into two camps, a minority led by Foreign Minister Motono,[108] Army Minister Tanaka and Privy Councillor Itō Miyoji, who supported the intervention, and the majority who opposed it, including Genrō Yamagata, Prime Minister Terauchi, leader of the opposition Hara Kei and Ambassador Uchida in Russia. Hara in particular, backed by Makino Nobuaki, was concerned about maintaining good relations with the United States. Hara argued that since 'the future of Japan depends on the close relationship with the United States, the only reason why there would be any problem between Japan and the United States would be because of their suspicion of Japan's aggressive ambitions'.[109] Apart from Motono, who was a keen supporter of the Tsarist regime, the military was clearly interested in having a pretext for going into Siberia.

International tension was eased by the American decision in late June 1918 to consider joint troop deployment with Japan as a response to Allied requests to aid the Czech forces against the Soviets. The Japanese troop deployment began on 12 August 1918, followed by the Americans on the 19th, and a general command office was established in Vladivostok under a Japanese official. As soon as the deployment started, there was a debate in Japan as to whether to restrict the number of troops around Vladivostok to 7,000 as had been agreed, or to go for a general deployment with the aim of establishing a pro-Japanese government near Lake Baikal which would have extended the geographical area of deployment from East Siberia (east of Baikal) to North Manchuria. Again the government split, with the military advocating a general deployment while Hara and Makino strongly criticised such a move. In the end, the government decided on a general deployment but with modifications to accommodate the criticisms. Consequently, the Japanese deployed 73,000 troops in three provinces of Russia.[110] It may be added that the Siberian troop deployment demonstrated not only the extent of American distrust of Japan, the changing allegiance of Britain from Japan to the United States as a future partner in the Pacific, but also the emergence of Hara, who was convinced that Japan should not be isolated internationally any more than it had already been and should pursue a more *ōbei kyōchō* (pro-Western, internationalist) approach in foreign policy.

Jinshuron in the First World War

Finally, *jinshuron* (racial discourse) resurfaced as a prominent feature in foreign policy debates during the war. In a sense, the rise and fall of *jinshuron* was an interesting barometer as to how secure or insecure the Japanese felt about their great power status. There appeared to be a corresponding rise in the frequency of *jinshuron* types of argument in domestic debates when Japan felt insecure about its relations with the other great powers. Under such circumstances, *jinshuron* claimed that Japan should prepare itself for a racial war (*jinshu sensō*) between the white and yellow races. *Jinshuron* offered an alternative at times when tension ran high in Japan's relations with the West, in that it assumed that China would always gladly join forces with Japan against the West out of racial kinship. It was necessary for Japan to rely on the most basic common denominator between it and China in order to obtain China's sympathy, because in reality Japan had betrayed China by behaving ruthlessly towards the latter as an imperialist power. Hence, the desire to foster *jinshuron* was partly a response to the fear that Japan was falling into an abyss of international isolation by recklessly following an imperialist policy (i.e. a *datsu-A* policy) in China, regardless of the international implications of these actions.[111]

Consider some of the examples of *jinshuron* propounded by some intellectuals during the war. There were a few who argued against a pan-Asian view of *jinshuron* by emphasising that the so-called racial antagonism was essentially an inter-group problem, because all races originate from the same source.[112] However, the views of the majority were alarmist in nature. In 1914, a prominent newspaper, *Asahi shimbun*, argued that the Western powers were suspicious of Japan partly because of their racial prejudice, since they tended to regard Japan as militarily strong but racially inferior.[113] Therefore, Japan should help to 'preserve China' in order to confront jointly the Western imperialists. In 1916, Tokutomi Sohō, a right-wing intellectual, warned of the existence of a white clique (*hakubatsu*) and argued that Japan had a mission to re-establish racial equilibrium by eliminating this white clique from Asia, and realise an Asian Monroe Doctrine.[114] In part, this was a pan-Asian backlash against the pre-eminence of *bummeiron*, which promoted the unity of Eastern and Western civilisations. It has been argued that Tokutomi's *hakubatsu* was a result of 'double-victim mentality' (*nijū no higaisha ishiki*) founded on the strength of distrust towards the West, and compounded by the feeling that the West was fundamentally suspicious of Japan.[115] In 1918, another writer warned that Japan should prevent the 'terrifying prospect of a racial war' by assisting the less developed countries in the East in order to achieve equality between the white and coloured races.[116]

It was not only the intellectuals who engaged in the *jinshuron* debate; mainstream politicians like Yamagata Aritomo did so as well. Interestingly, Yamagata had been previously critical of those pan-Asians who interpreted Japan's victory over Russia in 1905 as a victory of the yellow race against the white, arguing that the war had demonstrated that the yellow race could defeat the white race only with Western technology. Evidently, this argument underlined his *datsu-A ron* (escape Asia) perspective by including Japan as part of the West.[117] However, he seemingly reversed his position at the outbreak of the First World War by calling for a racial alliance between Japan and China in order to prevent the white race from uniting against the yellow race. It has been suggested that a detailed analysis of the circumstances surrounding this statement show that Yamagata had another agenda in calling for a racial alliance with China, which was to persuade the Chinese to become more pro-Japan in order to facilitate Japan's China policy at the time.[118] Notwithstanding his hidden agenda, the fact that Yamagata felt inclined to express such views demonstrates the complicated nature of the Japanese perception that the issue of race was intertwined with the political uncertainty surrounding Japan's position in China.

In the end, it can be said that *jinshuron* was a double-edged sword, an attempt to both justify Japan's expansion into China and rationalise Japan's insecurity *vis-à-vis* the Western powers. *Jinshuron* highlighted Japan's sense of racial alienation from the West, by appealing to the *ajia shugi* (pan-Asian) instincts of finding a rationale in Japan's relationship with China. Ultimately, it seems that the most important role played by *jinshuron* in foreign policy debates was to underpin Japan's sense of insecurity as non-white great power.

It has been illustrated thus far that, although it is generally accepted that Japan had attained great power status as early as 1905, this status was by no means secure. Japan faced a number of serious challenges from the Western powers throughout the period from the Sino–Japanese War of 1895 until the Paris Peace Conference of 1919. Surprisingly, even victory in the Russo–Japanese War of 1905 proved to be a mixed blessing, in that it led to unwanted suspicion and distrust of Japan in the West. Japan's experience in this period revealed the Western great powers' underlying distrust of Japan. Conversely, this heightened the sense in Japan that the West could not be trusted fully, as revealed in the continued prominence of pan-Asian thinking. Therefore, Japan continued to believe throughout this period that it was being isolated internationally (*kokusaiteki koritsu*), or more precisely, isolated by the West. The deterioration of Japan's relations with its ally, Britain, and with the United States during the First World War only confirmed and exacerbated this feeling. Seen in this context, the Japanese might have been led to believe that the only reason for the seemingly endless series of 'problems' which Japan encountered in its relations with other great powers was the racial difference between them.

The racial equality proposal and great power status

In the light of the above analysis, the explanatory category of great power status plays a crucial role in explaining the Japanese motivations for submitting the racial equality proposal. Japan felt insecure of its status as the only non-white great power before the First World War, because of a number of challenges previously posed by the Western great powers which had exposed the vulnerability of its newly acquired status. The situation deteriorated substantially during the First World War because of mutual suspicions which alienated Japan from Britain and the United States. Seen from this perspective, the racial equality proposal was Japan's expression of uncertainty and insecurity concerning the future international order and its position within it, in the light of its 'minority' status as the only non-white great power. It became essential for the Japanese to demand racial equality with the white great powers, as the racial difference became the last impediment to securing 'absolute' equality of status with the West. In so doing, the Japanese attempted, intentionally or unintentionally, to link the two separate issues of race and great power status in order to ensure the safety of their future status in the international organisation. As far as the Japanese were concerned, racial equality was an important, and indeed indivisible, part of great power equality.

Let us examine the above claim with reference to the origin of the racial equality proposal in the context of the Japanese government's peace policy at the peace conference. It seems that the key to explaining the claim made above can be found in the two particular clauses cited below from 'The Government's view on President Wilson's Fourteen Points' which formed part of the government's peace directive:[119]

> The Japanese Government is in favour of the ultimate aim of the League: but, in view of the racial prejudices which have not yet entirely been banished from among the nations, there is a danger, depending upon the nature of the measures taken to secure the objects of the League, that *its establishment will in practice produce results gravely detrimental to Japan.*
>
> Nevertheless, if a League of Nations is to be established . . . the Delegates will so far as the circumstances allow make efforts to secure suitable guarantees against the disadvantages to Japan which would arise as aforesaid out of racial prejudice.

It is evident that the original intention of the racial equality proposal was defensive in nature, a vague response made by the government to the uncertainty of Japan's future in the new international organisation proposed in the Wilsonian Fourteen Points. There can be no doubt that the government's racial equality demand, if it can be called as such, was a highly particularistic and nationalistic expression of Japan's desire to prevent itself and its nationals as a state from suffering the humiliation of racial prejudice in the League of Nations. It underlined the anticipatory fear that the new international order would continue to be disadvantageous to Japan, as was the existing one. It suggests strongly, therefore, that one of the motivations for the proposal was pre-emptory, to secure Japan's great power status in the League of Nations at its inception.

Moreover, the fact that Japan attended the peace conference as one of five principal powers implies that, in the strictest sense, the proposal was aimed at securing racial equality of Japan, not so much with the lesser powers, but with the Western great powers. Specifically, the Japanese government was apprehensive about being racially discriminated against by the Anglo-Saxon powers in the new international organisation because of its unpleasant historical experience, ranging from anti-Japanese immigration legislation to strong distrust of Japan during the First World War. Hence, the proposal had almost entirely to do with Japan's underlying sense of insecurity *vis-à-vis* Britain and the United States.

The fact that the aim of the proposal was so specifically geared towards securing Japan's own position indicates that it could not have been intended to have the altruistic objective of seeking universal racial equality. The passage quoted above makes it absolutely clear that the principal concern expressed is that the creation of the League might be 'gravely detrimental to Japan' because of racial prejudice. It does not remotely hint that the Japanese government might be concerned with the League having detrimental effects more widely due to racial prejudice. The racial equality proposal was thus never intended to have any universal implications. Accordingly, the argument put forward and assumed by some scholars, that the racial equality proposal was intended to promote a universal principle of racial equality, does not hold true.[120] This is attested by the Japanese government's sceptical attitude towards the universality of racial equality as a realisable and realistic objective.[121] For instance, Foreign Minister Uchida told the opposition party in June 1919 that the racial equality proposal was not intended to demand universal racial equality of all coloured peoples, but only for members of the League of Nations.[122]

The government's reluctance to be associated with the universal principle was revealed by its uneasiness with being associated with political movements such as the Pan African Congress.[123] Japan did not appreciate being perceived of as a champion of the coloured race because such a perception would conflict with its underlying desire to be more closely integrated with the West. For instance, Makino told a Liberian supporter of the racial equality proposal to go and see Clemenceau directly about racial equality.[124] As the government was not asking for universal racial equality, it saw no hypocrisy in its own position of demanding this proposal on the one hand, while continuing to discriminate against Koreans and Chinese on the other. The ironic twist came when the highly specific proposal geared towards ensuring a fair treatment of Japanese people became internationally known at the peace conference as a 'racial equality' proposal. Although the government was much alarmed by the universalist interpretation attached to its 'nationalistic' proposal, it was impossible to disclaim it, if Japan were ever to have any credibility as a non-white great power. So Japan had to silently endure being hailed in some quarters as 'the leader of the coloured and oppressed peoples'.

It has been pointed out that when Japan submitted this 'racial equality' proposal, it did not realise how challenging this was to the international order in the long run.[125] In a sense, Japan was, unknowingly and unwittingly, mounting a serious challenge to the existing norms which operated in the Western-dominated international system, by claiming that racial equality should be recognised as a fundamental principle of equality of status. The significance of this claim is undeniable, as evidenced by the incorporation of this principle as a fundamental principle of international justice in the United Nations Charter in 1945. Nonetheless, it must be stressed that although the proposal is significant in retrospect, in understanding the evolution of the racial equality principle as an important element of the international order, it would be a misrepresentation to claim that the Japanese government understood its universal implications when it was put forward. The fact was that the Japanese not only lacked the awareness that they were initiating such an important change in the existing international order, which incorporated elements of injustice, but they were themselves also guilty of a racially discriminatory attitude towards Chinese and Koreans.[126]

It was thus a considerable misconception on the part of those at the Paris Peace Conference that the Japanese proposal came to be known as the racial equality proposal, since its universalist label did not at all reflect its original intention. The most important point, which has been already been mentioned above, is that the original demand formulated by the Japanese government referred specifically to Japanese nationals. Therefore, whatever term is used to describe the proposal, it must always be understood within this context. The semantic origins of how the racial equality proposal came to be known as such are interesting. The Japanese term used by the Foreign Ministry was *jinshu sabetsu teppai*, which literally means 'abolition of racial discrimination'. Most of the official and unofficial debates used this term rather than 'racial equality' (*jinshu byōdō*). Similarly, the Japanese emphasised 'equal treatment' (*byōdō taigū*)[127] and 'discriminatory treatment' (*sabetsu taigū*), which shifts the focus of the principle substantively from the more open abstract notion of 'equality'. Hence, the Japanese government could, at least, not be blamed for attempting to name its particularistic interpretation of 'racial equality' by the universalist term.

CONCLUSIONS

As preliminary conclusions to the Japanese motivations, it can be stated that the racial equality proposal was a complicated issue which revealed the complex nature of Japan's status as the only non-white great power at the time. It has been argued that a combination of three explanations best explains why Japan needed to raise the issue at Paris. First, there were the political considerations of Prime Minister Hara, who believed strongly in the importance of Japan's being part of the West through joining the League, but who nevertheless had to convince the sceptics domestically about his vision of Japan's role internationally. Second, although the 'immigration' explanation has hitherto been treated as the most significant factor in much of the existing literature on the racial equality proposal, it has been demonstrated that this view was held predominantly by the Foreign Ministry, which had a vested bureaucratic interest in resolving the issue. Although the importance of the 'immigration' factor was chiefly symbolic for the Foreign Ministry, it nonetheless revealed the practical aspect of the deeper general problem which Japan had in coming to terms with its great power status. Therefore the explanatory category of great power status is the most significant. It explains the proposal in terms of Japan's need, as the only non-white great power, to secure racial equality in relation to the Western great powers. All in all, the racial equality proposal remains unique in the history of Japanese foreign policy as the only instance in which the less tangible aspects of Japan's predicament, as the only great power of Asian origin, were externalised in a concrete form.

5 Australia overwhelms the British Empire delegation

Having examined the Japanese motivations for raising the racial equality proposal at the Paris Peace Conference, we shall now analyse the response of the British Empire delegation. British opposition to the proposal was highly significant in setting the tone for the entire racial equality negotiation. The official reason for opposing the racial equality proposal was that it was 'encroaching upon the sovereignty of States members of the League' by interfering with domestic affairs of member states.[1] In order to understand the British opposition, two questions need to be addressed. First, why did the British let the Dominions take the lead in the negotiations? Second, why did Australia go to the extent that it did to oppose the Japanese proposal when other Dominions were willing to compromise? Answers to these questions indicate that the British government's perception of the proposal, as demanding unrestricted immigration of Japanese and other non-white immigrants, left the proposal in the hands of the Dominions and ultimately gave the power to Australia to reject it. Furthermore, analysis of the Australian opposition reveals that the racial equality proposal was vehemently rejected by Prime Minister Hughes for two main reasons. First, it was perceived to be a threat to the 'White Australia' policy, which was an integral and indivisible aspect of Australian domestic politics historically. Second, Hughes was manipulative in that his fight against the Japanese proposal at Paris was used as a political instrument to win votes in anticipation of the imminent Australian general elections.

Ultimately, the British accepted that the racial equality proposal might be sacrificed for the sake of imperial unity, especially as they did not perceive it as one of the more important issues at stake at Paris. All in all, the British opposition to the proposal can be best understood in terms of the explanatory categories of immigration and domestic politics.

RACIAL EQUALITY AS UNIVERSAL PRINCIPLE

To begin, let us examine whether the British ever seriously considered the possibility that the Japanese proposal was a demand of principle of universal racial equality. The British, on the whole, did not perceive the racial equality proposal as a demand of universal principle. As has been mentioned above, the initial motivation of the Japanese in submitting the proposal was nationalistically orientated, and sought to obtain guarantees of racial equality for Japanese nationals. Gradually, the proposal evolved to become more universal in its connotation because many changes were made in order to make it acceptable to the Dominions. It is interesting that the British government nonetheless never discussed the racial equality proposal as an issue of universal principle. This seems even more curious when, contrary to popular assumption, the racial equality principle would not have spelt an end to Britain's expanse of many non-white colonies.

First of all, let us elaborate on the claim that racial equality as a universal principle would not have caused problems theoretically for the British government. The British Empire professed to the imperial principle of equality of subjects as a basis for maintaining imperial unity of all subjects. Accordingly, racial equality as a principle was not problematic but, in fact, compatible with the British imperial government's fundamental principle of equality of imperial subjects:

> It would have been difficult for the United Kingdom delegates, in view of the established policy throughout the Empire under Imperial administration, to dissent from this clause, but the interests of the Dominions were, of course, paramount . . . [2]

In practice, the British government found the imperial principle difficult and arbitrary to implement, as there was an internal tension caused by the Dominions' practice of racially discriminatory immigration policies against other imperial subjects, especially Indian immigrants. Moreover, though the imperial principle was not strictly racialist in connotation, the implication was that some races – that is, the Anglo-Saxons – were innately more 'civilised' and 'democratic' because of their capacity of creating a superior political institutional framework in the form of parliamentary self-rule.[3] Hypothetically, even if racial equality were to raise problems by awakening the racial awareness of the non-white colonised peoples, the Imperial government could still fall back on its safe and unshakeable political principle of self-government as the most crucial defining factor to justify why some colonies (i.e. the self-governing Dominions) were more equal than others. Therefore, as the imperial principle of racial equality was nearly foolproof, the Japanese proposal certainly could not have been perceived by the Imperial government as posing a fundamental threat to British colonialism.

In the light of the above, the question that remains unanswered is why the British government did not discuss the racial equality proposal as a demand of universal principle. It seems that this could be explained as a general reflection of the British empirical tradition. There was an ingrained suspicion or uneasiness in Britain with 'ideas' which did not seem to have immediate practical implications. Cecil summarised succinctly the British attitude:

> . . . it is curious how all the foreigners perpetually harp on principle and right and other abstractions, whereas the Americans and still more the British are only considering what will give the best chance to the League of working properly.[4]

What Cecil found difficult to appreciate was the importance of discussing principles which did not have any direct practical relevance. Cecil, being an ardent advocate of the League, could understand the Americans preaching principles such as self-determination, democracy and open diplomacy, because they were all necessary elements to the practical framework of establishing an international organisation. In fact, an interesting contrast can be seen in the fundamentally different attitude towards 'principles' in Britain and France in the racial equality debate in the League of Nations Commission on 11 April. On the one hand, Cecil's rejection of the Japanese proposal underlined the British empirical thinking when he stated, 'One of two things must be true: either the points which the Japanese Delegation proposed to add to the Preamble were vague and ineffective, or else they were of practical significance.'[5] On the other hand, the French representative, Léon Bourgeois, exclaimed his support because 'it was impossible to vote for the rejection of an amendment which embodied an indisputable principle of justice'.[6]

Another interesting example of this, Balfour's reaction to Colonel House in early February 1919 when they were discussing the Japanese proposal, is worth quoting again in part:

> He [i.e. House] then showed me his last formula, which began with a recitation (quoted from the American Constitution) of the Eighteenth Century doctrine, that 'all men were born equal'.

> Colonel H's view was that such a preamble, however little it squared with American practice, would appeal to American sentiment, and would make the rest of the formula more acceptable to American public opinion. He did not give me a copy of it, but, like all its predecessors, it seemed to me to suffer from the defect of indicating a sympathy on the part of the League of Nations with the principle of equal and unrestricted Immigration laws, which it was not the present intention of either the United States or the British Dominions to carry into practical effect.[7]

This text is interesting because Balfour did not seem to register the implication of what House was saying, which was that the Americans would be more favourable of supporting the principle if it were to echo the sort of principles which were outlined in the American Constitution. Balfour's response was very pragmatic, since it did not occur to him that the proposal should ever be considered in a similar vein as the principles in the American Constitution because it was unquestionably related to immigration. Therefore, both Balfour and Cecil do not seem to have considered the Japanese proposal as a demand of universal principle of racial equality, in spite of the fact that racial equality was theoretically compatible with the imperial policy of equality of all subjects. No doubt, the British empirical tradition in foreign policy generally tended to rule out the possibilities of Britain being sympathetic to proposals which were not practically orientated.

However, it still does not explain fully why the British neglected to consider the proposal as demanding universal principle, because they could have at least debated it internally on the merits of such an interpretation. Quite possibly, the British did not consider it to be an important principle of international justice at the time. Apparently, the pejorative idea of racism as such was not really existent before the interwar period because Anglo-Saxon society was so deeply imbued with what we would consider today to be racist values.[8] For instance, it was universally recognised that there was some sort of scientific basis in believing in the differing capabilities of men. Accordingly, it would not have been too difficult to dismiss the principle as insignificant and not practicable in the contemporary intellectual climate.

All in all, the British were determined to interpret the Japanese proposal as pertaining to immigration, which precluded the possibility of seeing the proposal in any other light. This factor, in conjunction with the British understanding of the tradition of Japanese foreign policy as being primarily imperialistic and national interest orientated, could have made it more difficult for the British government to accept the idea that Japan was intending to demand a universal principle of racial equality. Indeed, the British were correct in assuming this as the Japanese were not contemplating universal principle when they first submitted the proposal in February 1919.

THE RACIAL EQUALITY PROPOSAL AS AN IMMIGRATION PROPOSAL

The racial equality proposal was a highly contentious issue for the Dominions precisely because it was perceived to be a demand for unrestricted immigration of non-whites into their territories. What this meant was that within British–Dominion relations, immigration belonged exclusively to the sphere of the Dominions; and, it was a highly politicised issue. It is necessary to understand the political importance of immigration in British–Dominion relations in order to appreciate the role which immigration played in the domestic politics of the respective Dominions, especially Australia.

It is important to stress the psychological preparedness of the British government for an immigration proposal to emanate from the Japanese at the peace conference. This fixation meant that the British were convinced that the racial equality proposal was nothing other than the immigration proposal which they had been expecting. London had received many signals from Ambassador Greene in Tokyo that the Japanese government might table some sort of proposal to redress their immigration problems:

> It is therefore unnecessary to do more here than to express my personal impression that the claim which has been put forward most prominently in the papers, possibly by a *mot d'ordre* from High Places, and the one which appears to have the deepest national interest for Japan, is that of the abolition of discrimination against her people in certain countries, and the acceptance of the doctrine of the equality of all races of no matter what colour. A disposition is shown to regard such acceptance as the touchstone of the sincerity of Western advocacy of a League of [N]ations.[9]

By January 1919, both the Foreign and Colonial Offices were privy to a highly confidential telegraph which set out the details of Japanese peace terms to be negotiated at Paris.[10] Although the British government were never entirely confident of its authenticity, they made the following comment on the section regarding the racial equality clause:

> The Japanese want to shelve the League of Nations, if it tends to perpetuate racial discrimination; but, if this cannot be done will try to secure guarantees against disadvantages arising out of race prejudice. Thus the question of discrimination against Asiatics in British Dominions may come up.[11]

London knew how sensitive the Dominion governments were on the question of immigration and decided against informing them of the content of the telegraph. In contrast to the preparedness of the Foreign and Colonial Offices, the Dominions were not informed from London of the possibility that such a proposal might be raised until they reached Paris.

Without a doubt, the Dominions' participation in the First World War and their subsequent attendance at the Paris Peace Conference marked a significant step forward in the evolution of British–Dominion relations. The most difficult aspect of this relationship was the degree of autonomy which the Dominions should have within the British Empire.[12] This is a highly complex issue, which is not within the scope of this study.[13] However, it is necessary to emphasise that the British government could no longer ignore the voice of the Dominions because of their decisive contributions to the British war effort.[14] For instance, out of the whole male populations, 19.35 per cent of New Zealanders, 13.48 per cent of Canadians, 13.43 per cent of Australians and 11.12 per cent of South Africans served in the war. The Indian contribution was numerically larger than all Dominions combined, totalling one million men and over £146 million. Consequently, the Dominions felt it their right to be involved more fully in British war policy and to have a say in the peace settlement. The breakthrough for the Dominions came with the question of their participation in the Paris Peace Conference. In signing the peace treaties, the British Empire delegation had sub-headings of Dominions which were signed by each Dominion representative, and Britain signed on behalf of all the Empire.[15] This allowed the Dominions to ratify the treaty in their respective parliaments before the final ratification was given by the King. It is not too difficult to imagine the expectation which the Dominions must have had of their 'potential' role at the Peace Conference, in the light of the last minute arrangement made by the British government regarding their representation. It will be seen that the racial equality proposal was the area where the Dominions, and especially Australia, were able to exercise their independence from the British government, and who, earlier on, had resigned themselves to take the back seat in the negotiations.

It had long been the policy of the British government to separate immigration from imperial defence and foreign policy. Britain had always been concerned about the negative impact which the discriminatory immigration policies of the Dominions would have on its relations with Japan. The Dominions considered that Japanese immigrants, along with the Chinese and Indians, destabilised the white settler societies economically and racially. For Britain, the maintenance of cordial relations with Japan became even more urgent after the signing of the Anglo-Japanese Alliance in 1902. Delegating responsibilities for immigration to the Dominions allowed for two things: on the one hand, it enabled Britain to detach itself from possible embarrassment caused by the discriminatory policies enacted by the Dominions towards Japan; on the other, it gave the Dominions the much desired sphere of autonomy to exercise 'independence' *vis-à-vis* the Mother Country.

Before 1890, the Dominions had been unable to devise an effective formula which excluded Asian immigration without impinging on imperial interests. However, the breakthrough came with the introduction of the 'Natal formula', which appeared to meet satisfactorily the concerns of the British government. The 'Natal formula' was an important and ingenious method which originated in South Africa in 1897, and was later adopted by the Australasian colonies to overcome imperial sensitivity.[16] Its central tenet was the application of non-racial criteria for discriminating against immigrants. Essentially, it entailed the use of a language test on would-be immigrants who were excluded if they failed to pass the test:

> Any person who when asked to do so by an officer fails to write out at diction and sign in the presence of the officer a passage of fifty words in length in a European language dictated by the officer.[17]

This was an ingenious device which served the implicit objective of excluding Asian immigrants without directly referring to their racial origins, and was adopted by South Africa, Australia and New Zealand. It was markedly different from the immigration policy practised in Canada, which was based on a quota system and tended to be more racially based, excluding 'any specified class of immigrants' or 'immigrants belonging to any race deemed unsuitable to the climate or requirements of Canada'.[18] The Colonial Office, which had been wary of offending Japan, could now be assured that the British government would not be singled out for racially discriminatory immigration legislation practised by the Dominions. For the time being, the British government were appeased by the 'Natal formula' and reduced their pressure on the Dominions.[19]

Throughout the decade 1910–20, the Foreign Office's official line of treating immigration as a Dominion issue became firmly entrenched. As mentioned, the British government declined Japanese naval assistance in January 1915 when it was revealed that a *quid pro quo* offered by the French and Russians to the Japanese was the solution to the racial problems in the British colonies:

> The third condition [the solution to racial problems] was one on which I could not say anything without consulting the Secretary of State for the Colonies and the Cabinet, and about which, even so, we could not say anything without consulting the Self-Governing Dominions. This would, in any case, take a long time, and there would be difficulties with regard to it. It was a matter in which the Self-Governing Dominions had hitherto made their own arrangements. Canada, for instance, had made her own special arrangement with Japan.[20]

The Foreign Office's anxiety prior to the peace conference that the Dominion governments should not find out about the possibility of the Japanese government bringing up 'the question of discrimination against the Japanese in America, Canada and Australia . . . at the Conference as arising out of the proposal for a League of Nations'[21] reveals how concerned Whitehall was about the Dominions negatively influencing the general position of the British government.[22] By the time of the Paris Peace Conference, the Dominions had practised at least two decades of independent immigration policies with little intervention from the British government. And as such, it was inevitable that the Dominions would guard jealously the one issue which was of crucial importance and of direct relevance to them at Paris.

In the light of the above, it can be said that the British government had neither the desire nor the will to intervene in the racial equality negotiation once the Japanese proposal was publicly acknowledged as an immigration proposal. As far as the British government was concerned, the Japanese proposal was not an issue of 'high politics', and, as a result, could be sacrificed for the sake of maintaining imperial unity. In fact, the British were frank about the primary role of the Dominions in these matters.[23] As previously mentioned, Cecil remained uninvolved despite repeated requests from Makino and Chinda to intervene to smooth out the Dominion opposition, and insisted throughout that it was a Dominion issue, eventually concluding that 'the question was essentially an Australian one'.[24] Hence, it becomes crucial to analyse why Australia remained resolutely opposed to the Japanese proposal even after the other Dominions came round to agreeing to it. We shall discover that the Japanese posed a twofold perceived threat to Australia – on the one hand, security, and on the other, political. However, these two types of perceived threat tended to merge into one in Australian domestic politics under the banner of 'White Australia'.

THE 'WHITE AUSTRALIA' POLICY AND AUSTRALIAN DOMESTIC POLITICS

What was the significance of the 'White Australia' policy in Australian domestic politics? The policy was singularly important to the Australians because, historically, they perceived it as being the mainstay of Australian life. In fact, there was an inseparable link established between the policy itself and Billy Hughes, whose longstanding commitment to it had become the hallmark of the Labour Party's political platform until 1916, when the party had split over the conscription crisis.[25] This connection should not be underestimated in the light of the centrality of Hughes's role in defeating the racial equality proposal at Paris. Hypothetically, it is highly plausible that had the leader of Australia been someone other than Hughes and who felt less personally committed to the policy, then it is likely that Australia would have acquiesced to the Japanese proposal. As it was, Hughes stood adamantly opposed to it because the perceived political benefit from opposition was much greater than the perceived cost of agreement. Hence, the fight against the racial equality proposal was portrayed in Australia as a fight to defend the 'White Australia' policy. More importantly, it was perceived by many as a *sine qua non* to Australia's national survival.

Without a doubt, Billy Hughes played the central role when he initially proposed the policy as part of his personal political platform in the early days of his political career. Hughes's political career ran parallel to the rise of the Labour Party, which was formed in 1891 as an exclusively working-class party.[26] The Australian Labour Party emerged, not as a result of any ideological conviction, but as a response to the practical need to reform the existing conditions of Australian workers.[27] It was nationalistic in orientation, being hostile to imperial federation, 'imported' governor-generals, overseas borrowings and the bestowal of imperial honours while, at the same time, strongly advocating a policy of protection.[28] In the early years, Labour parliamentarians were obliged to vote according to the majority of their respective caucuses (i.e. the trade unions) and not according to any federal Labour Party platform. On 24 January 1900, the founding conference of the Federal Labour Party was convened in Sydney, followed by the opening of the federal Parliament in Melbourne on 9 May, to which Hughes was elected as a member for West Sydney (New South Wales).[29] On 1 January 1901, Australia became a federation under the name of the Commonwealth of Australia.

The official birth of the 'White Australia' policy in 1901 was the result of the high degree of anti-Asian sentiment which existed in the country in the latter part of the nineteenth century. In the traditional Labour strongholds of Queensland and New South Wales, the idea of Asian exclusion was deeply rooted.[30] Apparently, Hughes's identification with the policy went back to January 1896 when his policy platform was adopted by the Australasian Federation of Labour as its official platform. It included as one of the seven commandments, 'the future exclusion from residence and citizenship within the federal territory of undesirable alien races'.[31] From then on, the official platform of the Federal Labour Party had two parts: first, the need to maintain the 'racial purity' of Australians, and second, collective ownership of monopolies. This twofold platform was readopted in 1915 and 1927.[32] Therefore, it is not an exaggeration to say that Hughes was, to a large extent, the embodiment of the values of the Labour Party. As is shown below, the 'White Australia' policy became an extremely important political weapon for the party, partly because of its ability to conjure up mass emotions. Hughes was one of its earliest proponents, as he stated in March 1901:

> Our chief plank is, of course, a vote Australia. There's no compromise about that. The industrious coloured brother has to go – and remain away![33]

The centrality of the 'White Australia' policy in Australian national politics meant that it was mercilessly politicised by the Labour Party for many years, as depicted in the party slogan, 'Special role of the Labour Party as the guardian of the ports'.[34]

Why was it so crucial for Australia to maintain 'White Australia'? At the bottom line, it was a means to confront Australia's hypothetical 'enemies'. In other words, the 'White Australia' policy was a symbolic manifestation of Australia's attempt to fight against all sorts of external threat, be it economic, racial, political or military. In order to understand the deeply rooted sense of 'threat' which seems to have existed collectively in Australia, it is important to emphasise the geographical location of Australia. There is no doubt that Australia felt very isolated from the rest of the 'white' world save New Zealand, as the last bastion of 'civilisation' in the South Pacific.[35] Canada did not feel the same degree of external threat from Japan because of its proximity to both the United States and to Britain; similarly, South Africa did not have a 'Japan' on its doorstep. As will become evident below, the sense of threat felt by the Australians evolved over time in response to the changing international environment.

Undoubtedly, the initial impetus to creating the 'White Australia' policy came from the sense of economic and racial threat which derived from the influx of cheap Asian labourers. These were seen to destabilise economic conditions by lowering the standard of living.[36] The Japanese were particularly disliked because of the threat of educated immigrants taking over the economy:

> . . . it is the educated Japanese that we fear . . . .There is no conceivable method by which the Japanese, if they once got a fair hold in competition with our own people, could be coped with. There is no social legislation by which we could sufficiently handicap them.[37]

However, this economic threat was coupled with the fundamental desire for the racial homogeneity of Australian society, which these non-white immigrants were threatening. As Hughes pointed out:

> The ideal of a 'White Australia', and one peopled in the main by men and women of British stock, reflects the traditions and achievements of our race. Racial purity pays in the long run. [In] Australia a certain percentage of the people of some European countries can be absorbed into our community, but we cannot assimilate these coloured peoples; their ways are not ours. The racial and economic barriers between us and them are insuperable. We cannot marry their women nor they ours without producing a race of half-castes at which both races would spit contempt.[38]

It is evident from the above that, in spite of protestations to the contrary by Australian leaders, there was a strong racist undertone in the policy. The racial superiority felt by the whites was fragile because it was undermined by the fear of the non-white race 'contaminating' the white settler society. Therefore, the sense of economic and racial threat felt in this period came from the presence of Asian immigrants in general, although the Japanese were beginning to attract special attention.

However, the turning point in the Australian sense of threat from the Japanese immigrants seems to have occurred with the Japanese victory in the Russo–Japanese War of 1905.[39] After this time, Japan became a real political and military threat for Australia and this somewhat overshadowed the perceived economic and racial threats. The theme of 'Japanese invasion southward' became common currency in Australian politics.[40] Hughes was convinced that Australia was the most vulnerable part of the British Empire, should British naval power decline.[41] For instance, the Labour Party's foreign policy was based on the view:

> . . . Australia, an outpost of European civilisation in an alien and hostile environment, can be secured against the coloured hordes only by alliance with and reliance upon a major power.[42]

This is why Australia's defence policy had always been to rely on a *pax Britannica* or, failing that, a *pax Americana*. Australia wanted to get Britain to underwrite the creation and maintenance of a *cordon sanitaire* which would effectively establish Australia's very own 'Monroe Doctrine' in the South Pacific.[43] In the Pacific, only Japan, in the discriminated category of immigrant countries, had any capability to reverse the white immigration policies, either militarily or diplomatically.[44] Needless to say, Australia's sense of vulnerability was heightened because of its perception that Britain was not responding sympathetically enough to Australia's regional defence needs in the light of greater threat emanating from Japan.[45]

There are numerous pieces of evidence which suggest that the security threat from Japan was very real for Billy Hughes in particular. Hughes was predisposed to be suspicious of Japan because of his Labour background. On the occasion of the renewal of the Anglo-Japanese Alliance in 1911, Australia expressed concern over the implications of Japan's wanting most-favoured-nation treatment for its immigrants.[46] In the end, however, Hughes came to realise the utmost importance of maintaining the alliance for Australian security interests, as a way of containing Japan in the Pacific. It is worth noting that Australia's fear of Japan was not totally unwarranted, since a systematic survey of imperial defence needs of British Dominions, conducted by the Admiralty in 1909–11 in the Pacific, concluded that, apart from Japan, there was no threat of external attack.[47] This conclusion was reinforced by the Jellicoe Report on Naval Defence in mid-1919.[48] In addition, Japanese military activities in the Pacific during the First World War naturally heightened this fear. In fact, Hughes felt threatened enough to ask Lloyd George for British protection from the Japanese naval fleet in the Pacific in October 1919.[49] Australia's position was again highlighted in 1920–1 during the imperial crisis over the renewal of the alliance.[50] Australia would not support termination unless the United States gave explicit guarantees to protect Australia against Japan. Evidently, then, Hughes felt acutely this sense of security threat from the Japanese, which coloured his general attitude towards Japan in the period.

It is significant that the 'White Australia' policy was used as a domestic political instrument by all parties to win voters in the highly controversial national referenda in 1916–17 over conscription.[51] Hughes strongly believed that Australia should give total support to the Allied war effort, through the introduction of conscription. However, this was not the view shared by the Cabinet nor the nation as a whole. When the first national referendum was held in October 1916, the pro-conscription group, which included Hughes, was defeated. The political crisis which resulted from this referendum led to the split of the Labour Party and the formation of a new coalition government under Billy Hughes as prime minister and Sir Joseph Cook, the leader of Liberals, as deputy prime minister. Hence, the first Nationalist government emerged. Hughes, who remained undaunted by this defeat, attempted another referendum in February 1917, only to be defeated for the second time.

During the conscription crisis, both the government and the opposition were guilty of politicising the fear of Japan as a means of defending 'White Australia'. Confidentially, Hughes gave the reasons for conscription to both Houses of Parliament as follows:

> Japan would challenge White Australia policy after the war, that Australia would then need the help of the rest of the Empire, and that if she wished to be sure of getting it she must now throw her full strength into the war in Europe.[52]

To make matters worse, counter-rumours were circulated by those who opposed Hughes and his policy, to the effect that conscription was a cloak to allow the breakdown of the 'White Australia' policy by allowing many Asian labourers into Australia, caused by the shortage of white labourers who would be conscripted.[53] In reality, the problem was serious enough for the Japanese Consul in Sydney to lodge an official complaint that the pro-conscriptionists were arguing that conscription was necessary to defend 'White Australia' against future Japanese challenges, while the anti-conscriptionists were arguing against it on the grounds that 'White Australia' must be maintained by keeping Australians in their jobs, instead of sending them off as troops only to be replaced by Japanese immigrants.[54] This debate illustrates three points: first, how central the 'White Australia' policy was to domestic politics; second, how deeply committed Hughes felt towards the policy; and third, how politicised was the fear of Japan. It should be remembered that all this took place during the war, in which Japan was an ally of the British Empire.

Therefore, Hughes was not far from telling the truth when he wrote in his memoir of the Paris Peace Conference that:

> The 'White Australia' policy . . . is an integral part of the national life of the Australian people, and although the subject of much hostile criticism, the geographical, racial and economic circumstances of the Commonwealth amply justify it. Australia, by her attitude towards Eastern peoples, does not arrogantly assert her superiority over other races: it is dictated by the instinct of self-preservation. The 'White Australia' policy is a gesture of defence, not of defiance. We do not regard Asiatics as inferiors, but as different from ourselves, believing that the ideals, traditions, and standards of living in the East are so incompatible with our own that we could never live with them as fellow-citizens.[55]

Over the years, the crux of the 'White Australia' policy had apparently shifted from emphasising the racial and economic undesirability of non-white immigrants to underlining the urgent need for defence and self-preservation. It seems that this was a realistic reflection of the changing perception of the threat felt by Australia of Japan, whose international status was rising rapidly.

THE POLITICAL SIGNIFICANCE OF THE RACIAL EQUALITY PROPOSAL FOR HUGHES

It does not, then, come as any surprise that Billy Hughes was overly anxious and excited about the racial equality proposal at the Paris Peace Conference. In the light of what has been said so far, it is clear that the 'White Australia' policy was an all-encompassing Australian national policy with multifarious implications. Thus, Hughes's opposition to the racial equality proposal must be understood in the context of his general approach to Australia's national interests at the Peace Conference. As we shall see, Hughes needed to capitalise on his success in Paris for the sake of his own political survival back home.

Australia, led by Hughes, fought for three aims at the peace conference: reparations, the acquisition of New Guinea and the rejection of the racial equality proposal. It would not be an understatement to say that Hughes was the personification of Australia as far as the rest of the conference was concerned, and that his personality played a decisive role in the way in which Australia played its part. One Australian newspaper depicted Hughes as follows:

> Mr Hughes aroused considerable ill feeling by his needless assertion that he did not mean to be muzzled when Australian affairs were under discussion. It would take a bold man to muzzle so fiery a political terrier.[56]

Hughes claimed that he was demanding Australia's right to New Guinea and the rejection of the racial equality proposal for the sake of defending the doctrine of 'White Australia'.

Hughes first entered the limelight at the peace conference over the issue of former German colonies in the Pacific. He had long been concerned about the future control of these colonies, which was the key to the stability of the region and the military security of Australia, by preventing the southward expansion of Japan. In November 1918, Billy Hughes reminded Lloyd George of Australia's interests:

> It only remains to remind you once more that Australia profoundly distrusts Japan, that its national welfare and its trade are alike seriously menaced by Japan. The recognition of Japan's claims to these islands will enable her to pursue much more effectively her policy which is directed towards securing for herself the trade which Britain and Australia have built up.[57]

Thus, he was decidedly against the imposition of the mandates system for these islands, and made a strong case for the annexation of New Guinea at the meeting of the British Empire delegation in February 1919.[58] Hughes considered it critical that Australia should obtain control over New Guinea as a buffer zone between itself and Japan. Hence, he argued that it was necessary to obtain a buffer state and expand Australia's outer boundary farther away from Australia proper as another aspect of defending 'White Australia'. Although this demand suggested an annexationist and expansionist motive, one cannot altogether dismiss the 'White Australia' argument which emanated historically from the perceived security threat posed by Japan. Typically, Hughes insisted on this demand with characteristic vehemence to the point of offending President Wilson, thereby causing problems for Lloyd George.[59] Only after having made a big scene did Hughes finally acquiesce and accept a 'C' class mandate on New Guinea. It seems that the difference in views over the former German islands and the British determination to honour the 1917 secret agreement with Japan had made Hughes resentful towards Britain.[60] Nonetheless, the British Colonial Office was of the view that Hughes's adamant behaviour over the mandates could be explained by his concern for his political future.[61]

In a similar vein, Hughes was determined to oppose the racial equality proposal because it was seen to threaten the 'White Australia' policy. As details of Hughes's negotiating position were given extensively in Chapter 1, it will suffice to reiterate that Hughes's intransigence over the issue became legendary, as no amount of pliability shown by the Japanese or coaxing by the other Dominions would induce him to change his position. He made the following statement to the Australian press on 28 March 1919:

> Australia cannot accept a proposal which strikes at the root of a policy we have long maintained and which is vital to our existence. The amendment, no matter how innocuous it may seem in form, is certainly aimed at giving the League control of questions relating to immigration, naturalisation, and matters which cannot be surrendered by any State without making it in effect a subject State. I feel sure that the people of Australia would not sign the Covenant, if it contains any such amendment as it is proposed.[62]

Therefore, the efforts made by Canada and South Africa in late March to persuade Hughes to agree to a compromise formula came to no avail because they had underestimated his determination to turn this proposal into a political vote winner in Australia.[63] Hughes made rejection of the racial equality proposal an important political message to the Australian public: first, as a symbol of independence *vis-à-vis* the British government,[64] and second, as a demonstration of his personal resolve to protect Australia's national interest, the 'White Australia' policy. His determination to fight for the defence of 'White Australia' did earn him praise from the Australian Senate for 'express[ing] the views of 90 per cent of the electors of Australia'.[65]

In spite of the bullish exterior, however, there was some concern within the Australian delegation over the fate of the Dominion as a result of the stance taken by Hughes on the proposal. Undeniably, his public display of unwavering determination to block the proposal was highly effective as he had managed to convince everyone at the peace conference, including Wilson, that he would wreak havoc, should the Japanese place the racial equality proposal for the final time at the plenary session on 28 April. In fact, Hughes himself admitted later that he did not know what he would have done, had all the other states turned against Australia at the plenary session.[66] Another delegate, J.G. Latham, claimed also that there would have been a very serious problem, had the Japanese resubmitted the proposal at the plenary session, because the vote at the 11 April League of Nations Commission meeting was a probable indication of what was to come.[67] Back home in Hughes's absence, E.L. Piesse, who was the Far Eastern adviser in the Prime Minister's Office, was deeply concerned about the negative repercussions on Australian–Japanese relations of Hughes's diplomacy at Paris.[68] In this sense, it seems that Hughes was gambling with high stakes in terms of Australia's reputation.

It must be stressed that Hughes's intransigence over the issue at Paris was not universally approved of in Australia. In fact, he was criticised by the Australian press for taking the issue of the Australian independence too far at Paris. This coincided with the strong and generally held suspicion that he was effectively conducting an electioneering campaign at the peace conference by making a big scene, first over the question of the mandates in New Guinea, and secondly over the racial equality proposal. In the Australian Parliament, even some Nationalist members, who did not wish to weaken Australia's links with Britain any further, protested against Hughes's unnecessarily strong insistence on Australia's independence.[69] The *Sydney Morning Herald* claimed that Hughes was embarrassing the country by his unstatesmanlike manner in insisting single-mindedly on Australian interests, and that he was essentially conducting 'a personal press campaign'.[70] Another paper, *The Argus*, was more explicit:

> He is apparently engaged in what is called in America 'a publicity campaign'. He knows that in the United States there is a Japanese problem, and without reserve he expresses what he calls the Australian opinion of the Japanese and of the future occupation of the colonies taken from Germany.[71]

Interestingly, the Australian press coverage of the peace conference tended to be generally more sympathetic to Chinese interests and, thus, fairly anti-Japanese, despite the wartime censorship in place, often echoing the views expressed in the American press.[72] It is also highly likely that Hughes was affected by the anti-Japanese sentiment sweeping the West Coast of the United States, as he travelled across the country on his way to Paris.[73]

In so far as it is possible to gauge the level of Hughes's popularity from the press comments, his political future in Australia was not as rosy as it may have, at first, seemed. Politically speaking, Hughes's domestic popularity during the war was much damaged by the conscription crisis. More importantly, the conscription crisis was simply a reflection of the deeper political divide within the old Labour Party, half of whose members did not share the enthusiasm which Hughes expressed in supporting the war unconditionally.[74] He had a small personal following in Parliament, and was intensely disliked by the Labour Party (now in opposition after the 1916 split), by many of the old Liberals and by the business community.[75] In a sense, the vehemence with which he had pursued and stood for Australian interests at Paris can be seen as a reflection of the insecurity of his position in Australia. It is almost certain that Hughes needed to bank on his performance at the peace conference in order to maintain his political leadership in Australia. Therefore, he had moved the general elections forward to December 1919 in order to capitalise on Australia's role in the First World War and the peace conference.[76] In a sense the only crime Hughes committed was to capitalise on his international statesmanship, as did all the other leaders who attended the Paris Peace Conference. The difference between him and the other leaders was that he was much more single-minded about it, possibly as single-minded as President Wilson had been, and President Wilson was equally determined to achieve his objectives, albeit in a more sophisticated manner.

In the end, Hughes's gamble at Paris, which was to reject outright the Japanese proposal at the expense of alienating the rest of the British Empire delegation, did pay off as he managed to remain in power after the general elections in December 1919, albeit at the cost of his party, the Nationalists, losing some seats. When he returned from Paris after fifteen months of absence, he received a tremendously enthusiastic welcome.[77] Immediately after his arrival on 10 September 1919, Hughes successfully introduced the peace treaty in Parliament for ratification. In the ensuing parliamentary debate on the treaty, he managed to influence the course of the debate on Australian gains from the peace conference by emphasising that he had defended 'White Australia' from Japan.[78] Needless to say, Japan was portrayed as untrustworthy and posing the greatest threat to 'White Australia'.[79] Not surprisingly, Hughes had no other important or new policy at the general elections, apart from the constitutional amendment.[80] Therefore, his achievements at the peace conference formed a major part of his party's election platform. For instance, Hughes made the policy of the National Party as 'adherence to the doctrine of a White Australia', and portrayed himself as the 'defender of the White Australia policy at the peace conference', a position which he claimed on the basis of defending Australia's rights to New Guinea and opposing the racial equality proposal.[81]

In retrospect, it seems reasonable to say that only Hughes's personality could have stood unwavering in the face of the immense pressure to compromise stemming from the fellow Dominions and the British government, not to mention Japan. His opposition caused endless problems for the British and the other Dominion governments, but he was determined to protect Australia's national interest and, by extension, his political future. Moreover, Hughes's statement to the Japanese press, explaining his position after the defeat of the proposal, nearly caused a diplomatic rift in Anglo-American relations since the Americans interpreted this as an attempt by the British government to throw the blame of the defeat on them.[82] Hence, it was truly Hughes's personal victory when he stated:

> But in the British Delegation we had a Court strongly sympathetic and ready to look at the question from the Australian point of view. Australia, as a portion of the Empire, was powerful enough to induce the Conference to support its national policy.[83]

In sum, it seems that Hughes's strength lay not only in his ability to wreak havoc, but also in having very little at stake in terms of possible negative repercussions when rejecting the racial equality proposal.

CONCLUSIONS

This analysis of the British position on the racial equality proposal shows that Hughes was able to influence the final position taken by the British Empire delegation, which was to oppose the racial equality proposal. This was possible due to a concatenation of factors which worked to his advantage. It was fortunate for Hughes that the British government did not perceive the Japanese proposal as a high priority issue, and was willing to concede it to the Dominions as a matter pertaining to immigration. This enabled Hughes to bulldoze his way through the negotiations because the proposal was not considered to be ultimately important enough, either for Britain or the other Dominions. For Hughes, the racial equality proposal provided an important political opportunity, together with the claims on New

Guinea, to push his personal political cause in advance of the up and coming general elections in Australia. This was only possible because any issue related to Japan was deemed to be a threat to the 'White Australia' policy, which Australia had long espoused as the central tenet of its national survival. The analysis of the Australian opposition to the Japanese proposal has demonstrated the importance of Australian domestic politics in affecting the position not only of Australia at the peace conference, but also of the British Empire as a whole.

Therefore, we can conclude from the analysis of the opposition of the British Empire delegation to the proposal that two categories of explanations – immigration and domestic politics – played the key role. Immigration was important in explaining the general attitude taken towards the proposal by the British government and, subsequently, by the Empire delegation as a whole. Also, the immigration factor explained why the Japanese proposal was so threatening to Australia because it was inextricably tied to Australian domestic politics, which was partly predicated on historical adherence to the 'White Australia' policy. Lastly, it is worth reiterating that the British Empire delegation did not perceive the racial equality proposal as a demand of universal principle.

6 The American opposition

This chapter analyses the American opposition to the racial equality proposal. The American position on the proposal was complex and multi-dimensional, as there was no single unifying voice which represented it. As a result, it is necessary to analyse three possible explanatory factors, immigration, domestic politics and the politics of bargaining at the peace conference, in order to illustrate the relative importance of each. First, the explanatory category of immigration is examined in the light of the historical sensitivity surrounding Japanese immigration into California, as witnessed in Chapter 3. However, Senator Phelan's arousal of anti-Japanese sentiment, by equating the proposal with unrestricted immigration of Japanese and other Asian immigrants, had managed to influence Colonel House, but not President Wilson. Second, it is argued here that Phelan's anti-Japanese agitation had a greater role in contributing to the domestic partisan politics against the Wilsonian League. In this sense, the racial equality proposal became an American domestic political issue; in spite of this, however, it does not seem to have been the decisive factor in President Wilson's final position on the proposal.

Finally, this chapter analyses the explanation of the politics of bargaining at the peace conference. There are two aspects to this explanation within the American context. First, there is the widely known 'bargaining chip' theory, expounded by the 'pro-China' sympathisers in the American delegation. This argument, although highly popular among American contemporaries, is not tenable because of contrary evidence. Instead, this chapter suggests that an understanding of the American opposition can be found in a second level of explanation, which argues that Wilson used the racial equality proposal as a political instrument to gain other ends at the peace conference. For Wilson, his unanimity decision on 11 April and his subsequent decision to rule on Shantung in Japan's favour were all a result of a rational calculation made in order to achieve his ultimate goal, the creation of the League of Nations. In the end, Wilson's perspective is the key to understanding American opposition.

ANTI-JAPANESE IMMIGRATION AND CALIFORNIAN POLITICS

As explained in Chapter 3, American sensitivity to Japanese immigration is historically evident as a cause of bilateral diplomatic friction between Japan and the United States. In light of this, there was a strong tendency domestically in the United States to view the racial equality proposal as demanding unrestricted immigration of Japanese and other non-white immigrants. The problem of Japanese immigration was, of course particularly acute in California, where it was used as a political weapon by some politicians, most notably by the Californian Democratic leader, Senator Phelan, who played a major role in the crisis over the 1913 Californian Alien Land Law. As is shown below, Phelan wanted to claim major credit for influencing American opposition to the proposal at Paris. However, he was only able to influence Colonel House, who, by mid-March, no longer had any real influence over Wilson and hence no longer possessed significant political clout within the American delegation.

Immigration had long been used as a political instrument in California, which bore the brunt of Oriental immigration. When the news of the racial equality negotiations reached Senator Phelan early in March 1919, he immediately took the opportunity to launch a propaganda campaign against the Japanese proposal. His objective in this campaign was to claim the credit for blocking the American adoption of the racial equality clause, by implying that the cablegrams he sent to Paris were strategically crucial in formulating the American opposition.[1] To this end, he sent many telegrams to Paris from early March onward, an example being the following:

> Any declaration in constitution of race equality or just treatment may be construed to give jurisdiction to League over immigration naturalisation elective franchise land ownership and marriage and should be avoided. An affirmative declaration that these are domestic question should be made in consonance – with established American policy. Believe Western senators and others will oppose any loop hole by which Oriental people will possess equally with white race in United States. It is vital question of self-preservation.[2]

Quite clearly, Phelan was determined to make political capital out of the Japanese proposal. In reality, however, Phelan's political manipulation of anti-Japanese sentiment was a well-known fact in the Wilson administration, which implies that it was highly unlikely that Phelan had the sort of influence which he claimed over the American decision on the Japanese proposal.[3] Notwithstanding Phelan's bid to monopolise the anti-Japanese platform, the Republicans moved in to frustrate his efforts in the Californian Senate.[4] On 4 April 1919, the Californian Senate voted against a resolution to introduce two anti-Japanese bills by the Democrat Senator Inman. Instead, it decided to defer to President Wilson on the timeliness of introducing these bills. This was an extraordinary feat by the Republican senators, who were determined to prevent the Democrats from getting all the credit for anti-Japanese immigration legislation.

Interestingly, the impact of the domestic anti-Japanese immigration lobby on the American position at Paris was not as conclusive as it might appear. It did have an effect on Colonel House's perception of the racial equality proposal. As previously discussed, House had considered the Japanese proposal principally in terms of its implication for immigration, or more precisely, as an attempt by Japan to solve the problem of its expanding population.[5] Initially House was sympathetic to the Japanese proposal, but his attitude began to change around mid-March 1919 when he realised that the strength of Australian opposition was such that the proposal could never be accepted by Britain. Furthermore, he became increasingly aware of the anti-Japanese agitation in California, which was fast consolidating domestic opinion against the Japanese proposal. In spite of the fact that House seemed more influenced by the strength of British opposition than by the domestic anti-Japanese immigration lobby, it is true that House did change his view to take into consideration American domestic objections based on anti-Japanese sentiment. To this extent, Phelan's efforts can be said to have paid off.

Nevertheless, there is very little indication that Wilson was much affected by the anti-Japanese immigration lobby in California. In fact, there is no circumstantial evidence to show that he considered the domestic anti-Japanese immigration movement as a significant factor affecting the racial equality proposal. Although Wilson was aware of the domestic situation, essentially he considered immigration to be a domestic issue, and it was obvious that the League would not intervene in the domestic affairs of states.[6] In this sense, the effect that Phelan and his supporters had on Wilson's position seems highly questionable, as will become evident in the discussion below on why Wilson had opposed the proposal.

In conclusion, the explanation that the Americans rejected the racial equality proposal because of the strength of the anti-Japanese immigration lobby in California does not ring entirely true, although the activities of the lobby do offer an explanation as to why American public opinion became so agitated over the proposal. Although the domestic anti-Japanese lobby did affect the perspective of House, it was a background consideration for the American decision makers at Paris, not the foremost reason for their opposing the proposal.

THE ANTI-LEAGUE MOVEMENT IN AMERICAN DOMESTIC POLITICS

In retrospect, it seems that Phelan's anti-Japanese agitation in California was more significant in contributing to the national anti-League campaign than specifically to his political agenda. While Phelan was hard at work in California working towards undermining the racial equality proposal, a parallel political movement on the national level also adopted opposition to the Japanese proposal as one of its platforms. This was the partisan anti-Wilson and bipartisan anti-League movement, which spread through the United States during the peace conference. This section explores whether the view that American opposition to the racial equality proposal was caused by the strength of the domestic anti-Wilson lobby holds true.[7] It appears that Wilson's hierarchical structure of decision making, his distance from domestic politics in Paris, and his personal agenda of creating the League of Nations at Paris meant that the influence of anti-Wilson and anti-League movement on Wilson's own attitude to the racial equality proposal was not as great as it seemed on the surface; again, this opposition was more of a background consideration. American domestic political opposition to the peace treaty was a complex phenomenon, and we attempt here simply to extrapolate those aspects which were relevant to understanding the racial equality proposal.

President Wilson's approach to the Paris Peace Conference created a sizeable anti-Wilson and anti-League lobby among domestic politicians. Regardless of political affiliation, their defining feature was their total commitment to the denunciation of what they perceived to be a peculiarly Wilsonian conception of the League of Nations; they wanted either to obliterate it, or to introduce changes to the covenant in order to better reflect American prerogatives. Broadly speaking, the predominantly Republican opposition[8] was divided into 'strong reservationists',[9] 'irreconcilables'[10] and 'mild reservationists',[11] depending on each group's degree of reservation about Wilson's conception of the League. At a fundamental level, what motivated the Republican opponents to oppose Wilson was their dissatisfaction with the way in which he had turned the peace conference into a partisan and personal issue. Once having adopted a partisan tone in discussing peace in 1918, it was impossible for Wilson to keep domestic politics and the peace separate, especially as the success of the peace treaty would be a decisive factor in the presidential elections in 1920.[12] Moreover, Wilson's autocratic method of decision making and his cavalier attitude towards Congress aggravated the tension. By failing consistently to consult Congress on matters relating to the peace, Wilson was circumventing the political machinery which supposedly represented the interests of the nation.[13] Marginalisation of Congress would cost him dearly in the end, and his method, based on the zealous personal conviction that he was acting in the best interest of the country, worsened anti-Wilson sentiment.[14]

The partisan resentment towards Wilson was such that the Republican leader of the Senate, Henry Cabot Lodge, presented to the Senate in March 1919, a document known as the Round Robin which 'announced to the world that the signatories did not find the Covenant of the League acceptable "in the form now proposed" '.[15] The significance of this document lies in the fact that it contained the signatures of thirty-nine Republican senators – more than the number of votes required to defeat the peace treaty. Quite clearly, Wilson's great weakness lay in his underestimation of the importance of domestic political forces, as he had assumed too much power directly from the popular mandate given to him to make peace.[16] Wilson's high-handed and exclusionary approach to decision making at Paris led to the criticism that 'It is Wilson's League not an American League.'[17]

Specifically, domestic opponents had identified the racial equality proposal and the Monroe Doctrine as bulwarks of the anti-League platform. The Republican opposition soon broadened the base of its political support by cleverly converting the anti-Wilson crusade into an anti-League movement; this enabled the Democratic League sceptics to join their cause.[18] The hardline 'irreconcilables' decided that the best tactic to defeat the Wilsonian peace was to vote in favour of adopting amendments to the covenant by joining hands with the reservationists and Democratic opponents of the League. First, the Monroe Doctrine,[19] a traditional American foreign policy doctrine, was considered most crucial to the American national interest.[20]

Secondly, the racial equality proposal was seen as a demand for unrestricted immigration. It was argued that since immigration belonged to domestic affairs of states, it should not be made part of the constitution for any international organisation. The United States should refuse to be part of an organisation which allowed its members to intervene in the domestic affairs of other member states. This issue became an important part of the anti-League platform because of its ability to manipulate anti-Japanese sentiment, as well as domestic sensitivity to non-white immigration. Essentially, this was a convenient political weapon used to manipulate the isolationist anti-foreign tendency domestically in the United States against Wilsonian internationalism. As such, the racial equality proposal brought Republican opponents together with the likes of Democratic Senator Phelan of California, who wanted to capitalise on the anti-Japanese immigration ticket.[21]

The importance of these two issues was such that William Howard Taft, who was a strong Republican League supporter, had repeatedly advised Wilson that a provision for the Monroe Doctrine in Article 10 of the covenant, together with some provision to be inserted in Article 15 to prevent Japanese immigration, would almost guarantee ratification of the treaty.[22] Similarly, Elihu Root warned House not to include the racial amendment in late March:

> Don't let it in, it will breed trouble. In any event, you're going to have hard ledding, with the racial provision, you will get nowhere in the Senate. And the people . . . ? On the Pacific coast, at least, they would think there lurked behind it a plan for unlimited yellow immigration.[23]

In any case, it would be incorrect to say that Wilson was completely oblivious to the strength of domestic opposition to the proposal. When he returned from his trip to the United States in mid-March, Wilson noted during an internal discussion on the Japanese proposal that the American Senate would never ratify a covenant which gave treaty powers the power to override internal state laws.[24]

One only needs to follow the unfortunate fate of the peace treaty in the United States to recognise the scope of the problem that Wilson had to confront. In the light of domestic anti-League politics, the racial equality proposal provided an ideal weapon for those waging the protracted battle to bring down Wilson and his peace plan, regardless of the cost and external implications. The strength of the domestic anti-League lobby put enormous pressure on Wilson to succeed in achieving the establishment of the League of Nations at Paris. However, as will be seen later, Wilson imposed the unanimity ruling not primarily because he had succumbed to the pressure from his domestic opponents, but because it was a price he had to pay to ensure the survival of the League at Paris. As the Japanese government had always suspected, the true nature of Japanese immigration problems in the United States had more to do with the politics than the economics of immigration.[25]

THE 'BARGAINING CHIP' THEORY AND THE 'PRO-CHINA' LOBBY

The 'bargaining chip' theory stands out, along with the 'immigration' explanation, as the other interpretation of the racial equality proposal most widely held by contemporaries in Paris. This was the predominant view in the American delegation, and was supported by the Chinese delegates. In the overall framework of explanatory categories employed in this study, this can be categorised as one aspect of the politics of bargaining at the peace conference. The basic idea behind the theory is simple. It claims that the Japanese government had intentionally concocted the racial equality proposal as a political instrument in order to defend its interest in Shantung. This works on the assumption that the proposal was a bargaining chip held by the Japanese, whose objective was not really to have the proposal adopted but to embarrass the American government and to gain leverage on the Shantung negotiations. Before delving into the details of this theory, it should be explained why some Americans at Paris interpreted the proposal in this manner.

The American and Chinese delegations in Paris enjoyed a close working relationship.[26] Essentially, China played the role of protégé to the United States.[27] For example, the Americans tended to consider the most important of China's interests, the Shantung settlement, as though it were one of their own interests at Paris. This was reflected in the fact that, with the exception of Colonel House, the delegation tended to be sympathetic to China.[28] The fact that the United States took China under its wing meant that the American attitude in general remained sympathetic to China while being wary of Japan. Public opinion in the United States was also antagonistic towards Japan.[29] Evidently, the crux of American distrust of Japan centred on the contested claim over the Shantung settlement.[30] This was compounded by rumours which circulated in February 1919 that the Japanese government was strongly pressurising the Chinese to concur with the

Japanese position on Shantung at the peace conference.[31] On the whole, the view expressed by Lansing was representative of the American delegation:

> Mr Lansing observed that the attitude of the Japanese was extremely disquieting, particularly in its relation to China, and that he felt that this was the time for us to have it out once and for all with Japan .... He also stated that it was America's duty to support China.[32]

The moral imperative to help their protégé, compounded by their innate suspicion of Japan, produced a hard core of anti-Japanese sentiment among the 'pro-China' Americans. This seems to have had a material effect on how the Americans generally viewed Japan and its racial equality proposal.

Notwithstanding their deep sense of distrust of the Japanese, it must be mentioned that there was also a feeling on the fringes of the American delegation that the racial equality proposal could have been a symbolic request to confirm Japan's great power status. For instance, the State Department's China expert, E.T. Williams, was of the opinion that racial equality should be regarded as a 'concession to her pride of race', which was a cheap price to pay in order to get Japan to be more accommodating on the Shantung settlement.[33] Thomas Millard, editor of the Shanghai-based *Millard Review*, saw the proposal principally as having a propaganda value for the Japanese and believed that the United States had nothing to fear from it as it was merely 'a placation of Japan and Asiatic peoples'.[34] Even Ray Stannard Baker, press officer in the delegation and a fierce opponent of giving Shantung to Japan, thought that Japan could have been seeking a 'complete recognition of her status as a great Power, equal to any other'.[35] However, it is important not to exaggerate the importance of these views as they remained in the minority, held by those who did not possess any political clout within the delegation. Consequently, the existence of such an implicit understanding in the margins of the American delegation did not influence the American position on this particular issue.

The 'bargaining chip' theory attracted considerable attention in the American delegation. The beginnings of the idea that the racial equality proposal could be traded for Shantung came from the State Department in March 1919. Like the British Foreign Office, the State Department had been aware since November 1918 that the Japanese government was contemplating the submission of a racial equality proposal at the peace conference.[36] Williams considered that the racial equality proposal was a cheap price to pay in order to buy Japan's goodwill in the up and coming Shantung negotiation. Hence, he attempted in March 1919 to persuade the peace commissioners, namely, Secretary of State Robert Lansing, General Tasker Bliss and Henry White, to accept racial equality for the following reason:

> If now we surrender to Japan our claims in those islands (the Pacific Islands) and further grant Japan our approval of the proposed amendment, a concession to her pride of race which she will highly appreciate, we are entitled to ask Japan to be equally conciliatory and to do justice in Shantung.[37]

Unlike the hardline peace commissioners, Williams realised that Japan could not be denied everything. In China's best interest, he proposed a trade-off of the two lesser demands made by Japan – racial equality and the Pacific islands – for Shantung. On 26 March, Williams showed impatience with the commissioners who failed to see the light:

> . . . the recognition in the League Constitution of a principle of racial equality does not necessarily imply a right to free immigration, or land ownership. Restriction in these matters can be advocated on economic grounds. The Japanese themselves have protested against this misinterpretation of their proposal.[38]

As far as Williams was concerned, it would be more practical and concomitantly less costly to cede to Japan a principle of racial equality which was a matter of national honour to them than to give them Shantung, which would have a far more injurious effect on China.[39]

However, when the racial equality proposal was defeated on 11 April and as the Shantung negotiation began in earnest, Peace Commissioners Lansing, Bliss and White began to suspect that the racial equality proposal was a political weapon contrived by the Japanese government to obtain their real objective, Shantung. This thinking stemmed from their strongly 'pro-China' inclination, which coloured their entire understanding of the Far Eastern question and made it into a simplistic black and white struggle of Japan versus China, with the United States supporting the latter. Thus, the emergence of the 'bargaining chip' theory coincided with the increasing difficulty which the Chinese were having over the Shantung negotiation in the Council of Four from mid-April onwards. Lansing, who was its most ardent supporter, used the 'bargaining chip' theory during the most intensive stage of the negotiation as an argument against giving Shantung to Japan:

> I concluded that Japs were promised satisfactory settlement if they would not press their 'race equality' amendment to Covenant. If this is so it was all immoral bargaining away of principle and of the right of China.[40]

Hence, the principal component of this theory is the distrust of the Japanese, which was essentially a reflection of the fundamental clash of interests between Japan and the United States over the future of China. The Shantung negotiations were a cause of great frustration for the American peace commissioners, who were largely excluded by Wilson from having any input into decision making. Lansing, Bliss and White all felt that it was America's duty to support the Chinese claims to the settlement. However, there was a suspicion that Wilson might be tempted to side with the other great powers to support the Japanese claim, on the basis that Japan had already been humiliated once over the racial equality proposal. Therefore, the 'bargaining chip' theory was a way of discrediting the Japanese claim to Shantung, and as such revealed more about the internal divisions within the American delegation, rather than their view on the racial equality proposal *per se*.

Interestingly, for the Chinese delegation, the greatest attraction of the 'bargaining chip' theory seemed to lie in its propaganda value. This can be seen in the paradoxical position of the Chinese delegation, whose official support for the racial equality proposal[41] was balanced by their retrospective contention after the defeat over the Shantung settlement that the Japanese had used the proposal as a bargaining chip to obtain favourable concessions in Shantung.[42] As such, C.T. Wang, who played an influential role in the Chinese delegation, used the theory frequently to explain why China did not win the Shantung settlement:

> China knows that equality of races forms the foundation of the League of Nations. Japan's demand to include such a phrase in the Covenant was pure camouflage. It was a smoke-screen to cover a real objective. The idea was to press this hard, knowing that President Wilson would refuse it; but after he had refused it the Japanese then pointed to Kiaochou, and said, 'Well, give us that anyhow.' And President Wilson said, 'Well, I guess we'll have to give those Japanese something'.[43]

In order to explain why Wilson, in whom the Chinese had so much confidence, had failed to deliver the promised goods, Wang argued that Wilson was 'bamboozled' in allowing Japan to have its way on Shantung in exchange for the racial equality clause.[44]

Although the 'bargaining chip' theory plays a role in depicting the climate of opinion within the American delegation, it loses credibility on two grounds. First, it was an *ex post facto* explanation, which emerged only after the defeat of the racial equality proposal in the League of Nations Commission, and moreover, was raised by the commissioners who did not have any influence over President Wilson at the time. Therefore, its worth lies more in its revealing the interpretation which the Chinese and the 'pro-China' American peace commissioners placed upon the racial equality proposal, than in providing an insight into what made Wilson impose the unanimity ruling on 11 April. Moreover, the crucial oversight made by the 'pro-China' lobby, the existence of the 1917 secret agreement between Japan and Britain, indicates that the Japanese demand for Shantung should have seemed secure as far as Japan was concerned.

As mentioned above, Japan had very promptly occupied the German territories in Shantung and the Pacific after entering the war in August 1914. The initial peace terms prepared by the Japan–Germany Peace Preparatory Committee established in September 1915 in the Japanese Foreign Ministry centred exclusively on the acquisition of the rights to these former German territories. On 27 January 1917, the Japanese government made a request to the British government to support its claims to the former German rights in Shantung and the Pacific islands north of the equator. Faced with a *fait accompli*, the British War Cabinet decided that there was no choice but to accede to the Japanese request and to ask for reciprocal support for British claims to the Pacific islands south of the equator.[45] The British reply to the Japanese government was despatched on 14 February 1917 as follows:

> Her Majesty's Government accede with pleasure to the request of the Japanese Government for an assurance that they will support Japan's claim in regard to the disposition of Germany's rights in Shantung and in possessions in Islands North of the Equator, on the occasion of a Peace Conference, it being understood that the Japanese Government will, in the eventual peace settlement, treat in the same spirit Great Britain's claims to the Islands South of the Equator.[46]

With this note, the Japanese had secured informally the most important concessions at the peace conference. The Japanese government subsequently successfully concluded a similar agreement with the French government on 1 May 1917, but without a reciprocal request from the French.[47] In addition, Japan exchanged similar notes with Italy and Russia.[48] Consequently, the Japanese claims to these territories were fairly secure, even in the eventuality of China's entry into war, which might otherwise have jeopardised them.[49] Therefore, Japan considered the peace conference's accession to these two demands as a matter of formality.

The above provides conclusive evidence against the 'bargaining chip' theory, that the Japanese government used the racial equality demand as a political instrument to obtain the territorial demands. Only the United States was not party to these secret agreements. This also explains why there was no reference at all to the use of the racial equality proposal as a political instrument by any of the key Japanese participants during the peace conference. Japan did not need to concoct a racial equality proposal for this purpose, because the acquisition of rights to Shantung was regarded by the Japanese as a *fait accompli*. Hence the 'bargaining chip' theory, which gained much currency among the contemporaries in the American delegation at Paris, must be ruled out as an explanation in understanding why President Wilson imposed the unanimity rule on 11 April.

THE STRUCTURE OF WILSON'S DECISION MAKING AT PARIS

In order to analyse Wilson's use of the racial equality proposal as a political instrument, it is first necessary to understand the nature of his role in the American delegation at Paris. Generally speaking, Wilson exercised overwhelming control over the delegation during the course of the peace negotiations, especially with regard to the League of Nations. The main internal characteristic of the American delegation was his autocratic and highly centralised method of decision making, which caused two major rifts between himself and Colonel House, and another with Secretary of State Lansing. His preferred structure of decision making meant that his own agenda, at the top of which was the creation of the League of Nations, became the most important goal of the United States at the peace conference.

Wilson's highly complex personality is often argued as being an important factor in understanding his politics. Wilson was both an idealist and a realist. These traits were not antithetical, as he was essentially an idealist in conviction and vision, but a realist in tactics.[50] His highly centralised decision making in Paris was not the result of any formal institution of such a structure, but a natural outcome of his tendency to weed out people who did not agree with his views.[51] Consequently, decision making in the American delegation largely reflected his personal inclination to rely heavily on a small number of advisors, and to exclude everyone else. This was aggravated by his conviction, derived from his immense popularity on his first arrival in Europe after the war, of having a moral mandate from the international public to create a better world.[52]

The nature of his exclusive executive control can be seen in his personal clashes with House and Lansing. House initially held a highly coveted position as special advisor to the president, until Wilson's brief trip to the United States from mid-February to mid-March 1919. This was a result of a very close friendship, bonding them from the time of their first meeting in November 1911.[53] In fact, Wilson regarded House as *de facto* head of the delegation during his absence, a fact which caused much resentment in the American delegation, especially on the part of Lansing, the official deputy head of the delegation, who felt 'surprised and humiliated'.[54] Thus the claims made by House concerning his influence on Wilson in this period are generally reliable. The rift between the two friends originated from House's 'overstepping the mark' in agreeing with Balfour and Clemenceau during Wilson's absence to speed up the peace by separating the treaty from the covenant. The other leaders were becoming impatient with the League, which was blamed for slowing down the peace process.[55] For Wilson, House's flirtation with such an idea was tantamount to a great betrayal and culminated in the gradual disintegration of the special relationship between them.

The rift between Wilson and Lansing developed earlier and was an established fact by the time of the peace conference, and was even acknowledged by other delegations.[56] Lansing was fundamentally at odds with Wilson's attitude to peace.[57] On the other hand, it appears that Wilson had a strong dislike of lawyers (Lansing being one) and the State Department generally, and only stopped short of sacking Lansing in the middle of the conference in fear of endangering America's credibility.[58] Wilson's alienation of Lansing extended to the other peace commissioners, particularly Tasker Bliss and Henry White. Wilson was criticised for not appointing a more respected Republican figure to the peace commission, such as William Howard Taft or Elihu Root, instead of a token Republican diplomat, Henry White.[59] Hence, the American delegation internally was divided and factional, with only a restricted number of delegates ever having access to the president.

In light of the above, after his special relationship with House ended in mid-March 1919, Wilson stood more or less alone in the delegation without any influential advisers or colleagues. By April, House was firmly excluded from Wilson's immediate entourage. The Japanese plenipotentiaries, of course, continued to consult House throughout the conference, most probably due to a lack of alternative access to Wilson. Effectively, the position of Lansing and the rest of the peace commissioners was so marginal in Wilson's perspective that their very presence in Paris seemed meaningless. For example, the other peace commissioners tried to convince Wilson not to give Shantung to the Japanese, a concession which they believed to be fundamentally against the American interest. But their argument fell on deaf ears.[60] It must be noted that Wilson's neglect of the other peace commissioners, who tended to be more representative of the views espoused by domestic opinion, though short-sighted, was very demonstrative of his singular attitude and the nature of his priorities, which were more personal than American. The internal dynamics of the delegation leads us to understand why Wilson's perception of issues, including the racial equality proposal, was so crucial to the overall American position at Paris. In the case of the racial equality negotiation, despite his low level of involvement in the day-to-day negotiation, his influence at the critical moments was decisive.

WILSON AND THE LEAGUE OF NATIONS

The League of Nations was Wilson's *raison d'être* at Paris, and his role in creating the League can be characterised as being largely symbolic and personal. It appears that Wilson was contemplating the idea of an 'association of nations', which would replace the balance of power system, as early as 1914.[61] Ever since his open commitment made in the Fourteen Points in January 1918, the League of Nations had been perceived internationally as President Wilson's project.

His prominent identification with the League was not reflected in the American government's preparatory work undertaken before the peace conference, however, which was overshadowed by Britain's Phillimore Commission report, finalised in July 1918.[62] In fact, Wilson maintained a curiously secretive and vague stance about the structure of the League, as shown in his successful intervention to prevent the British from publishing the Phillimore Report before the peace conference. He did this for the following reasons: first, publication would commit each country's stance on the League too early; second, it would 'be regarded as a sort of Holy Alliance against Germany'; and third, it might compromise his position domestically.[63] Wilson's position on the League before the peace conference remained abstract, as he insisted on 'Two main principles; there must be a League of Nations, and this must be virile, a reality, not a paper League of Nations.'[64]

Nevertheless, public opinion in the United States perceived the central role played by Wilson in creating the League at Paris,[65] and his advisers also were convinced of his singular 'obsession' with the League.[66] When he arrived in Europe to attend the peace conference, Wilson reiterated the importance of the League everywhere he went, as he did in London in December 1918: 'A League of Nations seems to me to be a necessity of the whole settlement. I accept it as a key to the whole settlement.'[67]

Wilson was personally determined to pursue the creation of the League at the Paris Peace Conference because he believed not only in the 'visionary' quality of such an organisation, but also in the practical necessity of it in order to deal with the kind of problems facing the world in the aftermath of the war.[68] At the peace conference, Wilson had to act swiftly to bring the creation of the League of Nations to the top of the agenda, which he did by presenting an agenda at the Supreme War Council's meeting on 13 January wherein he placed the League as the first of the five topics.[69] It was not until the 18th that Wilson's agenda was accepted by the conference. Having established the League of Nations Commission, he then got himself appointed as its chairman.

It is important to bear in mind that Wilson's obsession with the League was not necessarily shared by the rest of the American peace commission. In fact, it was acknowledged that Wilson was often acting against American interests by persisting with the League, and that he was paying a very high price to gain concurrence in the League from the other powers, as Lansing and White respectively testified:

> He was clearly convinced that the drafting and acceptance of the Covenant was superior to every other task imposed on the Conference, that it must be done before any other settlement was reached and that it ought to have precedence in the negotiations. His course of action was conclusive evidence of this conviction.[70]

> The fact is . . . that the League of Nations, in which he has been more deeply interested than anything else from the beginning,

> believing it to be the best if not the only means of avoiding war in the future, has been played to the limit by France and Japan in extracting concessions from him; to a certain extent by the British too, and the Treaty as it stands is the result.[71]

The fact that the League was, in reality, more Wilson's personal objective than that of the United States in general was revealed by House and Lansing, who confided as much to Cecil before the peace conference convened in early January 1919.[72] Hence, the situation was that Wilson himself was dedicated to his personal crusade to create the League, while other peace commissioners were highly concerned that such a crusade would leave the United States vulnerable to manipulation by other powers.

Although the British government's support for the League was a response to a growing domestic sentiment expressed by pacifists and liberals during the war,[73] many members of the British government perceived the intrinsic value of the League more in terms of consolidating Britain's relationship with the United States than for the pursuit of an ideal *per se*. They understood the importance of building a *pax Anglo–Americana* for the future stability of the international system, and were willing to cooperate with the Americans as far as possible over the League of Nations if this did not impinge on the more 'important' British objectives.[74] In practical terms, British contributions to the creation of the League of Nations were enormous. Cecil and Smuts were closely involved in the initial joint drafting of the covenant between the British and Americans in January 1919. Interestingly, while they claimed that Wilson did not have many concrete notions about the League,[75] Wilson counter-claimed that he withheld his personal programme for the League in order to let the British feel that their views were being incorporated.[76] In any case, the pragmatic approach which characterised the British position is best illustrated by Lloyd George who, though never really interested in the League,[77] 'was willing to tolerate the results coming from the League of Nations Commission as long as Wilson did not frustrate the realisation of other, more vital British interests'.[78] Britain and France did recognise the importance of appeasing Wilson over the League to extract specific concessions as well as to obtain overall peace terms.[79] Smuts best summarised the British government's attitude towards Wilson and the League:

> I suggest that we could best signalise that cooperation by supporting President Wilson's policy of a League of [N]ations, and

> indeed by going further and giving form and substance to his rather nebulous ideas. President Wilson has repeatedly and solemnly declared that America wants nothing for herself in this war, that she only desires to serve the great causes and ideals of humanity. In his mind the League of [N]ations is the root of the whole matter. If he could score a victory there, if he could go back to America with the League of [N]ations realised – not merely a formula, but a real substantive part of our future international system – I believe he will be satisfied, and will be prepared to drop some of the other contentious points he has unfortunately raised. My suggestion is that we should tell him quite frankly at the beginning that we are going to support him most fully on the League of [N]ations, and that in our opinion the League will be valuable not only from the point of view of future world peace but from the way it will enable us to solve some of the most difficult territorial and economic questions arising out of this war.[80]

At the peace conference, therefore, Wilson's personal resoluteness on the League of Nations had a material effect on the peace programme, and on how other powers perceived the American role.

Moreover, in spite of many denials made by Wilson and his supporters, there was no doubt that the successful creation of the League was crucial to strengthening the standing of both Wilson and his party for the next presidential elections.[81] As mentioned earlier, Wilson's policy generally at the peace conference, and especially on the League of Nations, became a highly partisan political issue in the United States. Cecil, who was closely working with Wilson on the initial drafts of the covenant in January 1919, attests to the political significance of the League for Wilson:

> He is also evidently a vain man, and still with an eye all the time on the American elections. He was very anxious therefore that the scheme which we should work on should be, nominally at any rate, his scheme, and did not mind that in actual fact it was very largely the production of others.[82]

By mid-March, Wilson faced problems on two fronts, at home and in Paris, with regard to his plan to have the League of Nations as an inseparable part of the peace treaty. First of all, as mentioned previously, Wilson became acutely aware of the strength of domestic political opposition against his peace plan during his brief return home in February and March 1919. The worst blow domestically came in the form of the Round Robin, led by Senator Henry Cabot Lodge, in early March.[83] Secondly, upon his return to Paris, Wilson discovered to his great dismay that House, together with the British and French, was agreeing to a fast peace which, against Wilson's fundamental conviction, excluded the League of Nations. In the meantime, he was receiving messages from his private secretary in Washington, Joseph Tumulty, that in spite of the growing political opposition to the League, American public opinion increasingly favoured the League as being the basis of a just peace.[84] As Wilson believed that he had a moral mandate from the people, all these political obstructions to his objective most likely had the effect of strengthening his determination and conviction that it was absolutely vital to create the League, at any cost.[85] By the time of the ruling over the racial equality proposal in the League of Nations Commission in April 1919, therefore, it had become crucial politically for Wilson to succeed in creating the League of Nations.

In sum, it can be said that the League of Nations was a high-profile and highly political goal for President Wilson. To him, the League came to represent everything: his personal vision to create a new international order based on the international mandate from all 'peoples'; his conviction that it was necessary practically as a new framework to deal with postwar problems; and his political fight to win over the American public against partisan opponents of his peace. Essentially, he put all his eggs in one basket, the League of Nations.

WILSON'S DECISION TO IMPOSE THE UNANIMITY RULING

Having emphasised the crucial importance of the League for Wilson, it becomes evident that the racial equality proposal was also affected whenever Wilson intervened, by his tendency to view issues in terms of their relative importance in promoting his personal cause. This can be illustrated by the three instances in which he intervened in the racial equality negotiation: the initial rejection of the religious article amendment, the unanimity ruling on 11 April, and the final phase of the negotiation from mid-April to 30 April, when the Shantung settlement was made. In the first case, it was established above that Wilson was not averse to the racial equality proposal, as was shown by his initial offer to assist in drafting and submitting it as part of his religious freedom article in early February. However, his religious freedom article was voted down in the League of Nations Commission, particularly by the British whose opposition to the racial equality amendment part of the article had begun to be widely known.[86] Wilson's immediate reaction was to drop the controversial article. The only plausible reason for his decision is that he was not willing to stall the commission at this early stage over an article which, though he personally perceived it to be compatible with the League, was not an important enough issue over which to upset the majority including Britain. It must be noted that Wilson was keenly aware of the necessity of courting Britain's support for the League,[87] which was ironic, given the British desire to keep Wilson happy by abiding as much as possible to his wish to create the League in exchange for his generally favourable understanding of other interests at Paris. Therefore, it can be said that for Wilson to realise his primary objective, it was imperative for him to have British backing as he was convinced that only with an Anglo-Saxon consensus could the League deliver the promises made of a new international order:

> We, Anglo-Saxons, have our peculiar contribution to make towards the good of humanity in accordance with our special talents. The League of Nations will, I confidently hope, be dominated by us Anglo-Saxons; it will be for the unquestionable benefit of the world. The discharge of our duties in the maintenance of peace and as a just mediatory in international disputes will redound to our lasting prestige. But it is of paramount importance that we Anglo-Saxons succeed in keeping in step with one another.[88]

In turn, this underlined his distrust of the French and Italians as being fundamentally incapable of sharing his vision of the League.[89]

The case of the unanimity ruling imposed by Wilson as chairman of the League of Nations Commission on 11 April over the racial equality proposal is highly significant. It has been shown above that Wilson was not overly influenced by domestic agitation about the impact of the proposal on Japanese immigration, nor was he personally committed to racial equality as a universal principle. He was not even involved in the racial equality negotiation after his initial interest faded in early February. In other words, it is fair to state that Wilson was, in the final analysis, fairly indifferent about the racial equality clause as it stood. In light of this, it is intriguing that he should impose a unanimity ruling on the racial equality amendment on 11 April even when the majority of the members (eleven out of seventeen) voted for its adoption. Since House's claim that he was the one responsible for influencing Wilson's decision is not entirely reliable, due to the rift in the personal relationship between himself and the president, the only explanation is that Wilson himself had reasons for wanting to reject the proposal. Although Wilson was aware of the strength of domestic opposition to the proposal and to his version of the League, it is unlikely, from his past record of dealing with the opposition, that he would have relented under the pressure.[90] Instead, it is more likely that the opposition would have actually hardened his resolve to push through the League.

However, even Wilson could not ignore the Australian opposition, which was having a decisive impact on the overall British position on the racial equality proposal. Wilson had realised by then that a racial equality proposal in any form was totally unacceptable to the Australians, in spite of the efforts made by other Dominions to achieve a compromise. It must be borne in mind that Hughes's opposition was so virulent that it was conceivable to all concerned that he would carry out his threat of disrupting the peace conference if necessary. Moreover, it had been clear from 13 February that Britain would have no choice but to oppose the racial equality amendment if Australia continued to do so, in order to maintain unity within the delegation. By then, Wilson was well aware that without Britain's support it was not possible to create the League of Nations, since the French and Italians clearly had a more pragmatic understanding of it as a means to manipulate him. In light of these circumstances, it is not unreasonable to suggest that Wilson considered the option of supporting the British position on the racial equality proposal as a relatively cheap gesture of Anglo-American solidarity, if it meant that Britain would continue to show general support for Wilson's League.[91]

There is no reason to suppose that Britain would not have continued its support for the League, had the racial equality proposal been adopted.[92] However, the possibility of damage from Hughes's threat to disrupt the plenary session over the racial equality issue, not only exposing an inner division within the British Empire delegation and thus humiliating Britain but also questioning the moral value of the League in the eyes of the world, was incalculable. Moreover, Wilson did attempt to persuade the Japanese to drop the demand on 11 April 'with a view to the eventual discussion of these articles', by strongly emphasising that the League was based on the principle of equality of nations.[93] Evidently, Wilson had realised by then that the Japanese would not simply 'give up' their racial equality proposal, and that it would have to be 'put on hold' until after the creation of the League. He was willing to concede that racial equality could be dealt with in the League at a later date, should the Japanese desire to raise it again. In any case, it seems that Wilson, for the moment, was not willing to take the risk of offending and alienating Britain, whose commitment to the League was essential to its success, over a racial equality proposal which he doubtless regarded as a dispensable issue.

Nevertheless, Wilson was not straightforward in his support for the British position, as he decided to impose the unanimity ruling without declaring American opposition to the proposal.[94] It can be construed that Wilson was simply being politically manipulative in not declaring American opposition and in imposing the ruling. There was little need for the United States to declare its opposition to the racial equality proposal when the British had already been identified as the chief opponent to the proposal.[95] It made little political sense for Wilson to side officially with the British at this stage and be branded as one of the objectors to the principle of racial equality, which was increasingly gaining support from the other powers including France and Italy, when he could defeat the proposal effortlessly by imposing unanimity. Diplomatically, the Japanese would not be able to blame the United States for the defeat of the proposal if the Americans were perceived as playing the role of an arbiter, which Wilson was effectively able to do as chairman.[96] This disappointed Cecil because, effectively, the British Empire delegation was singled out as the source of opposition to the racial equality proposal.[97]

It can be said that Wilson's decision in the League of Nations Commission on 11 April was not determined by his perception of the proposal *per se* as implying immigration or universal principle, but by his *realpolitik* concerns of sustaining Britain's support for the League by acting in such a way that the British opposition would prevail in the commission. This was characteristic of the decisions he took at the peace conference, and demonstrates the difficulty he had in dissociating any given issue from the implication it might have for the prospect of realising the League. In this sense, it is true that Wilson was influenced by the British position and, by extension, the Australian opposition to the racial equality proposal. As is shown below, Wilson was personally much affected by the unanimity ruling which he himself imposed on 11 April, as he became consciously aware of having humiliated the Japanese over the issue; and this in turn had a profound effect on how he conducted his Shantung settlement.

WILSON, RACIAL EQUALITY AND SHANTUNG

It seems that in his own mind, Wilson made a trade-off between the racial equality proposal and the Shantung settlement as a means of maintaining Japan's support for the League. As previously mentioned,

Shantung was the most contentious issue between Japan and China at the peace conference. The contention involved certain rights over the railway, police and other properties in the Shantung province, which were formerly held by the Germans but were subsequently taken over by the Japanese during the war. It is widely known that the Americans generally took an extraordinary interest in the Shantung settlement and overwhelmingly backed the Chinese position.[98] By April 1919, however, there was increasing disillusionment on the American side that the promise of a new international order was being overshadowed by the reality of great power diplomacy at Paris.[99] This disillusionment was compounded when Wilson ruled on Shantung in Japan's favour on 30 April.

In retrospect, it appears that Wilson himself was the person most affected by the decision to impose the unanimity ruling on 11 April. It has been argued that Wilson's reason for the ruling was to maintain British support for the League, at the cost of humiliating the Japanese. When the Shantung negotiation took place, he remained conscious of the negative effect his racial equality ruling must have had on the Japanese government, whose determination to obtain Shantung had hardened.[100] In the circumstances, Wilson perceived three interrelated problems which needed to be resolved urgently. First, there was the Japanese threat of withdrawal from the peace conference over Shantung.[101] Second, the Japanese had already lost face over racial equality. Third, without Japan and Italy, the League of Nations might have to be aborted altogether. Thus, it became a question of how to resolve the Shantung settlement without damaging the League of Nations which, to his mind, was more fundamental to the stability of the international order than giving Shantung back to China and, in the process, aggravating Japan. This thinking was reinforced by the underlying reproach that Japan had been 'wronged' once over racial equality. Inadvertently, the earlier defeat of the racial equality proposal had an indirect but causal effect on his decision on Shantung.

In spite of his decision to favour the Japanese claim, Wilson was essentially 'pro-China' in sentiment.[102] What made him distinct from the other 'pro-China' sympathisers was his belief in the credibility of the Japanese threat of withdrawal over Shantung. He believed that the Japanese could not be marginalised on every issue, as they had already been humiliated with the rejection of the racial equality clause.[103] He was anxious not to alienate them because he believed that a crucial component of an effective League of Nations was great power cooperation. Just as he had to first appease the British by imposing unanimity voting on the racial equality proposal, he now felt obliged to give concessions to Japan, since the Japanese threat of withdrawal, coupled with Italian departure from the conference over Fiume, would most certainly spell the end of the League.[104] Evidently, Wilson was aware of the logical inconsistency in his decision to hand over Shantung to the Japanese when he had so doggedly opposed giving Fiume to Italy.[105] But the deadlock over Fiume probably precipitated his desire to resolve the Shantung question without further complication, which benefited Japan:

> Concerning Japan, it is necessary to do everything to assure that she joins the League of Nations. If she stands aside, she would do all that she could want to do in the Far East. You heard them this morning saying clearly that they will not sign the treaty if the obligations contracted *vis-à-vis* them are not respected.[106]

The Shantung decision presented a moral dilemma for Wilson as he saw the situation as choosing between the two extremes:[107] on the one hand, the choice of giving Shantung to China which he would naturally have liked to do; and on the other hand, the need to obtain Japanese adherence to the League of Nations.

Essentially, Wilson acted much against his advisers on the Shantung question. His private secretary, Joseph Tumulty, cabled him frequently from Washington urging him not to yield to Japan.[108] Ray Stannard Baker, who by then had become disillusioned with the conference, made a final plea to Wilson in a memorandum dated 29 April, that 'The Japanese proposal amounts to "offering China the shell and securing for Japan the oyster"'.[109] Interestingly, Wilson was dissatisfied with the advice given by his experts which only allowed him the option of abiding by the principles, being completely unappreciative of the reality of the situation in which the decision had to be made.[110] As Wilson's alienation from his staff increased, so too did his conviction that Shantung must be given to Japan if the League of Nations were to be salvaged, regardless of the intensity of opposition. He justified his case by pointing out the greater international justice which would result through the creation of the League of Nations as opposed to immediate justice of granting Shantung to China.[111] His decision, though taken out of the necessity of attaining a higher ideal, was a devastating blow to China.[112] In the event, Wilson's single-handed decision, taken against the majority view of the American delegation as well as domestic opposition, cost him his most highly prized objective when the American Senate refused to ratify the peace treaty.[113]

It must be said that the environment in which the decision was made (the Council of Four consisting of Wilson, Lloyd George, Clemenceau and Orlando, whose attendance was interrupted with the dispute over Fiume) did have a psychological effect on Wilson. Minutes of the Council of Four suggest that Wilson was under pressure from Lloyd George and Clemenceau, particularly the former, to support the Japanese claims.[114] Effectively, Wilson's resistance to the Japanese claims ran against the interests of Lloyd George and Clemenceau, as both Britain and France were party to secret agreements which recognised Japan's right to Shantung, in Britain's case, in exchange for similar assurances for territorial claims to the Pacific islands to the south of the equator.[115] Thus Wilson faced another dilemma: while a territorial concession to Japan over Shantung touched a raw American nerve, it was nevertheless acceptable to Britain and France. In the end, Wilson acquiesced to great power pressure and concluded that:

> . . . we thought it was the best that could be got, in view of the definite engagements of Great Britain and France, and the necessity of a unanimous decision, which we held to be necessary in every case we have decided.[116]

Even Makino concluded later that Shantung was the price paid by China for Wilson's obsession with the League.[117]

Wilson was, first and foremost, motivated by his personal desire to create the League. Having appeased the British over the racial equality proposal, Wilson now had to appease the Japanese over Shantung in order to maintain token great power solidarity behind the League. This he felt he had to do despite going against the general American position on the issue, as well as against China's vested interests, which the United States was supposedly protecting at Paris. Admittedly, it would have been very difficult for any American president to ignore the secret agreements in 1917 made by France, Italy, Britain and Japan. However, Wilson's overriding priority made him seem like a victim rather than the manipulator of peace conference politics. At least one participant thought highly of his conduct over Shantung:

> Some people have depicted President Wilson as a headstrong, uncompromising idealist; others, as a wavering idealist, easily turned away from his purpose by the Machiavellis of the Old World: on the occasion of the Adriatic problem, we shall find him making his appeal to the Italian nation, against the advice of his French and British partners and with most ill-advised obstinacy; but we

shall also find him anxious to learn and to understand, taking carefully into account what he had learnt, and evincing a tenaciousness combined with a sense of practical possibilities for which he has not been given enough credit: an instance of this was his attitude in the course of the negotiations with the Japanese over Shantung.[118]

WILSON AND UNIVERSAL RACIAL EQUALITY

The Americans, like the Japanese and the British, did not take seriously the view that the racial equality proposal demanded universal racial equality. As previously discussed, House generally tended to perceive the Japanese proposal as implying immigration.[119] With regards to Wilson, however, he failed to express his standpoint clearly on the issue, which can be said to be indicative of his ambivalent attitude towards the principle. As has already been mentioned, Wilson saw the Japanese amendment as being compatible with his religious freedom article (Article 21) at the very beginning of the racial equality negotiations. However, Wilson's support was not based on a strong personal commitment to the principle, and subsequently he quite readily discarded his religious freedom article, together with the racial equality amendment, in the face of opposition from some members, most notably Britain, in the League of Nations Commission. The incident showed that neither religious freedom nor racial equality for Wilson was an essential component of the League; they were principles which would have been compatible with the general notion of the League, but dispensable all the same.

Moreover, Wilson did not seem to consider the possible implications of the racial equality proposal for domestic racial problems in the United States. Basically, his views on race reflected those held by the majority of white Americans at the time, that racial problems were not relevant to the fundamental equality or inequality of men.[120] To be fair, Wilson did recognise the enormity of the racial problem in the United States, but was resigned to the fact that he was not the one to change the situation, as evidenced in his rejection of a recommendation given by Oswald Garrison Villard in 1913 to create a National Race Commission with the objective of promoting better race relations: 'I say it with shame and humiliation, I have thought about this thing for twenty years and I see no way out. It will take a very big man to solve [it].'[121]

It is not at all surprising that Wilson did not conceive of racial equality as having any 'universal' implications for the domestic racial situation in the United States, as the most important underlying assumption was that 'universal' principles would not interfere with domestic affairs of states. This is why the claim made that Wilson regarded the Japanese proposal as a 'human rights' proposal, demanding the equality of all races in the United States,[122] does not hold ground. The proposal was never discussed at Paris with reference to domestic racial equality. The determination of the great powers to distinguish clearly between the internal and the external was a defining feature of their understanding of what was acceptable as universal. All in all, Wilson's understanding of the racial equality proposal as implying universal principle was limited in many respects. Certainly, he did not regard racial equality as a principle of the same importance as self-determination.

CONCLUSIONS

In this chapter, an attempt has been made to demonstrate the complexity of the American position on the racial equality proposal. Although the argument that the Americans opposed the proposal because of the long-standing problem of Japanese immigration in California seems highly plausible, this opposition was not at all decisive, as Senator Phelan's propaganda campaign to attempt to influence the decision makers at Paris had only limited success. He managed only to influence the views of Colonel House, who was not in a position to influence Wilson at the time. Phelan's propaganda against the Japanese proposal had more success in influencing American domestic partisan opponents to President Wilson's League, and the Japanese proposal became embroiled in American domestic politics; but even then, its material effect on Wilson's final decision seemed marginal.

The chapter then looked at the explanatory factor of the politics of bargaining at the peace conference. As the first level of this explanation, the popularity of the 'bargaining chip' theory among American contemporaries is unwarranted. The Japanese did not need to concoct a racial equality proposal to gain Shantung, as the theory claimed, because of the existence of the 1917 secret agreements between Japan and the major Western powers save the United States, which supported Japan's demand for Shantung and the Pacific islands at the peace conference. In light of this, it is crucial to understand why President Wilson had decided to impose unanimity ruling on 11 April, which effectively defeated the Japanese proposal. In the final analysis, it is argued here that the American opposition can be best explained as Wilson's need to use his opposition to the racial equality proposal as an implicit trade-off to ensure the survival of his ultimate objective, the League of Nations. Implicit in this calculation was his conviction that it was crucial to prevent the isolation of Britain over the racial equality issue, because Britain's general support for the League of Nations was considered paramount to its ultimate success. In a sense, the extent to which Wilson was determined to ignore the other American perspectives, those of his domestic opponents as well as almost everyone else in the American delegation at Paris, was a remarkable contrast to both the Japanese and British governments, whose positions on the racial equality proposal were very much affected by the respective 'domestic' considerations. In the end, all this revealed that Wilsonian idealism did not take into account the possibility that the proposal had anything to do with universal racial equality.

7 Conclusions and reflections

This chapter attempts to do three things: to offer conclusions to the main body of the study, to delineate the possible effects of the racial equality proposal on Japan's interwar politics and diplomacy, and to reflect on the historical significance of the principle of racial equality in the context of what has been argued in this study.

CONCLUSIONS

The main purpose of this study has been to make a detailed analysis of the racial equality proposal at the 1919 Paris Peace Conference. In order to understand the proposal, it has been necessary to explain not only the Japanese motivations but also the responses of the British and American delegations. The analysis of Japanese motivations and the Anglo-American responses has shown that internal mechanisms for determining the position taken by each country were not as one-dimensional or straightforward as they appeared on the surface. The study used the five categories of explanation, outlined in the introductory chapter, in order to understand the positions taken by the three protagonists: universal principle, great power status, immigration, domestic politics and the politics of bargaining at the peace conference.

In the analysis of the Japanese motivations, the three explanations of great power status, immigration and domestic politics proved valid. Interestingly, in the process of examining these explanations, it became clear that the racial equality proposal was not really about the principle of universal racial equality, as has been assumed by some scholars. First, the explanation of domestic politics suggested that the racial equality proposal, as Japan's condition for accepting the League of Nations, played the role of justifying the pro-League policy of Prime Minister Hara and his close supporters. The League was considered to be an important signal of Japan's willingness to cooperate with the

West in order to prevent the further international isolation of Japan, underlining the *ōbei kyōchō* (pro-Western, internationalist) attitude of Hara's foreign policy. Hara and his *ōbei kyōchō* supporters had to contend with two groups that were sceptical of the League. First, there existed a number of sceptics within the government and the Diplomatic Advisory Council, who had an ingrained suspicion that the League was simply another form of political alliance to maintain the *status quo* to the advantage of the West, or more to the point, the Anglo-Saxons. In view of the urgency of the situation, Hara managed to extract a compromise from the sceptics. The condition was that if Japan were to join the League, then it would do so by securing some means of protecting itself from being racially discriminated against within the organisation. The second type of scepticism which the pro-League supporters of Hara had to appease was public opinion in Japan. Much pressure was put on the government by the wider public to succeed at the peace conference, especially over the question of the racial equality proposal, which was regarded to be the *sine qua non* of Japan's joining the League. The public were sceptical of the League for reasons similar to those expressed by the sceptics within the government; only the liberal intellectuals shared Hara's pro-League perspective. In the light of the above, racial equality could be seen as a condition that would make Japan's acquiescence to the League at least slightly more tolerable to its opponents.

Secondly, the explanation which has been most widely cited hitherto, that the proposal was a means of resolving the long-standing problems of Japanese immigration into the Anglo-Saxon territories, was important but not the dominant reason. It has become clear that this was the view chiefly espoused by the Foreign Ministry but not necessarily endorsed by the government as a whole. In the absence of detailed guidelines from Tokyo, the racial equality proposal was worded to reflect the particular perspective of those with an immediate input into its drafting in Paris. The substance of the proposal reflected the bureaucratic priorities of the Foreign Ministry, which for historical reasons was anxious to resolve once and for all the issue of anti-Japanese immigration practices in the United States and the British Dominions. It can be said that immigration was such an important issue for the Foreign Ministry which tended to perceive it not only as a practical problem, but also as a symbolic manifestation of Japan's 'unequal' status. In fact, anti-Japanese immigration policies in the Anglo-Saxon territories meant a 'loss of face' for the Japanese government, which was anxious to protect as well as to further its great power status by securing racial equality. Significantly, it became clear in the analysis that the so-called immigration explanation in reality belonged more accurately as part of the explanation of great power status, insofar as it was a concrete manifestation of the most important explanatory factor. In this sense, the immigration factor, though treated independently in this analysis because of the weight given to it by the existing literature on the proposal, can be seen to represent one highly important aspect of the problems associated with Japan's great power status.

Lastly, the most important explanation is that of great power status, which referred to Japan's insecurity as a non-white great power. In the period from the Sino–Japanese War of 1895 until the First World War, the West posed three major challenges to Japan. These were the Triple Intervention of 1895, the 'Yellow Peril' after the Japanese victory over Russia in 1905 and the 1913 Californian Alien Land Law. It has been argued that these events contributed to undermining Japan's confidence as the only non-Western great power at the time. Moreover, public interest in foreign policy debates, as evidenced in the continuing existence of the *ajia shugi* (pan-Asian) versus *datsu-A ron* (escape Asia) debate from the mid-Meiji period onwards, testified to the importance and awareness of the problem of Japan's international status from its early modern days. The experience of the First World War had heightened Japan's sense of isolation internationally, as is seen in the deterioration of its relations with both Britain and the United States. These provided the general understanding of the fragility of Japan's perception of its great power status. Importantly, there was an inclination domestically to connect this insecurity to the racial aspect of Japan's identity as seen in the prominence of *jinshuron* (racial discourse). This insecurity was reflected in the Hara government's peace policy towards the League of Nations which specified that Japan should secure measures to prevent itself from being racially discriminated against in the new organisation. Thus, the origins of the racial equality proposal can be associated with Japan's insecurity as a non-white great power in a League that would be dominated by the Western powers.

One of the interesting results of the analysis was that the proposal was not intended as a demand for universal racial equality. It was clear from the original clause relating to 'racial prejudice' in the peace policy that the intention was to secure racial equality for Japanese nationals. There was no discussion of it ever as a universal principle in the official record. Moreover, the Japanese continued to practise discrimination against the Chinese and Koreans.

The British Empire delegation's position on the racial equality proposal can be best explained in terms of the two explanatory categories of immigration and domestic politics. First of all, the British government's interpretation of the proposal as an immigration measure had effectively made the proposal an 'internal' problem within the British Empire delegation. This was because immigration historically belonged to the Dominions' sphere of influence in British–Dominion relations. In practice, the British government did not have much control over the immigration policies of the Dominions and was, moreover, very unwilling to enforce its imperial prerogative over the Dominions. This enabled Australia to influence the overall position adopted by the delegation, which was to oppose the proposal. The Australian premier, Billy Hughes, had vested interests in defeating the proposal for domestic political reasons. Essentially, Hughes opposed the proposal because of the possible negative implications it had for the 'White Australia' policy. Historically, Australia had exercised immigration policies which were designed specifically to restrict the flow of non-white immigrants. The fear of Japanese immigrants was also related to the issue of defence, again particularly in the case of Australia, which felt threatened by the military strength of Japan as a power in the Pacific. It seems that Billy Hughes's persistent opposition was a reflection of how important the protection of the 'White Australia' policy, with its large anti-Japanese component, had become in Australian politics. Moreover, it was crucial for Hughes to perform well at Paris by fighting for the protection of Australian national interests because he was effectively conducting an election campaign for the up and coming Australian general elections while at the peace conference. Thus he made rejection of the proposal into a symbol of resistance to the British government, with the hidden agenda of demonstrating to the Australian public his personal resolve to protect Australia's vested interests so as to increase his own domestic support. The ultimate victory of Hughes is significant because it showed how far the Dominions could go in influencing the foreign policy of the British imperial government.

It appears that the British did not seem to have considered at all the possibility that the racial equality proposal was a demand for a universal principle of racial equality. It was the strength of conviction held by the British, that the proposal was, without any doubt, about immigration, which basically determined how the proposal was to be treated within the British Empire delegation. Although it has been argued by some that the British had to oppose the proposal because of its universal implications for the British Empire with its many non-white colonised peoples, this is not a correct assumption to make; the principle of racial equality was actually theoretically compatible with the imperial principle of equality of subjects. Therefore, the fact that the British had completely neglected the universal aspect of the proposal could only be explained by their avowed conviction that it had nothing to do with it.

The American position was just as complex because a number of perceptions operated simultaneously at different political levels. First of all, in the domestic political arena in the United States, the high level of anti-Japanese sentiment demonstrated why there was so much American domestic agitation over the proposal. The history of antagonistic anti-Japanese immigration policies in the United States resulted in a strong tendency to view the proposal as demanding unrestricted immigration of Japanese and other non-white immigrants. The problem was particularly acute in California, where the fear of Japanese immigration became an important political issue extensively manipulated by politicians such as Senator Phelan. The Californian anti-Japanese immigration lobby managed to stir up much heated debate in the United States, with the desired effect of influencing Colonel House, who became concerned about the domestic implications of the Japanese proposal. This explanation was important in understanding why the American public responded so strongly against the proposal, but its ultimate impact on decision making at Paris was not as effective as it was in the case of Britain.

Interestingly, the racial equality proposal was adopted by the anti-Wilson and anti-League movement in the United States as one of their platforms alongside the Monroe Doctrine. Republican opponents mounted united opposition to Wilson as a result of their dissatisfaction with the way in which he had turned the peace conference into a partisan and personal issue. In effect, the racial equality proposal provided an ideal weapon for those waging a protracted battle to bring down Wilson and his peace plan regardless of the cost and its external implications, with the added benefit of manipulating anti-Japanese sentiment. However, just as in the case of immigration, its impact on the decision making of Wilson was questionable.

The explanatory category of the politics of bargaining at the peace conference produced two competing perspectives. First, there was the well-known 'bargaining chip' theory expounded by the 'pro-China' commissioners, namely, Secretary of State Lansing, General Tasker Bliss and Henry White, backed by domestic public opinion. This theory held that Japan had intentionally concocted the racial equality proposal as a political instrument in order to obtain a favourable settlement over Shantung. This view was shared by some of the Chinese delegates, who attempted to explain Wilson's failure to support them over Shantung in terms of Wilson's being 'bamboozled' by the Japanese. However, this explanation was made *ex post facto* and did not seem to influence what Wilson thought about the proposal. Moreover, the fact that the Japanese government had signed the secret agreements of 1917 to gain Shantung and the Pacific islands at the peace conference meant that the 'bargaining chip' theory was invalidated. Accordingly, Japan did not need to invent racial equality to press these claims, because it did not expect any difficulties in obtaining these demands at the peace conference.

The most important reason for the American rejection of the racial equality proposal lay in the suggestion made that Wilson had used the racial equality proposal as a political instrument to gain other ends, namely the establishment of the League of Nations. Wilson's *raison d'être* at Paris was to create the League of Nations, and everything else was subordinated to achieve this end. In order to attain his objective, Wilson considered British support as being imperative because of his belief that only Anglo-Saxon solidarity could guarantee the success of the League. When Wilson realised the irrevocable nature of British opposition to the proposal thanks to Australia's attitude, he considered supporting the British position on the racial equality proposal to be the only possible option. This would show solidarity with the British, which hopefully would guarantee Britain's continued general support for the League. Thus he imposed a unanimity ruling on the 11 April meeting without declaring American opposition, and managed to defeat the proposal. It must be mentioned that Wilson, in his capacity as chairman of the League of Nations Commission, was entitled to insist on a unanimity ruling. Indirectly, Wilson's decision was affected by Hughes's persistent opposition. Wilson's fixation with creating the League affected the vital decision over the Shantung settlement, as he was forced to take into account Japan's threat of withdrawal from the conference. To his mind, it was more important to save the League, which would secure a safer world, than to secure Shantung for China, even if this meant going against the wishes of the American public. Hence, it was Wilson who had used the Japanese proposal as a bargaining instrument to gain other ends, that is to protect the League of Nations, at the peace conference.

Finally, the Americans, like the Japanese and British, did not interpret the proposal as one of universal principle of racial equality. Apart from House, who flirted with the idea for a day or two, the American delegation did not seriously consider the Japanese proposal as a demand for a universal principle. This was interesting, because one of the main reasons given by the Japanese public for supporting the racial equality proposal was that it was compatible with the Wilsonian international order. However, such thinking had hardly any effect on the Americans. Although Wilson initially was sympathetic to the proposal, his interest was marginal and he certainly did not regard it as being of the same order as his principle of self-determination.

THE EFFECTS ON JAPAN IN THE INTERWAR PERIOD

This section will examine briefly the implications that the defeat of the racial equality proposal in 1919 might have had on Japanese foreign policy in the interwar years. By necessity, what follows is not a detailed analysis of the important events in the 1920s and 1930s, but a more general and possibly somewhat speculative attempt to understand how the proposal, which was obviously important to Japan, could have affected the policy and the thinking of those leaders who played a prominent part in interwar Japanese politics and diplomacy. It is argued that the proposal played a more significant role than has been thought in the past. The failure of the racial equality proposal had two main implications for interwar Japan. First, it contributed to the general disillusionment which pervaded in Japan in the 1920s, a belief that the Anglo-Saxon West[1] had created an international system which was fundamentally 'unfair' and 'unjust' at the Paris Peace Conference. Second, it had a symbolic importance as a means of justifying the increasingly 'independent' – that is, Japan-centric and pan-Asian – foreign policy, especially in the 1930s.

Before we proceed, let us first finish the story of the racial equality proposal, which did not end at the Paris Peace Conference. Having failed there, the Japanese government decided to make a speech at the opening of the League of Nations on 30 November 1920 in order to signal to the world that it had not completely given up on the proposal.[2] Ambassador Ishii, who was posted to the League of Nations in Geneva, suggested that Japan should resubmit the proposal at the commission in order to amend the covenant in 1921. But in April 1921, the government instructed him to abandon the idea altogether for the time being.[3] The reasons given were that the racial equality debate at the peace conference had affected negatively Japan's relations with the United States, Britain and the Dominions, and hence it had turned into a problem with diplomatic implications. Moreover, there were many obstacles to achieving the success of the proposal, which were compounded by the present negotiations on the revision of the Anglo-Japanese Alliance, and the treatment of the Japanese in the South Pacific islands under the mandatory system. All in all, it was considered best not to disrupt the rather 'delicate' relationship between Japan, Britain and United States by resubmitting the proposal. It was this sort of 'weak-kneed' (*nanjaku*) attitude of not wanting to upset the allies which later became the focus of criticism of the 'Shidehara diplomacy' (*Shidehara gaikō*)[4] in the late 1920s.

Japan's disillusionment with the West

Let us examine the proposition that the rejection of the proposal contributed to deepening Japan's sense of disillusionment with the West in the 1920s. This can be explained in terms of three factors: disillusionment with the League of Nations, increasing Anglo-American solidarity in East Asia and the Pacific, and the diplomatic row over the 1924 Alien Immigration Act in the United States. It seems that the disillusionment contributed to undermining eventually Japan's attempt to pursue the 'Shidehara diplomacy'.

First, it can be said that the rejection of the racial equality proposal played an important role in influencing Japan's general underlying attitude towards the newly created League of Nations. The proposal revealed Japan's fundamental uncertainty about the League and, more widely, international society, which was perceived to be dominated by the Anglo-Saxon powers. Generally speaking, the Japanese public was disappointed with the results of the Paris Peace Conference.[5] As stated previously, the fact that Japanese public opinion on the whole tended to measure the equity of the League of Nations and, by extension, the Anglo-Saxons on the basis of acceptance or non-acceptance of the racial equality proposal meant that the rejection of the proposal by the Paris Peace Conference left an indelible mark on Japan and its postwar relations with the West.[6] The rejection created much deeper psychological implications for the Japanese than has generally been assumed. It proved what the Japanese had always feared and suspected – that the Anglo-Saxons were not capable of practising what they preached especially in terms of what they implied by 'international justice'. Their rejection of the Japanese proposal implied to the Japanese, who were sceptical of the League, that the West intended to continue with the *status quo*, which was to practise double standards in dealing with Japan. More symbolically, it meant that the West was unwilling to acknowledge Japan as an equal on the basis of race. This is an important yet not fully recognised factor, which coloured Japan's attitude towards the world in the interwar period.

However, the Japanese government, through the Foreign Ministry, attempted to deal with the problem of Japan's international isolation in a pragmatic way. In the early 1920s, the government supported the 'Shidehara diplomacy', which stressed the importance of pursuing a policy of international cooperation, especially with Britain and the United States, as the best means of furthering its national interests in East Asia.[7] It emphasised economic diplomacy rather than the military diplomacy of the past. Essentially, the 'Shidehara diplomacy' rested on the assumption that Japan should not be isolated from the Anglo-Saxon West. In a sense, this was a highly pragmatic policy which acknowledged the limits of Japan's national strength at the time, conceding that Japan could not antagonise the United States because it did not have the means of going to war against it. However, this was couched in liberal, internationalist expressions, such as 'the age of geopolitical manoeuvrings and aggressive policies is now over, and diplomacy has begun marching the path of justice and peace'.[8] Clearly, the policy was influenced by the 'new diplomacy' of the United States, with an implicit intention of integrating more closely with it.

Moreover, the new international order created in the post-1919 world based on the League of Nations became *de facto* obsolete in East Asia, due to the failure of the United States to ratify the Treaty of Versailles. This meant that a new system had to be created in the region in order to maintain international stability. The forum in which this new order took place was the new Anglo-American nexus which emerged at the Washington Conference of 1921–2.[9] At the Washington Conference, the Four Power Treaty between Japan, Britain, the United States and France was signed in December 1921, instituting a system of 'conference' among the signatories. This had the effect of displacing Japan from the pre-eminent position of power in East Asia, hitherto held jointly with Britain through the Anglo-Japanese Alliance. In reality, the naval ratio negotiated for the Five Power Treaty of 5:5:3:1.75:1.75 (US, Britain, Japan, France, Italy respectively) showed that Japan's status was not only less than that of the United States and Britain, but was also measurably diluted, being now juxtaposed against France and Italy whose primary imperial interests were not in East Asia. From Japan's perspective, then, the downgrading of Japan's status constituted 'a dishonourable action' on the part of Britain[10], and the anticipation that Japan would become isolated due to the Anglo-Saxon domination of world affairs appeared to come true.[11] Needless to say, the acceptance of this new order based on the dual hegemony of Britain and the United States in the Pacific was much criticised by the younger generation of leaders.[12]

For Japan, it seems that the problem with the *pax Anglo-Americana* now ruling East Asia and the Pacific was twofold. First, in spite of the fact that Japan recognised the necessity of cooperating with the United States, it nevertheless felt threatened by the negative attitude of the Americans towards Japan. As a reflection of the American tendency to adopt a moralistic undertone in foreign policy, the Americans were highly critical of many of the Japanese actions in China especially during the First World War.[13] American foreign policy of the time saw China as its *protégé*, to be guided and tutored to become the Asian equivalent of democratic America[14] – a sentiment not shared by Britain.[15] Naturally, this sense of mission towards China tended to colour the general American perception of Japan as the dangerous 'other' in East Asia, which was threatening China's emergence as a modern democracy. Hence, the American attitude to Japan was characterised by an underlying sense of distrust, thinly veiled by the necessity of having to recognise Japan's importance as a great power. This became manifestly clear when the 'bargaining chip' theory emerged in the American delegation in 1919. Clearly, the existence of a Sino–American 'conspiracy' against Japan at the Paris Peace Conference had made the Japanese government doubly anxious about the recurrence of an anti-Japanese campaign at the Washington Conference. As an illustration of the high level of mutual distrust, Foreign Minister Uchida sought to influence the American decision on the composition of the delegation by attempting to relay the message that Japan did not favour E.T. Williams, who had been appointed as special advisor, on the basis that 'being a one-time missionary to China, [he] had the tendency to be innately prejudiced against us'.[16] No doubt, the underlying mutual distrust continued to be prevalent and influenced the basis of bilateral relations in the 1920s.

Secondly, Japan increasingly felt betrayed by Britain, especially as the result of the decision to terminate the Anglo-Japanese Alliance at the Washington Conference.[17] The fact that Britain was the first Western power to recognise Japan as a great power by signing the Anglo-Japanese Alliance in 1902 became deeply engraved in Japanese public memory. When the question of the renewal of the alliance came up in 1921, a majority of the Japanese were overwhelmingly in favour of continuing it. According to a memorandum from the Asia Bureau of the Foreign Ministry, the alliance was symbolically important because 'Japan alone out of the five great powers was of the different race'.[18] On the British side, too, the government was in favour of some sort of continuation. However, Nish succinctly summarises the difficulty of the British position at Washington: 'It was not that the Japanese had greatly offended but rather that the Japanese alliance did not fit in with Britain's need for American goodwill and understanding.'[19] However, this left the impression with the Japanese of the existence of an Anglo-American collusion to exclude them from the new equation.[20] Quite possibly, the Japanese were, in reality, being hypersensitive about not being liked by Britain, as the British tended to view Japan in the 1920s 'with cordiality, moderated by a dash of mistrust and suspicion'.[21]

The third factor which seriously endangered Japanese–American relations in the 1920s was the 1924 Immigration Act. The 1924 act was extremely damaging because the Japanese government had perceived it as one of challenging the prestige and reputation of Japan as a great power. In fact, it has been shown in this study that the problem of Japanese immigration remained unresolved, and moreover, that the racial equality proposal had the effect of making it manifestly worse in the United States during 1919. Because of the success with which Californian State Senator Phelan was able to stir up anti-Japanese sentiment in late March 1919, the new California Oriental Exclusion League was founded in late 1919, reorganised in September 1920 into the Japanese Exclusion League of California with State Senator Inman as president.[22] In 1920, California adopted another Alien Land Law with the objective of strengthening the 1913 Alien Land Law, due to the threat caused by the rise of the adult Japanese population within California from 32,785 in 1910 to 47,566 in 1920.[23] As evidence of the importance that the Japanese and American governments attached to finding a satisfactory solution to the problem of immigration, regular consultative sessions were undertaken by Ambassadors Shidehara and Morris in their respective postings from September 1920 to January 1921.[24] However, such efforts did not bear fruit. The Japanese remained the group which encountered the longest sustained attack by American society 'north of the Mason-Dixon line', because they were of a distinct racial group, they challenged the white American middle class, and their country of origin became increasingly unpopular.[25]

The 1924 Immigration Act, instead of having a general quota for all immigrants, introduced individual national quotas under which Japan was allowed one hundred persons per annum, the lowest quota and on a par with countries such as Egypt, India and Samoa.[26] This constituted a 'loss of face' to the Japanese government, which saw the act as essentially one which was targeted against Japan as a country:

> To Japan the question is not one of expediency, but of principle. To her the mere fact that a few hundreds of thousands of her nationals

> will or will not be admitted into domains of other countries is immaterial, so long as no question of national susceptibilities is involved. The important question is whether Japan as a nation is or is not entitled to the proper respect and consideration of other nations. . . . The manifest object of the [exclusion clause] is to single out the Japanese as a nation, stigmatizing them as unworthy and undesirable in the eyes of the American people.[27]

Ironically, it was Ambassador Hanihara Masanao's letter to Secretary of State Charles Hughes, written in April 1924, which gave the necessary ammunition to the anti-Japanese lobby which ensured the successful passage of the bill. In the letter, Hanihara warned of 'the grave consequences' which the enactment of this bill would have on American–Japanese relations.[28] This wording caused a furore when it was taken up by Senator Cabot Lodge, and presented as evidence of Japan's 'veiled threat'. To counter this, the Japanese government lodged an official diplomatic complaint to the American government, stating that it could no longer continue with the gentlemen's agreement which effectively had been nullified by the new act.[29] Evidently, one of the major problems with the Japanese immigration issue was that the American government refused to take responsibility for actions taken by state governments, even if these very actions constituted a legitimate case of diplomatic intervention.[30] This was not uniquely an American problem, however, as a similar position was taken by the British government during the racial equality negotiation at Paris, when Lord Robert Cecil insisted that Britain could not intervene in the Dominions which had the right to control immigration policies. Whatever the American justifications might have been, the Japanese could only see the enormity of the damage caused by this action.[31] The 1924 Immigration Act was the last major point of contention in the bilateral relationship over immigration, but there continued to be a string of minor incidents throughout the rest of the decade and into the 1930s.[32]

The failure of the racial equality proposal contributed to Japan's general sense of disillusionment with the West, and especially the Anglo-Saxon powers, in the early 1920s. Contrary to this underlying sentiment, the early postwar governments under the banner of the 'Shidehara diplomacy' adopted the policy of emphasising international cooperation with the United States and Britain. However, it became evident in the process of pursuing this policy that Japan was becoming secondary to the Anglo-American hegemony in East Asia and the Pacific, which emerged as a result of the Washington Conference of

1921–2. Moreover, the 1924 Immigration Act undermined to some extent the 'Shidehara diplomacy' by questioning the wisdom of cooperating with the Americans, who had not been hesitant about humiliating the Japanese. Overall, it appears that the apparent domestic consensus over the 'Shidehara diplomacy' was possibly not as strong as has been suggested in the past. In retrospect, it is ironic that the racial equality proposal, which was originally created by the pro-internationalists within the Japanese government in order to demand greater equality of Japan with the West, had indirectly contributed to making their pro-Western policy increasingly less tenable in the 1920s.

The importance of the proposal to Pan-Asianists

The second major implication of the rejection of the proposal is that it was perceived as being symbolic of the rejection of Japan by the West. This view was espoused especially by the pan-Asianists and other apologists in the 1930s. Increasingly during this period, the proposal was used retrospectively as a justification for Japan's 'independent' path in foreign policy. We can attempt to analyse the impact of that rejection by examining very briefly the resurgence of pan-Asianism in the immediate aftermath of the First World War, the importance of race and racial equality in pan-Asian thinking in the late 1920s and the 1930s, and the changing domestic consensus in the mid-1930s.

One of the most important revelations from the racial equality debate in 1919 was the depth of pan-Asian feeling in public opinion, which did not necessarily reflect the views of the elite group of pro-internationalists in the Foreign Ministry and the government. It has been demonstrated in previous chapters that the pan-Asianists, through pressure groups and intensive public campaigns, had used the proposal to challenge the Hara government's pro-Western internationalist outlook in foreign policy. Without a doubt, this was an important factor for the pan-Asian lobby because it underlined the importance of racial and cultural affinity of Japan with Asia. What the defeat of the proposal did, therefore, was to confirm the pan-Asian claim that the West was not treating Japan with the respect that it deserved, because of racial difference. The rejection provided a fertile ground for those Japanese who increasingly began to perceive that Japan had been wronged at Paris by the Anglo-Saxon powers. This connection between Japan as the 'wronged' nation and the Anglo-Saxons as the perpetrators was used by the pan-Asianists in an attempt to steer public opinion away from a foreign policy which sought to integrate Japan further with the West. Although it is not possible to say that the proposal was decisive in influencing the resurgence of pan-Asianism in the 1920s, there is little doubt that it did act as a catalyst for the increasing feeling that Japan was being badly treated, and in some cases wronged, by the West.

It was no coincidence that the end of the First World War saw a resurgence of pan-Asianism, and in particular, the rise of the radical nationalist wing of pan-Asian thinking. For instance, it was in the immediate aftermath of the war that the two iconoclastic pan-Asian thinkers, Kita Ikki (1883–1937) and Okawa Shūmei (1886–1957), came into national prominence. Okawa saw the racial significance of the war as a struggle between the white and the yellow races;[33] in fact, he was a committee member of a minor pressure group, Zen ajia kai (All Asia Society), which fought for the adoption of the racial equality proposal in 1919.[34] For Okawa, the advocation of *ajia fukkō* [revival of Asia] from white domination became one of the most important objectives in his brand of pan-Asianism. He became especially anti-West after the 1924 Immigration Act, and in 1925 preached in his book *Asia, Europe and Japan* that Japan, as leader of Asia, and the United States, as leader of the West, were bound to clash in the future. Indeed, one of the objectives of his pan-Asian organisation, Gyōchisha, was the liberation of coloured peoples in order for them to belong to a new, morally based international system.[35]

Similarly, Kita Ikki[36] wrote the 'Principles of a Plan to Reorganise the State' [Kokka kaizō-an genri taikō] in 1919, later published in 1923, based on his understanding of the peace conference. What Kita called for was a reorganisation of the Japanese state, to bring the people closer to the emperor by removing the oligarchs in between. In terms of the basic outline, it was strikingly similar to Konoe's New Order Movement of the late 1930s, with the idea of a national defence state (*kokubō kokka*).[37] In 1919, Kita joined Okawa's organisation *Yūzonsha*, whose manifesto stated:

> We the Japanese people must be the cyclone centre of a war to liberate mankind. Therefore the Japanese state is the Absolute which will bring about the establishment of our idea of world revolution. . . . We do not consider it sufficient to pursue reorganisation and revolution for Japan alone, but because we really believe in the Japanese nation's destiny to be the great apostle of mankind's war or liberation we want to begin with the liberation of Japan itself.[38]

Both Okawa and Kita were convinced that Japan should play the leading role in the new world order, which was yet to be constructed. Although the partnership of these two extremist ideologues did not last long, it is highly significant that they were heavily influenced by Japan's participation in the First World War and the Paris Peace Conference, leading them to consolidate their respective ideological tenets.[39] What they represented was disillusionment with the existing order, both domestically and internationally. They became the key thinkers in the 1930s, as the country plunged into the 'Valley of Darkness'.

It is quite clear that the idea of race and racial equality continued to play an important role in pan-Asian thinking, especially in terms of its imperialistic aspirations on the continent. Interestingly, the Japanese increasingly used the term 'racial equality' to legitimise their continental expansionism. For instance, the Manchurian Youth League (Manshū seinen remmei) declared in 1928 that:

> The only way to survive [for the Manchurian Japanese] . . . would be to join hands with the various racial groups living in Manchuria . . . to devote themselves to the harmony of races . . . and to bring about a paradise-like republic to the land of Manchuria–Mongolia backed by Japanese civilisation.[40]

This reflected the thinking of Ishiwara Kanji, one of the architects of the Manchurian incident in the Kwantung Army, who sought a 'forging of racial cooperation among Asian peoples' by creating a 'racial paradise', Manchukuo.[41] Essentially, the message was that Japan was different from any other Western imperial power because it was an Asian power, and that it was willing to recognise, first and foremost, racial harmony of all peoples residing in Manchuria in order to create a 'racial paradise'. This can be seen as a repudiation of the Western acceptance of Japan on the basis of great power status, which failed to extend that acceptance to racial equality of the Japanese and the Western great powers. In fact, the Japanese were using 'racial equality' as a weapon against the West, and in order to make the Japanese more palatable to other Asians who were about to come under Japanese imperial control. Of course, this was essentially a propaganda exercise and Ishiwara and his colleagues in the Kwantung Army were under no illusion that 'the interest of Japan and the Japanese shall, as a general rule, be given primary consideration' in the newly created Manchukuo in 1932.[42] It is worth noting that this idea of 'racial harmony' became an intrinsic aspect of Japan's propaganda for the Greater East Asia Co-Prosperity Sphere in the 1940s.[43]

One interesting barometer of pan-Asian thinking on the question of racial equality can be traced through Konoe Fumimaro, who attended the Paris Peace Conference as Saionji's private secretary and who became a key figure in Japanese politics in the 1930s. It must be remembered that Konoe was disgruntled by the treatment meted out to Japan by the West even before attending the peace conference as witnessed in his article, 'Eibei hon'i no heiwashugi o haisu' (Abolish the Anglo-Saxon Based Peace). After the peace conference, Konoe continued to feel that the international order in the post-1919 world, which was largely an Anglo-Saxon invention, was not based on fairness and justice. Konoe saw the world in terms of the 'haves' and 'have-nots', the former representing powers which favoured the *status quo*, namely Britain and the United States, and the latter including Japan, wanting to break with the *status quo*.[44] In fact, it seems that the failure of the peace conference to establish the basis for a true peace plagued Konoe for the rest of his life. He tended to see the West's rejection of the racial equality proposal as symptomatic of the Western dictated definition of *status quo* which perpetuated unfairness in the world.[45]

Japan's withdrawal from the League of Nations in 1933 proved to be an ideal opportunity to trumpet the failure of the racial equality proposal of 1919 as a justification for leaving such an 'unfair' international order. In February 1933, one month before Japan's withdrawal from the League of Nations, Konoe wrote:

> In thinking about it, the Paris Peace Conference was the ideal opportunity to correct the existing irrationalities in the world and to establish a true world peace. This conference was held immediately after the war and the politicians who attended it had all experienced much pain with the horrors of the war. However, the Paris conference did not recognise the blatant irrationality of discriminating against people by skin colour.[46]

Matsuoka Yōsuke, the Japanese representative who executed the dramatic withdrawal from the League, also referred to the failure of racial equality as an example of the West's bullying of Japan at the peace conference.[47]

Needless to say, Konoe's views became highly influential in the 1930s, as both leading political parties, Seiyūkai and Minseitō, abandoned the policy of international cooperation and supported expansion into China and throughout Asia.[48] In fact, it has been argued that the reason why party politicians pursued the policy of international cooperation in the 1920s was the perception that this policy was the best way of safeguarding Japan's imperialistic ambitions.[49] The idea that Japan had been putting up with the existing international order because of the lack of national strength to fight against the white race was widely prevalent.[50] By the mid-1930s, even the hitherto stalwart pro-Western Foreign Ministry began to reflect more the line taken by Konoe: that Japan saw as part of its mission the need to redress the unfairness which existed in the present international system. Shigemitsu Mamoru, who served as Vice Foreign Minister from May 1933 to April 1936, held the view that Japan was the only power capable of stabilising East Asia, and that it was important for the Western powers to recognise this.[51] It can be said that by the late 1930s, the racial equality proposal became a highly useful propaganda tool, used by Japanese politicians as a means of justifying whatever positions they took against the Anglo-Saxon West.[52]

It is worth noting that the Japanese sensitivity was such that even Nazi Germany became concerned about not offending Japanese sensibilities over race, although the Japanese sensitivity was such that even the Japanese remained unconvinced of German efforts.[53] In fact, the Nazis went so far as to issue the following press directive in February 1935:

> The Yellow Peril must no longer be made out as a picture of horror, for Germany's attitude toward other races leaves completely open the question of the worth of other races – especially when these races must not, for political reasons, be offended.[54]

The German Ambassador in Tokyo was so concerned about the adverse effects the racial policy of the German government would have on German–Japanese relations that he was ready to emphasise to the Japanese that 'Germany's only racial problem was a Jewish one'.[55]

Thus it can be seen that the failure of the racial equality proposal contributed importantly to Japan's perception of its role in the interwar international order. The rejection of the proposal contributed to disillusionment in Japan as it had entered the new era of the 'Shidehara diplomacy' in the 1920s; the international order, which it was supposedly supporting, was not entirely based on justice and fairness. The fear of Anglo-Saxon domination, and the resultant marginalisation of Japan, played a predominant part in such thinking. The pan-Asianists took a defiant stance against the pro-Western 'Shidehara diplomacy' in the 1920s, and dominated mainstream thinking in the 1930s. For them, the rejection of the proposal constituted vital evidence that the West had been fundamentally unfair to Japan. In the end, the Japanese effectively used the rejection as a weapon against the West, in the course of their own bid to create an alternative world order in the late 1930s.

As a conclusion to the effects of the proposal on interwar Japan, we shall end with what the Shōwa Emperor had to say retrospectively in 1946 about the racial equality proposal. There exists a confidential 'monologue' record by the Shōwa Emperor on his 'thoughts' concerning the years leading up to the Second World War. In it, the very first topic the emperor refers to is 'The Background Causes to the Greater East Asia War' in which he states:

> If we ask the reason for this war, it lies in the contents of the peace treaty signed at the end of the First World War. The racial equality proposal demanded by Japan was not accepted by the powers. The discriminatory sentiment between the white and the yellow remains as always. And the rejection of immigrants in California. These were enough to anger the Japanese people.[56]

The above passage acts as a preamble to the monologue. Interestingly, after this preamble, the emperor next talks about the assassination of Chang Tso-lin in 1928. In this sense, the preamble was used to 'set the scene' or to explain the underlying dissatisfaction which the Japanese nation harboured towards the Anglo-Saxon West after the Paris Peace Conference. The fact that the emperor felt the need to mention this underlines how hateful the experience of 'racial discrimination' was to the Japanese, and that this sentiment was felt not only by the pan-Asianists and ultra-nationalists, but more widely in society. The greatest significance of this testimony lies in the fact that the Shōwa Emperor recognises the rejection of the racial equality proposal as one of the foremost underlying reasons for Japan's decisions leading to the Greater East Asia War. Since we know that the proposal was not the direct cause of the war, it seems fair to say that its importance was symbolic for the emperor.

REFLECTIONS ON THE PRINCIPLE OF RACIAL EQUALITY

Surely one of the most significant findings of this study has been the conclusion that the major protagonists – Japan, the British Empire and the United States – did not interpret the racial equality proposal as a demand for the universal equality of all races. Hence, the assumption made by some scholars recently that the proposal was indeed an attempt by the Japanese to demand universal racial equality is anachronistic, and not true to the substance of what had been debated in 1919.[57] In the light of this finding, three general observations can be made of the 'place' which racial equality occupied in international society of the time: first, the seeming lack of recognition of racial equality as a universal principle of international importance by the three main protagonists; second, the principle of racial equality as a variation of the principle of equality of states; and third, the limited conception of the principle in terms of applicability.

What we consider today to be the principle of racial equality, with all its universalist baggage of moral, political and civic values, did not seem to hold true in 1919 when the Japanese racial equality proposal was debated at the Paris Peace Conference. Interestingly, it was not only the objectors who did not ascribe to the universalist connotation; neither did the proponents. Why was this the case? Quite simply, the world was different then. In fact, if we consider the moral, political and social climate of the time, we should be asking the opposite question. Why should racial equality be accepted and encouraged in a world of European imperialism, when multi-racial empires, which stretched literally across and around the globe, were governed by the dominant white race? It was certainly logical to hold the view that it was not in the interest of these imperial powers that there should be equality of all races; nor was there any inclination to believe that that was a 'desirable' value to be pursued.[58] This was especially true in the case of Britain, which might have held a more paternalistic view about developing the concept of 'self-rule' as the first step towards independence, though as a concept this was applicable only to the white Dominions at this time. At any rate, it would appear that any issue involving 'racial equality', such as immigration, was treated as an internal matter for states and empires, and not an international issue. No doubt, the Japanese would not be impressed by racist views such as those expressed by Quincy Wright of the American Naval Intelligence unit in 1921:

> Although it is not possible to grade races in a single ascending scale, it must be recognised that races differ greatly in natural capacity both physical and mental. One race will rank high in qualities in which another ranks low, while in other qualities, they will be reversed. Thus a recognition of racial differences no moral stigma.[59]

However, it is important to make the qualification that we are principally concerned here with Japan, Britain and the United States. As we saw, the French did not object officially to the racial equality proposal on the basis that it was 'an indisputable principle of justice', nor did the Italians, whose purpose appeared underneath the surface to be more politically motivated.[60] Perhaps it is worth noting that Japan was closest to Britain at the time in terms of how it defined its interests as a great power.

Having said that, we still need to answer why Japan did not want to recognise universal racial equality, given that it was the only great power not belonging to the dominant 'white' race. The simple answer is that Japan was not interested in the universal principle of racial equality. This study has shown that the Japanese approach to this proposal was made not from an altruistic angle but a nationalistic one. In fact, one consistent strand in the Japanese position was that it did not seek universal racial equality. The label of the 'racial equality' proposal which it inadvertently acquired at the peace conference was thus ironic and unintentional. However, the fact that the Japanese had often used both terms, 'the racial equality proposal' and 'the proposal for the abolition of racial discrimination', interchangeably seems to imply that they did not see much substantive difference between the two. The Japanese did not see any contradiction in demanding a racial equality proposal without pushing for universal racial equality, precisely because the proposal did not carry that implication.

The domestic debate on racial equality in 1919 revealed that the Japanese had a complex view of race and racial equality. Although there were the left-wing intellectuals who espoused universal racial equality, it can be said that the majority – both internationalists and pan-Asians – tended to ascribe to the view that the Japanese remained different and special from the rest of the Asian peoples. This social Darwinistic view of the Japanese race implied that the Japanese were not equal to the other coloured races, but superior. Elsewhere, I have described this categorical distinction of Japan's world view based on race as 'two-tiered',[61] and I have argued that this 'two-tiered' conception of race allowed the Japanese, especially those of pan-Asian persuasion, to reconcile the seemingly contradictory position of, on the one hand, appealing to the pan-Asian racial alliance with the Chinese and Koreans against the West, while on the other, placing Japan clearly in the position of leadership in Asia (*Ajia no meishu*). In other words, 'race' meant two things: the more Gobineaurian conceptualisation of the world according to the three races of white, yellow and black, which the Japanese utilised to pitch themselves together with China and Korea against the white race; and the more 'nation' based concept of differentiating the Japanese from the Chinese and Koreans within the yellow race, in order to stake out their special position of leadership.[62]

It is possible to suggest, then, that the three principal powers locked into the racial equality debate at Paris did not recognise the importance of racial equality as universal principle. The Western world was still imbued with the nineteenth-century notion of race as a 'respectable scientific category', which regarded racial differences as biological, a 'matter of fact, not of prejudice'.[63] Not until the early 1930s did the scientists – mostly anthropologists and biologists – in Britain and the United States begin to discredit racialism as untenable scientifically, though as a social category it remains potent even today.[64] Needless to say, although this new consensus would have no doubt become the basis of the intellectual foundation eventually, the rise of Nazism and its racialist policies in extreme form did precipitate the consolidation of opposition against any continuance of legitimising scientific categorisation of race.[65] Therefore, the principle of racial equality was not considered to be so important to contemporaries in 1919, whose sense of political and moral universalism rested on other values. Racial equality was a new idea, and consequently was still underdeveloped as a concept in 1919. International society still lacked moral consensus on the importance of this principle as a universal value. In the light of this, the acceptance of racial equality as one of the fundamental principles of the United Nations Charter in 1945, only two and a half decades after the rejection of racial equality as a principle in the covenant of the League of Nations, stands out as a striking testimony to the level of social and political upheaval which international society and its ruling Western states underwent in the interwar period.

The second observation is the connection which the Japanese made between the proposal and their own great power status. This is a significant point of departure from the existing literature because it shows that the Japanese saw racial equality in terms of great power equality, or more precisely, the equality of status among great powers regardless of racial difference. Therefore, the Japanese government wanted to have racial equality of the Japanese people, Japanese nation and Japanese state with the Western great powers, because their immediate past experience had taught them that this was an essential component of absolute equality with the West. In this sense, racial equality was a purely political demand, imbued with a sense of insecurity but also arising out of national pride and sensibilities.

Moreover, the fact that Japan sought greater equality with its peers illuminates the workings of international society[66] in coping with the expansion of its members. According to Hedley Bull, there are two main levels in the expansion of international society. The first level comprises non-members becoming members of the society: that is, the acceptance of non-Western states as members of international society. Although this is indisputably a significant step in the process of expansion, it is preliminary in nature as new non-Western members are incorporated as peripheral members and, on the whole, do not make a significant contribution to the core decisions of the society. The second level of expansion occurs when a new peripheral member becomes part of the core group of states, or the great powers, having a decisive influence on the workings of the society.

It is commonly perceived that Japan's entry into international society, first as a peripheral member and subsequently as a core member, was a textbook example of how a non-Western state could integrate into the mainstream international system. It is true that Japan worked diligently towards gaining great power membership by complying with the membership criteria which had been laid out informally by the Western states, which were mostly centred on political and military power.[67] In effect, the Japanese case, as underlined by the racial equality proposal, demonstrates the complex nature of integration which belied the apparent smoothness of the transition. Racial equality with peers was an assumption that Japan made in joining the ranks of great powers. Great power membership for Japan meant equality, at least nominally, with other great powers. Japan, as a non-white power, was justifiably concerned with its racial difference with the rest of the group. Therefore, one fundamentally important principle for the Japanese was that Japan should be equal to all other great powers, or more precisely, equal to white great powers. Hence by incorporating Japan into the great power club, the Western states unwittingly introduced a new element in great power membership.

However, the Japanese soon discovered that not only was racial equality not to be taken for granted, but also that equality of status among the great powers did not in any way imply equality of power,[68] as there was a hierarchy even at the top. In other words, there was equality only in so far as the members met the minimum criteria set out for membership; in reality, the strength of each state varied considerably. At the Paris Peace Conference, the implicit hierarchy was in the order of the United States, Britain, France, Italy and Japan.[69] Possibly it was easier for Britain to accept this pecking order, since Britain perceived this weighting purely on the basis of the relative strength of states, whereas Japan could never be sure that its low-ranking position within the great power club was the result of a lack of strength or was due to race. In essence, it can be said that as far as Japan was concerned, the racial factor was something that was inherent and indivisible from its other national attributes; and the Western great powers, with no prior experience of dealing with racial issues within the exclusive club, had to confront the new challenge. Hence, Japanese entry into the club questioned the precise nature of great power membership and tested the capacity of the core group's ability to evolve in line with the changing composition of its membership.

Thus, Japan's racial equality proposal can be interpreted as a challenge to the 'club' of Western great powers by the newcomer, attempting to introduce new 'rules of the club' which would make the newcomer's position more comfortable. Seen in this light, it was a daring proposal because it sought to change the *status quo*. Furthermore, the intimate linkage between great power status and racial equality indicates that the principle of racial equality was seen, in a sense, as an additional aspect of the principle of equality of states. What we can infer from the Japanese demand is that the principle of equality of states as applied to equality among the great powers was deficient in failing to recognise explicitly Japan's special status as a non-white great power. In a way, Japan was seeking a more refined definition of great power status which took into account its special requirement.

Thirdly, it is interesting that the principle of racial equality as proposed by the Japanese government only sought a limited application of the principle. In fact, the Japanese only wanted to apply the principle to themselves, and not to anyone else. Japan was only able to make this demand because of its privileged status as great power. More to the point, there was a monopoly over the 'dispensation' of any principle of any importance by the elite in international society. The events of 1919 took place in a world in which only the voice of the very small elite group of great powers mattered. At the Paris Peace Conference, the most notable example of the imposition of principles from above with the intention of limited applicability was the Wilsonian principle of self-determination. For President Wilson, the principle was synonymous with 'popular sovereignty', based on the American democratic tradition.[70] However, it appears that he had not been fully aware of the difficulties of application until he had reached Paris; nor had he fully contemplated the difficulty of supplying a satisfactorily containable definition of what constituted a nation:[71]

When I gave utterance to those words I said them without the

> knowledge that nationalities existed, which are coming to us day after day. . . . You do not know and cannot appreciate the anxieties that I have experienced as a result of many millions of people having their hopes raised by what I have said.[72]

It is interesting that Britain and France acquiesced to supporting the principle despite the fact that it had seriously damaging implications for their imperial holdings, possibly as damaging as universal racial equality or even more so. There seems to have been an implicit understanding among the great powers that the principle of self-determination, just as any other principle discussed at the Paris Peace Conference, would have to be contextualised; that is, its applicability was 'universal' only within strict confines determined by the great powers who were deciding the rules of the game. In truth, there was a strong resistance to the idea at the peace conference once the participants had realised the potential political scope of the principle.[73] Therefore, Wilson had to compromise by reassuring the powers that its applicability was solely restricted to the territories held by the defeated powers in Europe, and not even applicable to the former German colonies which were divided as mandates among the Allied Powers.[74] Wilson defended his contradiction as follows:

> It was not within the privilege of the conference of peace to act upon the right of self-determination of any peoples except those which had been included in the territories of the defeated empires.[75]

The hypocrisy of the self-contradictory positions taken by the great powers is remarked on by Harold Nicolson, who explained to Sir Eyre Crowe that:

> . . . we are left in a false moral position if we ask everyone else to surrender possessions in terms of Self-Determination and surrender nothing ourselves . . . . He [Crowe] says, 'Nonsense, my dear Nicolson. You are not being clear-headed. You think that you are being logical and sincere. You are not. Would you apply self-determination to India, Egypt, Malta and Gibraltar? If you are *not* prepared to go as far as this, then you have no right to claim that you are logical. If you *are* prepared to go as far as this, then you had better return at once to London.' Dear Crowe – he has the most truthful brain of any man I know.[76]

This was the kind of hypocritical logic required to accept the principle which would so clearly be disadvantageous to a great power such as Britain.

Both self-determination and racial equality, which became two of the important universal principles in the latter twentieth century, saw their origins in 1919. The degree of importance and general acceptability attached to them differed considerably because of the disparity in political power held by the Japanese and Americans. Had racial equality been advocated by President Wilson instead of self-determination, then it would certainly have been the most important principle to come out of the peace conference. As it was, Makino and Chinda were no Wilsons, and Japan as a new great power simply did not have the same clout as the United States. From the dexterity exhibited in the example of self-determination, it would seem that the great powers could have coped adequately with the principle of racial equality even if it were to have been adopted. In the end, general principles like any other issue at the peace conference were subject to politics. Although it is unfair to blame Wilson for the compromises he made on the principle of self-determination, it is still reasonable to say that it showed the limits of Wilsonian idealism.

Having said all this, however, we can still conclude on a positive note. In spite of all the seeming problems attached to the racial equality proposal, they still do not negate the fact that the proposal was an important milestone in terms of the evolution of the principle of racial equality in the twentieth century. This study has revealed that the original substance of the principle, as debated by statesmen and others in the early twentieth century, differed from what we would understand by the principle today. Nevertheless, it is highly significant that 'racial equality' was the preferred term used by contemporaries, regardless of the fact that the original Japanese term translated more accurately as 'abolition of racial discrimination'. This seems to indicate that there was a nascent recognition that racial equality could possibly become an important principle, though the time was not yet ripe in 1919. Although the Japanese had motives other than altruism in proposing the idea, it still needed a 'Japan' to sponsor the principle in the international forum as Western powers probably would have been more reluctant to forward something potentially explosive to their national interests. Thus, history has shown that the racial equality proposal of 1919 stands as an important landmark in that it challenged the existing universalist values upheld by the hegemonic great powers of the time. The irony of it all was that the contender seemed to have done so without truly recognising the inherent importance of the challenge.

Notes

INTRODUCTION

1 In fact, from the non-Western world excluding Latin American countries, one can only count four others: China, the Hedjaz, Liberia and Siam. F.S. Marston, *The Peace Conference of 1919: Organisation and Procedure*, Oxford: Oxford University Press, 1944, p. 264.
2 Japan signed 'unequal' treaties with the United States in March 1854, Britain in August, and Russia in October of the same year, and France and the Netherlands in 1855.
3 Iriye calls this '*mu-shisō no gaikō*'. Iriye Akira, '*Nihon no gaikō: Meiji ishin kara gendai made*', Tokyo, Iwanami, 1966, p. 27.
4 Arno J. Mayer, *Politics and Diplomacy of Peacemaking: Containment and Counterrevolution at Versailles, 1918–1919*, London: Weidenfeld and Nicolson, 1968; F.S. Marston, *The Peace Conference of 1919: Organisation and Procedure*, Oxford: Oxford University Press, 1944; H.V.W. Temperley (ed.), *A History of the Peace Conference of Paris*, 6 vols, London: Henry Frowde and Hodder & Stoughton, 1924, to name but a few.
5 Ikei Masaru, 'Pari heiwa kaigi to jinshu sabetsu teppai mondai', *Kokusai seiji*, 1962, vol. 23, pp. 44–58.
6 D.C.S. Sissons, 'The Immigration Question in Australian Diplomatic Relations with Japan, 1875–1919', History Section 26/821, Australian and New Zealand Association for the Advancement of Science, 1971.
7 Paul Gordon Lauren, *Power and Prejudice: The Politics and Diplomacy of Racial Discrimination*, Boulder, Colorado: Westview Press, 1988.
8 Mamiya Kunio, 'Okuma Shigenobu to jinshu sabetsu teppai mondai', *Waseda daigakushi kiyō*, 1989, vol. 22, pp. 213–37; Nakanishi Hiroshi, 'Konoe Fumimaro "Eibei hon'i no heiwashugi o haisu" rombun no haikei', *Hōgaku ronsō*, 1993, vol. 132, pp. 225–58.
9 Onuma Yasuaki, 'Haruka naru jinshu byōdō no risō', in Onuma Yasuaki (ed.), *Kokusaihō, kokusai rengō to nihon*, Tokyo, Kōbundō, 1987. Coincidentally, Onuma's and my own interest in the issue ran parallel, as I had first started looking at the Japanese perspective on the racial equality proposal in an M.Phil. thesis in International Relations entitled 'The Racial Equality Proposal at the 1919 Paris Peace Conference', submitted to the University of Oxford in April 1986.

10 Ikei, op. cit.
11 Onuma, op. cit. This view is also shared by Mamiya, op. cit.
12 L.F. Fitzhardinge, *William Morris Hughes: A Political Biography*, 2 vols, Sydney: Angus & Robertson Publishers, 1964 and 1979.
13 This was the term apparently coined by Asada Sadao in 'Nichibei kankei to imin mondai', in Saitō Makoto *et al.* (eds), *Demokurashi to nichibei kankei*, vol. 2, 1973, quoted from Nakanishi, op. cit.
14 Hedley Bull and Adam Watson (eds), *The Expansion of International Society*, Oxford: Oxford University Press, 1984.
15 John Vincent, 'Racial Equality', in ibid., p. 245.
16 Lauren, op. cit., p. 84.
17 Ikei, op. cit., p. 57.
18 Onuma, op. cit., p. 477.
19 There are four criteria suggested by Hedley Bull and Martin Wight: military strength, having general interests, the recognition by others of having the status of great power and self-imposed role as managers of the international system in conjunction with other great powers. Martin Wight, *Power Politics*, Leicester: Leicester University Press, 1978, p. 46, p. 50; Hedley Bull, *The Anarchical Society: A Study of Order in International Politics*, London: Macmillan, 1977, pp. 201–2, p. 207.
20 R.H. Fifield, *Woodrow Wilson and the Far East: The Diplomacy of the Shantung Question*, New York: Thomas Y. Crowell, 1952.
21 Onuma, op. cit.
22 Onuma, op. cit.; Nakanishi, op. cit.; Mamiya, op. cit.
23 Onuma, op. cit., pp. 450–1.
24 See, for instance, Robert Lansing's *The Peace Negotiations: A Personal Narrative*, London: Constable and Company Ltd., 1921; also R.L. Buell, 'The Development of the Anti-Japanese Agitation in the United States II', *Political Science Quarterly*, 1923, vol. 38, no. 2, pp. 57–81.
25 25 July 1919, *Annales de la Chambre des Députés: Débats Parlementaires: 11me Législature*; D.H. Miller, *The Drafting of the Covenant*, vol. 2, New York, privately printed, 1928, p. 390.
26 29 August 1919, *Annales*, op. cit.
27 Miller, op. cit., p. 390.

1 NEGOTIATING RACIAL EQUALITY AT THE PEACE CONFERENCE

1 The commission consisted of the following members: two members from the United States (Wilson, House), the British Empire (Cecil, Smuts), France (Bourgeois, Larnaude), Italy (Orlando, Scialoja) and Japan (Makino, Chinda), and one member each from Belgium, Brazil, China, Czechoslovakia, Greece, Poland, Portugal, Romania and Serbia. It had fifteen meetings in total from 3 February to 11 April 1919.
2 Newfoundland did not have a separate representation, and was represented by the British government.
3 The exception to this was General Jan Smuts of South Africa, who was appointed to the British War Cabinet in June 1917.
4 M.L. Dockrill and Z. Steiner, 'The Foreign Office at the Paris Peace Conference in 1919', *International History Review*, 1980, vol. 2, no. 1, p. 83.

5 ibid., p. 65, p. 67; V.H. Rothwell, *British War Aims and Peace Diplomacy 1914–1918*, Oxford: Clarendon Press, 1971, p. 9.
6 Rothwell, op. cit., pp. 10–11.
7 ibid., p. 18.
8 Max Beloff, *Britain's Liberal Empire 1897–1921*, vol. 1, London: Macmillan, 1987, p. 203.
9 Robert Lansing, *The Peace Negotiations: A Personal Narrative*, London: Constable and Company Ltd., 1921, p. 14; Inga Floto, *Colonel House in Paris: A Study of American Policy at the Paris Peace Conference 1919*, Princeton: Princeton University Press, 1980, p. 70.
10 Even House eventually fell out of Wilson's favour after mid-March. This will be discussed in Chapter 6.
11 It must be noted that Lloyd George made his pronouncements a few days earlier in January 1918, outlining very similar principles to those enunciated by Wilson in his Fourteen Points. The failure to come up with a joint Anglo–American statement underlined the sense of distrust in the relationship between Britain and the United States. For a detailed treatment of Anglo-American relationship in this period, see S.P. Tillman, *Anglo-American Relations at the Peace Conference of 1919*, Princeton, Princeton University Press, 1961.
12 Parts of the Memorandum of a Conversation between Robert Lansing and Hu Weide, Alfred Sze, and Koo, 18 December 1918, box 1, *Wellington Koo Papers*.
13 R.S. Baker, *Woodrow Wilson and World Settlement*, vol. 1, London: William Heinemann Ltd., 1923, p. 239. The importance of the League for Wilson will be discussed in Chapter 6.
14 Greene to Balfour, 23 January 1919, *PRO*, FO 608/211, f 475.
15 The Americans thought that the selected plenipotentiaries were 'moderately liberal' and sympathetic to the present international system. Morris to Secretary of State, 29 November 1918, SDR 763.72119/2830, reel 388, National Archives Microfilm Publications (hereafter NAMP), M367.
16 22 November 1918, Hara Keiichirō (ed.), *Hara Kei nikki*, vol. 8, Tokyo: Kangensha, 1950; Koizumi Sakutarō, *Saionji Kimmochi jiden*, Tokyo: Kōdansha, 1949, pp. 168–9.
17 According to Makino's report on the peace conference made to Hara on his return from Paris. 13 September 1919, *Hara Kei nikki*, vol. 8. This was possibly caused by the difference in political culture, since in Japan it was considered just as prestigious, if not more, to send Saionji and Makino who had an impressive record of experience in foreign affairs and domestic politics.
18 Matsui to Uchida, 23 January 1919, doc.19, *Nihon gaikō monjo*, 1919, part 1, vol. 3; Hankey's Notes of Council of Ten, 22 January 1919, *Wilson Papers*, vol. 54.
19 The original Japanese version can be found in doc. 538, *Nihon gaikō monjo*, 1918, vol. 3. This is an English translation of the original which was found in the British Colonial Office files. It came with the following note: 'These excerpts are from a document which is believed to represent the intentions of the Japanese at the Peace Conference'. See Foreign Office to Colonial Office, 13 January 1919, *PRO*, CO 532/139, f 2719.

20 Makino Nobuaki (1861–1954) of the Satsuma clan was a diplomat and politician with a strongly liberal inclination. He joined the Iwakura Mission, studied in the United States, joined the Foreign Ministry in 1891, became Minister of Education 1906–1908, Privy Councillor 1908–1911, Foreign Minister 1913–1914, and acting chief plenipotentiary at the Paris Peace Conference. Later he became head of Imperial Household Agency and then Lord Keeper of the Privy Seal.
21 This will be analysed in Chapter 3. Makino Nobuaki, *Kaikoroku*, vol. 2, Tokyo, Chūō kōronsha, 1978, p. 204.
22 Although the Japanese sources do not elaborate on this point, House's record shows that the Japanese had come to ask advice concerning the race question because of public interest in Japan for the new international organisation to embrace some broad principle of race equality. Charles Seymour (ed.), *The Intimate Papers of Colonel House*, vol. 4, London: Ernest Benn Ltd., 1928, pp. 320–1.
23 In fact, he was praised by his friends and condemned by his critics for these qualities. Allan Nevins, *Henry White: Thirty Years of American Diplomacy*, New York: Harper and Brothers Publishers, 1930, p. 385; Paul Birdsall, *Versailles Twenty Years After*, Hamden, Connecticut, Archon Books, 1962, p. 20; G. Clemenceau, *Grandeur and Misery of Victory*, London: George G. Harrap & Co. Ltd., 1930, p. 139.
24 Seymour, op. cit., vol. 4, p. 324.
25 House to Wilson, 6 July 1918, *Wilson Papers*, vol. 48.
26 Seymour, op. cit., vol. 4, pp. 320–1.
27 These meetings were not recorded in the Japanese sources. Seymour, op. cit., vol. 4, pp. 322–4; Binder 15, series II, collection group 466, *House Papers*; D.H. Miller, docs 362 and 363, vol. 5, and diary, 11 February 1919, vol. 1, *My Diary: At the Conference of Paris*, New York, privately printed, 1924.
28 The text of the proposal read: 'The equality of nations being a basic principle of the League of [N]ations, the High Contracting Parties agree that concerning the treatment of aliens in their territories, they will accord them as soon and as far as practicable equal treatments and rights in law and in fact without making distinction on account of race or nationality.' Interestingly, House claims that Makino and Chinda did not want to submit the proposal as their own, whereas the Japanese sources do not mention this and claim instead that Wilson had offered to propose the amendment as his own. Seymour, op. cit., vol. 4, p. 321; Matsui to Uchida, 15 February 1919, doc. 363, *Nihon gaikō monjo*, 1919, part 1, vol. 3.
29 Seymour, op. cit., vol. 4, p. 323.
30 D.H.Miller, *The Drafting of the Covenant*, vol. 1, New York: G.P. Putnam & Sons, 1928, pp. 183–4.
31 'Japanese Immigration into the U.S.: Recommendations as to the handling of the problem,' doc. 465, reel 25, NAMP, M1107.
32 Matsui to Uchida, 16 February 1919, doc. 364, *Nihon gaikō monjo*, 1919, part 1, vol. 3.
33 Note dictated by Balfour on 10 February 1919 on conversation with House, Additional Manuscripts 49751, *Balfour Papers*.
34 This will be discussed in Chapter 5.

35 P.J. Baker to Cecil, 10 February 1919, *PRO*, FO 608/240, file no. 1613/1/1.
36 Matsui to Uchida, 16 February 1919, doc. 364, *Nihon gaikō monjo*, 1919, part 1, vol. 3.
37 ibid.
38 Kikuchi Takenori, *Hakushaku Chinda Sutemi den*, Tokyo: Kyōmeikaku, 1938, pp. 207–8.
39 For an English text of the speech see Matsui to Uchida, 15 February 1919, doc. 363, *Nihon gaikō monjo*, 1919, part 1, vol. 3.
40 Miller, *Drafting of the Covenant*, vol. 1, p. 268.
41 ibid., vol. 2, p. 325.
42 Matsui to Uchida, 16 February 1919, doc. 364, *Nihon gaikō monjo*, 1919, part 1, vol. 3.
43 Miller, *Drafting of the Covenant*, vol. 2, p. 325.
44 ibid., vol. 1, p. 269.
45 The only evidence direct uncovered was that Wilson apparently called the Japanese proposal as an 'absurdly mild' recognition of racial equality. Diary of Ray Stannard Baker, 8 March 1919, *Wilson Papers*, vol. 55.
46 13 February 1919, binder 15, series II, collection group 466, *House Papers*.
47 This was one of the principle foreign policy-making organs in Japan at the time of the peace conference. For details, see Chapter 2.
48 3 February 1919, *Hara Kei nikki*, vol. 8.
49 Itō Miyoji (1857–1934) was a politician whose career spanned the Meiji, Taishō and Shōwa periods. As a *protégé* of Itō Hirobumi, he was involved in the drafting of the Meiji constitution. In December 1885, he became Private Secretary to Itō Hirobumi in the Itō cabinet, Secretary of the Privy Council in 1889, member of the House of Peers in 1890, chairman of *Tokyo nichi nichi shimbun* in 1891–1904, Agriculture Minister in the third Itō cabinet in 1898, and Privy Councillor in 1899. He was partly instrumental in the fall of the Okuma cabinet and the rise of the Terauchi cabinet, and was appointed as member of the Diplomatic Advisory Council.
50 Minutes of the Diplomatic Advisory Council, 19 and 22 February 1919, Kobayashi Tatsuo (ed.), *Suiusō nikki: Itōke monjo*, Tokyo, Hara shobō, 1966.
51 19 February 1919, *Hara kei nikki*, vol. 8.
52 Minutes of Diplomatic Advisory Council, 19 February 1919, *Suiusō nikki*.
53 'Jinshuteki sabetsu teppai ni kansuru mondai', 2.4.2.2, *Kokusai remmei: Jinshu sabetsu teppai*, vol. 3, Diplomatic Record Office, Tokyo.
54 Uchida to Matsui, 4 March 1919, doc. 371, *Nihon gaikō monjo*, 1919, part 1, vol. 3.
55 ibid., Uchida to Ishii, 3 March 1919, doc. 370.
56 ibid., Ishii to Uchida, 14 March 1919, doc. 379. For the text of the speech, see ibid., Ishii to Uchida, 19 March 1919, doc. 385; 16 March 1919, *The New York Times*. Lord Reading in Washington supported the view that the speech had been seized upon by those opposing the League, in Reading to Curzon, 15 March 1919, *PRO*, FO 608/241, f 4841. Interestingly, Ishii defended his position in his later telegram to Uchida that there had not been a negative reaction to his speech apart from a few

senators. Ishii to Uchida, 24 March 1919, doc. 391, *Nihon gaikō monjo*, 1919, part 1, vol. 3.
57 6 April 1919, *Tokyo nichi nichi shimbun*; Niizuma Kōdō, 'Beikoku no han nihon fū', *Nihon oyobi nihonjin*, 1919, no. 756, pp. 35–7; 'Sabetsu teppai to kokumin no kakugo', *Nihon oyobi nihonjin*, 1919, no. 754, p. 39.
58 12 March 1919, *Hara Kei nikki*, vol. 8.
59 Uchida to Matsui, 4 March 1919, doc. 371, *Nihon gaikō monjo*, 1919, part 1, vol. 3.
60 ibid., Matsui to Uchida, 15 March 1919, doc. 381; L.F. Fitzhardinge, *William Morris Hughes: A Political Biography*, vol. 2, Sydney: Angus & Robertson Publishers, 1979, p. 403.
61 Matsui to Uchida, 25 March 1919, doc. 392, *Nihon gaikō monjo*, 1919, part 1, vol. 3.
62 ibid., Matsui to Uchida, 20 March 1919, doc. 387.
63 ibid.
64 ibid., Matsui to Uchida, 25 March 1919, doc. 392.
65 ibid., Uchida to Matsui, 16 March 1919, doc. 382.
66 In fact, Australia was generally regarded as a colony which should have been 'suppressed' and 'tamed' by Britain. 20 April 1919, *Tokyo nichi nichi shimbun*.
67 Four formulas were as follows: 1. Makino: 'By the endorsement of the principle of equality of all nationals of states members of the League'; 2. Borden: 'By the endorsement of the principle of equality between nations and just treatment of their nationals'; 3. Smuts: 'By the recognition of the principle of open equal and honourable relations between nations and just treatment of their nationals within the territories of other nations'; 4. Cecil: 'The members of the League agree that they will grant equal treatment to all foreign residents being nationals of other members of the League, within their territories'. Henry Borden (ed.), *Robert Laird Borden: His Memoirs*, vol. 2, London: Macmillan, 1938, pp. 925–7.
68 ibid. The proposal now reads, 'By the endorsement of principle of equality of all nationals of States members of the League'.
69 According to Borden, two more proposals besides his and that of the Japanese were considered at the meeting: one from Smuts, and another from Cecil. Fitzhardinge, op. cit., vol. 2, p. 404.
70 Matsui to Uchida, 30 March 1919, doc. 396, *Nihon gaikō monjo*, 1919, part 1, vol. 3; Maida Minoru, 'Jinshu sabetsu teppai hiketsu ni tsuite', *Gaikō jihō*, 1919, vol. 29, no. 10, p. 11.
71 Matsui to Uchida, 30 March 1919, doc. 396, *Nihon gaikō monjo*, 1919, part 1, vol. 3.
72 According to Borden, this was either the one proposed by Borden above or another proposed by Smuts which was: 'By the recognition of the principle of open equal and honourable relations between nations and just treatment of their nationals within the territories of other nations' in Borden, op. cit., vol. 2, pp. 925–7.
73 Hughes claims that the Japanese could not accept it on the strength of public opinion in Japan. William Morris Hughes, *The Splendid Adventure: A Review of Empire Relations Within and Without the Commonwealth of Britannic Nations*, London: Ernest Benn Limited, 1929, p. 359.

74 Matsui to Uchida, 2 April 1919, doc. 400, *Nihon gaikō monjo*, 1919, part 1, vol. 3.

75 ibid.

76 M.P. Lissington, *New Zealand and Japan 1900–1941*, Wellington: A.R. Shearer, 1972, p. 37.

77 ibid.

78 Maida, op. cit., p. 10.

79 Bonsal, who was House's private assistant, had a comical account of the last attempt made by House to reason with Hughes on 5 April when Hughes apparently came out of the meeting mumbling, 'We "Ossies" are going to fetch away from Paris what we came here to git.' House lamented to Bonsal, 'I have just had my Waterloo. I may as well admit it. What a man! What a man!' Diary, 5 April 1919, container 19, *Stephen Bonsal Papers*.

80 Minutes of Diplomatic Advisory Council, 30 March 1919, *Suiusō nikki*.

81 30 March 1919, *Hara Kei nikki*, vol. 8.

82 Uchida to Matsui, 30 March 1919, doc. 395, *Nihon gaikō monjo*, 1919, part 1, vol. 3.

83 It read as follows: 'In proceeding this day to the signature of the Covenant of the League of Nations, the Japanese Plenipotentiaries declare their earnest expectation that having particular regard to the basic principles of the League of Nations, each of the States, Members of the League, will refrain from exercising discriminatory treatment either in law or in fact in respect of nationals of any other State, which is a member of the League, on grounds of race or nationality'.

84 Matsui to Uchida, 5 April 1919, doc. 401, *Nihon gaikō monjo*, 1919, part 1, vol. 3.

85 Borden records meetings with other Dominion premiers and the Japanese on 25 and 31 March, 7, 9 and 10 April 1919. Borden, op. cit., vol. 2, pp. 925–7.

86 Matsui to Uchida, 13 April 1919, doc. 405, *Nihon gaikō monjo*, 1919, part 1, vol. 3.

87 ibid., Chinda to Lloyd George, 7 April 1919, doc. 402.

88 British Empire Delegation Minutes 17, 3 April 1919, F126, *Lloyd George Papers*.

89 Matsui to Uchida, 13 April 1919, doc. 405, *Nihon gaikō monjo*, 1919, part 1, vol. 3.

90 ibid. By the end of March 1919, *The Times* predicted that the Japanese amendment in the revised form would likely be adopted. See 27 March 1919, *The Times*.

91 Cecil to Lloyd George, 15 April 1919, F6/6/29, *Lloyd George Papers*.

92 Matsui to Uchida, 14 April 1919, doc. 406, *Nihon gaikō monjo*, 1919, part 1, vol. 3.

93 Miller, *Drafting of the Covenant*, vol. 2, p. 389.

94 ibid., vol. 2, p. 390.

95 ibid.

96 13 April 1919, *Corriere della Sera*; Extract from *Idea Nazionale* of 28 April 1919, entitled 'The League of Nations is a Fraud', Erskine to Curzon, 6 May 1919, *PRO*, FO 608/241, f 9694. In late April, when the Italians realised that Wilson was being soft to the Japanese by giving

them Shantung whilst refusing Fiume to Italy, public opinion in Italy turned against Japan and claimed that the Japanese had been devious in accomplishing their diplomatic triumph at the expense of Italy. See 3 May 1919, *Corriere della Sera*.

97 Miller, *Drafting of the Covenant*, vol. 2, p. 390.

98 Matsui to Uchida, 13 April 1919, doc. 406, *Nihon gaikō monjo*, 1919, part 1, vol. 3.

99 Miller, *Drafting of the Covenant*, vol. 2, p. 391. The Japanese Foreign Ministry telegraph simply stated that 'also the Chinese delegates supported our proposal' in Matsui to Uchida, 13 April 1919, doc. 406, *Nihon gaikō monjo*, 1919, part 1, vol. 3.

100 This is an analysis based on Chinese position leading up to the 11 April voting. See, for instance, diary, 29 March 1919, Add.51131, f.64, *Cecil Papers*; Miller, *Drafting of the Covenant*, vol. 1, p. 336.

101 After the 11 April ruling and during the Shantung negotiation, the Chinese position on the racial equality proposal becomes more complicated because, in spite of Koo's declared support for it, many in the Chinese delegation, especially C.T. Wang, began to circulate the view that the Japanese had used it as a 'bargaining chip' to obtain favourable settlement on the Shantung issue. The division seems to reflect the internal political division of the Chinese delegation into those from the North (Koo) and those from the South (Wang). For the Sino-American 'bargaining chip' theory, see Chapter 6.

102 Matsui to Uchida, 13 April 1919, doc. 406, *Nihon gaikō monjo*, 1919, part 1, vol. 3.

103 Miller, *Drafting of the Covenant*, vol. 2, p. 391.

104 Matsui to Uchida, 13 April 1919, doc. 406, *Nihon gaikō monjo*, 1919, part 1, vol. 3.

105 Miller, *Drafting of the Covenant*, vol. 1, pp. 462–3.

106 Matsui to Uchida, 13 April 1919, doc. 406, and Horiguchi to Uchida, 1 May 1919, doc. 411, *Nihon gaikō monjo*, 1919, part 1, vol. 3. This error nearly caused a diplomatic incident between Brazil and Japan.

107 To the French, the American position seemed conspicuously contradictory for supporting a league based on the so-called Wilsonian ideals, but turning a blind eye to an obvious principle of universal importance. 14 April 1919, *Le Matin*, Paris; also see 29 August 1919, *Annales de la Chambre des Députés: Débats Parlementaires: 11me Législature*.

108 Miller, *Drafting of the Covenant*, vol. 2, p. 392.

109 ibid.

110 Miller, diary, 11 April 1919, *My Diary*, vol. 1.

111 Miller, *Drafting of the Covenant*, vol. 1, pp. 462–3.

112 ibid.

113 ibid., pp. 464–5.

114 Diary, 11 April 1919, Add.51131, f.71, *Cecil Papers*.

115 12 April 1919, binder 15, series II, collection group 466, *House Papers*.

116 Miller, doc. 767, *My Diary*, vol. 8.

117 Diary of Grayson, 15 March 1919, *Wilson Papers*, vol. 55.

118 Matsui to Uchida, 13 April 1919, doc. 406, *Nihon gaikō monjo*, 1919, part 1, vol. 3.

119 Minutes of Diplomatic Advisory Council, 21 April 1919, *Suiusō nikki*.

120 ibid.
121 Onuma Yasuaki, 'Haruka naru jinshu byōdō no risō', Onuma Yasuaki (ed.), *Kokusaihō, kokusai rengō to nihon*, Tokyo, Kōbundō, 1987, pp. 452–3.
122 Uchida to Matsui, 4 March 1919, doc. 371, *Nihon gaikō monjo*, 1919, part 1, vol. 3.
123 Minutes of Diplomatic Advisory Council, 21 April 1919, *Suiusō nikki*.
124 Diary, 26 April 1919, Add.51131, f.75, *Cecil Papers*.
125 British Empire Delegation Minutes 29, 28 April 1919, F126, *Lloyd George Papers*.
126 Diary, 15 and 26 April 1919, binder 15, series II, collection group 466, *House Papers*.
127 British Empire Delegation Minutes 29, 28 April 1919, F126, *Lloyd George Papers*.
128 Correspondence between Tokyo and the Japanese delegation now concentrated almost exclusively on the Shantung question, leaving very little room for racial equality.
129 Minutes of Council of Four, 28 April 1919, *FRUS*, 1919, Paris Peace Conference, vol. 5.
130 Matsui to Uchida, 28 April 1919, doc. 223, *Nihon gaikō monjo*, 1919, part 1, vol. 3.
131 This perspective will be discussed in Chapter 6.
132 Cecil to Lloyd George, 15 April 1919, F6/6/29, *Lloyd George Papers*.
133 Makino, op. cit., vol. 2, p. 210.
134 Matsui to Uchida, 29 April 1919, doc. 410, *Nihon gaikō monjo*, 1919, part 1, vol. 3.

2 DOMESTIC POLITICS AND THE LEAGUE OF NATIONS

1 Hara Kei (1856–1921) was a Christian, journalist, diplomat and politician. He pursued his journalistic career at *Yūbin hōchi shimbun* and *Daitō nippō* until 1882 when he entered the Foreign Ministry. Hara Kei becam consul at Tientsin, then First Secretary at Paris, before being appointed as Private Secretary at the Ministry of Agriculture and Commerce in 1889–1892. As a *protégé* of Mutsu Munemitsu, Hara went back to the Foreign Ministry when Mutsu became Foreign Minister in the second Itō cabinet. He then became editor of *Osaka mainichi shimbun*, and subsequently joined Seiyūkai in 1900. He served twice as Home Affairs Minister in the Saionji cabinets 1905–1912, then, for the third time, in 1913 in the Yamamoto cabinet. He became head of Seiyūkai in 1914 and prime minister in 1918.
2 Its members during the peace conference were Hara Kei (Prime Minister), Uchida Yasuya (Minister of Foreign Affairs), Tanaka Giichi (Minister of Army), Katō Tomosaburō (Minister of Navy), Makino Nobuaki (Privy Councillor), Itō Miyoji (Privy Councillor), Hirata Tōsuke (Privy Councillor), Inukai Tsuyoshi (leader of Kokumintō), Terauchi Masatake (ex-Prime Minister), Gotō Shimpei (ex-Foreign Minister) and Motoda Hajime (Privy Councillor).
3 Kobayashi Tatsuo, 'Rinji gaikō chōsa iinkai no setchi', *Kokusai seiji*, 1964, vol. 28, p. 67.
4 Apparently, the newspapers such as *Nichi nichi*, *Asahi* and *Hōchi* were all

dissatisfied with its creation. Greene to Balfour, 7 June 1917, *PRO*, FO 371/2951, f 144032; Gaimushō hyakunenshi hensan iinkai (ed.), *Gaimushō no hyakunen*, vol. 1, p. 663. For criticisms, see Makino Nobuaki, *Kaikoroku*, vol. 2, Tokyo: Chūō kōronsha, 1978, pp. 144–5; Kobayashi Tatsuo (ed.), *Suiusō nikki: Itōke monjo*, Tokyo: Hara shobō, 1966, p. 9; Kojima Kazuo, *Ichi rōseijika no kaisō*, Tokyo: Chūō kōronsha, 1951, pp. 161–7; Kobayashi, 'Rinji gaikō chōsa iinkai no setchi', p. 65.

5 *Gaimushō no hyakunen*, vol. 1, p. 658.

6 For a history of the Foreign Ministry, consult *Gaimushō no hyakunen*, vol. 1.

7 Iriye Akira, *Nihon no gaikō: Meiji ishin kara gendai made*, Tokyo: Iwanami, 1966, p. 80.

8 Uchida Yasuya (1865–1936) was a diplomat and politician. He was appointed foreign minister first in 1911 in the second Saionji cabinet, then again in 1919, and retained the post after Hara's assassination in the Takahashi Korekiyo and Katō Tomosaburō cabinets. In 1925, he was appointed Privy Councillor, in 1931 Chairman of the Manchurian Railway, and foreign minister for the third time in the Saitō Makoto cabinet in 1932. In the early 1930s, he gained notoriety for his 'scorched-earth diplomacy' (*shōdo gaikō*) in Manchuria.

9 See, for instance, Greene to Balfour, 15 December 1916, *PRO*, FO 371/2951, f 14332.

10 Uchida Yasuya denki hensan iinkai (ed.), *Uchida Yasuya*, Tokyo, Kajima kenkyūjo shuppankai, 1969, p. 230. Interestingly, he became increasingly pan-Asian in his thinking in his later years. See Ikei Masaru, 'Uchida Yasuya – shōdo gaikō e no kiseki', *Kokusai seiji*, 1976, vol. 56, no. 2, p. 19.

11 *Gaimushō no hyakunen*, vol. 1, pp. 665–6.

12 Basically, there only existed nine *genrō* in the history of Japan who were Kuroda Kiyotaka (1840–1900), Itō Hirobumi (1841–1909), Yamagata Aritomo (1838–1922), Matsukata Masayoshi (1835–1924), Inoue Kaoru (1836–1915), Saigō Tsugumichi (1843–1902), Oyama Iwao (1842–1916), Katsura Tarō (1847–1913) and Saionji Kimmochi. Saionji was, of course, the chief plenipotentiary to the Paris Peace Conference.

13 This was much curtailed by the Okuma cabinet, which stopped the tradition of sending confidential diplomatic documents to the *genrō*.

14 After 1892, it was the *genrō* who recommended and effectively appointed the successive governments Oka Yoshitake, *Kindai nihon no seijika: Sono seikaku to unmei*, Tokyo, Bungei shunjūsha, 1960, p. 221; Leslie Connors, *The Emperor's Adviser: Saionji Kimmochi and Pre-war Japanese Politics*, London: Croom Helm, 1987, p. 46.

15 Yamagata Aritomo (1838–1922) was an influential Chōshū clan army general and *genrō*. He was prime minister twice in 1889 and 1898. His famous declaration of December 1890 of Japan's need not only to defend *shukensen* (national boundary) but also *riekisen* (the area in between the enemy and national boundary) became the mainstay of the early Japanese defence policy. Although keen to strengthen the military, he was nevertheless aware of the importance of cooperating with the great powers, especially Britain and the United States.

16 There were three main political parties in Japan in this period – Seiyūkai (headed by Hara Kei), Kenseikai (Katō Kōmei), and Kokumintō (Inukai

Tsuyoshi). Seiyūkai had been out of power for the most of the war as the Okuma cabinet was of Dōshikai which was a predecessor of Kenseikai, and the Terauchi cabinet was a militarist, non-party government.

17 The newly inaugurated Hara cabinet on 29 September 1918 consisted of the following: Hara Kei (Prime Minister and Minister of Judicial Affairs), Uchida Yasuya (Minister of Foreign Affairs), Tokonami Takejirō (Minister of Interior and head of Railways), Takahashi Korekiyo (Minister of Finance), Tanaka Giichi (Minister of Army), Katō Tomosaburō (Minister of Navy), Yamamoto Tatsuo (Minister of Agriculture), Nakabashi Tokugorō (Minister of Education).

18 Kikuchi Gorō and Mizoguchi Hakuyō (eds), *Hara Kei zenden*, vol. 2, Tokyo, Nippon hyōronsha, 1922, pp. 262–5.

19 Hayashi Shigeru and Tsuji Kiyoaki (eds), *Nippon naikaku shiroku*, vol. 2, Tokyo, Iwanami, 1981, p. 305.

20 In fact, Hara's foreign policy based on economic diplomacy became the mainstay of Japanese foreign policy in the 1920s under the name of 'Shidehara diplomacy'. Uchiyama Masakuma, *Gendai nippon gaikōron*, Tokyo, Keiō daigaku hōgaku kenkyūkai, 1971, p. 24.

21 Hara reportedly said, he 'keenly desire[s] to see Japan and America brought closer together and every shadow of misunderstanding removed'; 21 October 1918, *The New York Times*.

22 *Gaimushō no hyakunen*, vol. 1, pp. 681–2.

23 Iriye, op. cit., p. 77; Hosoya Chihiro, 'Makino Shinken to berusaiyu kaigi', *Chūō kōron*, 1965, vol. 80, no. 5, p. 369.

24 Press conference given by Foreign Minister Uchida, 7 October 1918, *Nihon gaikō monjo*, vol. 3, 1918.

25 Ian Nish, *The Anglo-Japanese Alliance: The Diplomacy of Two Island Empires 1894–1907*, London: Athlone Press, 1966, p. 250; Hosoya, op. cit., p. 368.

26 Banno Junji, 'Rikugun no ōbeikan to chūgoku seisaku', in Hosoya Chihiro and Saitō Makoto, eds, *Washinton taisei to nichibei kankei*, Tokyo, Tokyo daigaku shuppankai 1978, p. 457; Hayashi and Tsuji, op. cit., vol. 2, p. 306.

27 17 November, 2 and 8 December 1918, 30 March 1919, Hara Keiichirō (ed.), *Hara kei nikki*, vol. 8, Tokyo: Kangensha, 1950. Also 'Memorandum: Collection of press clippings from certain Japanese papers to April 26, 1919, regarding Japan and the Peace Conference', SDR 894.9111/3, reel 563, National Archives Microfilm Publication (hereafter NAMP), M820.

28 Minutes of the Diplomatic Advisory Council, 2 and 8 December 1919, *Suiusō nikki*.

29 Seki Shizuo, *Nippon gaikō no kijiku to tenkai*, Tokyo: Mineruba shobō, 1990, p. 222.

30 Hara was criticised in the Diplomatic Advisory Council for not giving enough priority to the peace conference. Minutes of the Diplomatic Advisory Council, 13 November 1919, *Suiusō nikki*.

31 Unno Yoshirō, *Kokusai remmei to nihon*, Tokyo, Hara shobō, 1972, p. 7.

32 This was very preliminary in nature as Foreign Minister Katō ordered the assembly of information to prepare for peace. Unno Yoshirō, 'Pari kōwa kaigi to gaimushō', *Rekishi kyōiku*, 1967, vol. 15, no. 1, p. 47.

33 The committee was headed by the Vice Foreign Minister and included chiefs of political and commercial divisions of the ministry as well as representatives from the Navy and Army Ministries. It had the following special sub-committees: i) Shantung Railway, ii) German South Pacific territories, iii) Shantung lease, peace drafting, iv) international law relating to the peace and v) control of industrial rights. Nagaoka Harukazu, *Nihon gaikō monjo: Nihon gaikō tsuikairoku 1900–1935*, Tokyo: Diplomatic Record Office, p. 318.
34 Unno, 'Pari kōwa kaigi to gaimushō', p. 47.
35 Shidehara Kijūrō heiwa zaidan (ed.), *Shidehara Kijūrō*, Tokyo: Shidehara Kijūrō heiwa zaidan, 1955, pp. 135–6; Minutes of Diplomatic Advisory Council, 13 November 1918, *Suiusō nikki.*
36 Diary of Itō, 26 October and 6 November 1918, *Suiusō nikki.*
37 Unno, 'Pari kōwa kaigi to gaimushō', p. 47.
38 Doc. 538, *Nihon gaikō monjo*, 1918, vol. 3.
39 Nakano Yasuo, *Seijika: Nakano Seigō*, vol. 2, Tokyo: Shinmitsukaku shoten, 1971, p. 262; 'Gaikō butai tōmen no sanhanagata', *Chūō kōron*, 1918, no. 364, p. 57.
40 'Gaikō butai tōmen no sanhanagata', p. 57.
41 See, for instance, 24 January 1919, *Teikoku gikai kizokuin giji sokkiroku*, vol. 35, Tokyo: Tokyo daigaku shuppankai, 1981; 3 February and 21 March 1919, *Teikoku gikai shūgiin giji sokkiroku*, vol. 35, Tokyo: Tokyo daigaku shuppankai, 1981.
42 'Dai yonjū-ikkai gikai hōkokusho', *Kensei*, 1919, vol. 2, no. 3, pp. 5–6; 'Katō sōsai no enzetsu', *Kensei*, 1919, vol. 2, no. 6, p. 13.
43 Makino, op. cit., vol. 2, pp. 173–4; Hosoya Chihiro, 'Makino Shinken to berusaiyu kaigi', *Chūō kōron*, 1965, vol. 80, no. 5, p. 365.
44 Hosoya, 'Makino Shinken to berusaiyu kaigi', *Chūō kōron*, 1965, vol. 80, no. 5, pp. 366–7.
45 The British government created the Phillimore Commission to study the idea as early as December 1916. An interim report was produced in May 1918, and the final version in July 1918. This was confidentially communicated to the United States and the British Dominion governments. French Premier Ribot set up a committee under Léon Bourgeois in July 1917 to study the League, which completed the final report in June 1918 and sent it to the allies in July. However, the American government preferred not to appoint commissions to pursue the idea and, accordingly, a draft made by Colonel House in the summer of 1918 was subsequently used as an initial basis for the covenant. The Italians only considered a study committee as late as mid-January 1919. Final Report by the Committee on the League of Nations, 3 July 1918, 'P' (War) Series, *PRO*, CAB 29/1, pp 439–55; David Stevenson, *French War Aims against Germany 1914–1919*, Oxford: Clarendon Press, 1982, p. 78, p. 109; Drummond to Balfour, 15 November 1917, *PRO*, CAB 24/32, G.T. 2667; D.H. Miller, 'Memorandum regarding the Covenant', *My Diary: At the Conference of Paris*, vol. 1, New York, privately printed, 1924, pp. 331–69; Orlando to Bonin Longare, 14 January 1919, doc. 864, *I Documenti Diplomatici Italiani*, vol. 1, 6th Series, Italian Foreign Ministry.
46 Unno, *Kokusai remmei to nihon*, p. 7.

47 Shidehara, op. cit., p. 136.
48 In April 1919, the report entitled, 'Issues relating to the League of Nations' was published. To show how outdated it was, it included the following documents: i) a memorandum by the allied powers on the peace terms issued by Wilson in December 1916; ii) a comment by former Foreign Minister Motono; and iii) a record of conversation with Foreign Minister Uchida. See *Gaimushō kōwa jumbi iinkai chōsho*, vol. 7, Tokyo, Ministry of Foreign Affairs.
49 Chinda to Uchida, 16 October 1918, doc. 542 and 9 November 1918, doc. 545, *Nihon gaikō monjo*, 1918, vol. 3.
50 ibid., Makino to Uchida, 14 December 1918, doc. 557.
51 Unno, *Kokusai remmei to nihon*, p. 8.
52 Makino, op. cit., vol. 2, p. 174.
53 ibid., vol. 2, p. 179.
54 Minutes of Diplomatic Advisory Council, 19 November and 8 December 1918, *Suiusō nikki.*
55 Morris to Secretary of State, 27 November 1918, no. 299, *FRUS*, 1919, Paris Peace Conference, vol. 1.
56 Minutes of Diplomatic Advisory Council, 2 and 8 December 1918, *Suiusō nikki.*
57 This document became the basis for the supplement on the Wilsonian Fourteen Points attached to the three peace principles mentioned above. ibid., minutes of Diplomatic Advisory Council, 13 November 1918.
58 ibid., minutes of Diplomatic Advisory Council, 2 and 8 December 1918.
59 ibid., minutes of Diplomatic Advisory Council, 8 December 1918.
60 Foreign Office to Colonial Office, 13 January 1919, *PRO*, CO 532/139, f 2719.
61 Minutes of Diplomatic Advisory Council, 19 and 22 February 1919, *Suiusō nikki*; *Gaimushō no hyakunen*, vol. 1, p. 710.
62 Uchida to Matsui, 31 January 1919, doc. 356, and 6 February 1919, doc. 360, *Nihon gaikō monjo*, 1919, part 1, vol. 3.
63 ibid., Uchida to Matsui, 6 February 1919, doc. 360, and Uchida to Saionji, 8 February 1919, doc. 361.
64 ibid., Uchida to Matsui, 15 March 1919, doc. 380.
65 ibid., Uchida to Matsui, 24 March 1919, doc. 391.
66 ibid., Uchida to Matsui, 1 April 1919, doc. 398.
67 ibid., Uchida to Matsui, 25 April 1919, doc. 408.
68 1 May 1919, *Hara Kei nikki*, vol. 8.
69 Nakano Seigō, *Kōwa kaigi o mokugeki shite*, Tokyo, Tōhō jironsha, 1919, p. 123.
70 Nakanishi Hiroshi, 'Konoe Fumimaro "Eibei hon'i no heiwashugi o haisu" rombun no haikei', *Hōgaku ronsō*, 1993, vol. 132, pp. 239–40.
71 *Suiusō nikki*, pp. 790–1.
72 Uchida to Matsui, 26 March 1919, doc. 393, *Nihon gaikō monjo*, 1919, part 1, vol. 3.
73 ibid., Uchida to Matsui, 2 April 1919, doc. 399.
74 ibid., Uchida to Matsui, 24 March 1919, doc. 391.
75 Nakanishi, op. cit., pp. 225–58. Pan-Asianism will be looked at more detail in Chapter 4.
76 The military, on the whole, expressed no objection to Japan's joining the

League although they did oppose some aspects of the covenant such as abolition of conscription. General Tanaka to Nara, 7 March 1919, doc. 34, *Nihon gaikō monjo*, 1919, part 1, vol. 3; Takeshita to Navy Vice-Minister, 7 February 1919, telegram no. 9, Bessatsu Takeshita kaigun chūshō hōkokushū, (January 1919–), 2.3.1./17–1, *Pari heiwa kaigi*, Tokyo, Diplomatic Record Office; Kazushige Ugaki, *Ugaki Kazushige nikki*, vol. 1, Tokyo, Misuzu shobō, 1968, p. 194; Roger Dingman, 'Nihon to Wirusonteki sekai chitsujo', in Satō Seizaburō and Roger Dingman (eds), *Kindai nihon no taigai taido*, Tokyo, Tokyo daigaku shuppankai, 1974, p. 108.

77 Nakano, *Kōwa kaigi o mokugeki shite*, p. 123.

78 Charles Seymour (ed.), *The Intimate Papers of Colonel House*, vol. 4, London, Ernest Benn Ltd., 1928, p. 324.

79 The British Embassy in Tokyo viewed the Japanese newspapers as being essentially all 'pro-Japanese', being 'hypersensitive' about anything which was regarded as tarnishing Japan's prestige. Greene to Balfour, 28 February 1918, *PRO*, FO 410/67, Confidential Print 11580, no 4.

80 Polk to Ammission, 20 March 1919, SDR 185.111/161, reel 321, NAMP, M820.

81 Apart from the three mentioned here, references to the other papers namely *Hōchi shimbun*, *Kokumin shimbun*, *Chūgai shōgyō shimpō*, *Yamato*, *Yorozu chōhō*, *Jiji shimpō* have been taken from the following unless otherwise cited. 'Memorandum: Collection of press clippings from certain Japanese papers to April 26, 1919, regarding Japan and the Peace Conference', SDR 894.9111/3, reel 563, NAMP, M820.

82 These three papers represented the respectable, middle-of-the-road views; in other words, they were not irresponsible gutter press. The British Embassy had classified *Asahi shimbun* as pro-ally and anti-Terauchi and *Tokyo nichi nichi shimbun* as fairly impartial except on the China question, where it tended to be jingoistic. Greene to Balfour, 28 February 1918, *PRO*, FO 410/67, Confidential Print 11580, no 4.

83 Greene to Balfour, 12 November 1918, *PRO*, CO 532/139, f 4086.

84 15 and 30 November 1918, *Asahi shimbun*.

85 Polk to Lansing, 26 April 1919, SDR 185.111/257, reel 322, NAMP, M820.

86 24 and 30 January 1919, *Tokyo nichi nichi shimbun*.

87 ibid., 19 March 1919.

88 These topics will be discussed at length in Chapter 4.

89 30 January 1919, *Tokyo nichi nichi shimbun*.

90 27 March 1919, *Yomiuri shimbun*.

91 For instance, 17 April 1919, *Asahi shimbun*.

92 9 April 1919, *Tokyo nichi nichi shimbun*; 9 April 1919, *Yomiuri shimbun*.

93 For example, 14 March 1919, *Tokyo nichi nichi shimbun*.

94 12 March 1919, *Asahi shimbun*.

95 25 and 27 January, 5 February 1919, *Tokyo nichi nichi shimbun*.

96 ibid., 7 February 1919.

97 ibid., 17 and 18 February 1919.

98 ibid., 1, 3 and 6 April 1919.

99 ibid., 14 April 1919.

100 17 April 1919, *Chūgai shōgyō shimpō*.

101 29 March, 3 and 20 April 1919, *Tokyo nichi nichi shimbun*.
102 ibid., 20 April 1919; 17 April 1919, *Asahi shimbun*; 15 April 1919, *Hōchi shimbun*; 9 April 1919, *Jiji shimpō*; 16 April 1919, *Osaka mainichi shimbun*.
103 27 June 1919, *Tokyo nichi nichi shimbun*.
104 ibid., 5 May 1919.
105 ibid., 27 June 1919.
106 ibid., 20 April 1919.
107 6, 10, 15 April 1919, *Kokumin shimbun*; 24 April 1919, *Yamato*; 15, 20 April 1919, *Hōchi shimbun*; 7 April 1919, *Yorozu chōhō*.
108 6 April 1919, *Kokumin shimbun*.
109 ibid., 19 March 1919; 17 April 1919, *Asahi shimbun*.
110 25 April 1919, *Tokyo nichi nichi shimbun*.
111 ibid., 20 April 1919.
112 ibid., 8 May 1919.
113 12 May 1919, *Asahi shimbun*.
114 9 June 1919, *Tokyo nichi nichi shimbun*.
115 ibid., 25 June 1919.
116 19 April 1919, *Yorozu chōhō*.
117 30 March and 3 April 1919, *Tokyo nichi nichi shimbun*; 10 April 1919, *Hōchi shimbun*.
118 3 April 1919, *Tokyo nichi nichi shimbun*.
119 16 May 1919, *Asahi shimbun*.
120 22 February and 6 May 1919, *Tokyo nichi nichi shimbun*.
121 13, 16, 17 April 1919, *Kokumin shimbun*; 9 April 1919, *Yamato shimbun*.
122 16 and 30 March 1919, *Yomiuri shimbun*.
123 ibid., 2 April 1919.
124 ibid., 20 April and 23 May 1919.
125 Kizaka Jun'ichirō, 'Taishōki minponshugisha no kokusai ninshiki', *Kokusai seiji*, 1974, vol. 51, p. 59.
126 ibid., p. 75.
127 Ishibashi Tanzan, *Ishibashi Tanzan zenshū*, vol. 3, Tokyo, Tōyō keizai shimpōsha, 1970, pp. 126–7.
128 ibid., pp. 68–70.
129 In 1919, those who paid tax of over ten yen had the right to vote, which only amounted to three per cent of the male working population.
130 Takayoshi Matsuo (ed.), *Ishibashi Tanzan hyōronshū*, Tokyo, Iwanami, 1986, pp. 86–90.
131 ibid., pp. 44–6.
132 For studies of Taishō democracy, consult, for instance, Mitani Taichirō, *Taishō demokurashīron*, Tokyo, Tokyo daigaku shuppankai, 1974.
133 Kizaka, op. cit., pp. 63–4.
134 ibid., p. 72.
135 Yoshino Sakuzō, 'Sekai no daishuchō to sono jun'ōsaku oyobi taiōsaku', *Chūō kōron*, 1919, no. 365.
136 Dingman, 'Nihon to Wirusonteki sekai chitsujo', p. 100.
137 Yoshino Sakuzō, 'Jinshuteki sabetsu teppai undōsha ni ataeru', *Chūō kōron*, 1919, no. 367, pp. 70–2.
138 Yoshino Sakuzō, 'Jinshuteki sabetsu teppai mondai ni tsuite', *Chūō kōron*, 1919, no. 370, p. 95.

139 Nakano Yasuo, *Seijika: Nakano Seigō*, vol. 2, Tokyo, Shinmitsukaku shoten, 1971, p. 250.
140 ibid., vol. 2, pp. 249–50; Nakano Seigō, 'Teikoku gaikō no kiki', *Nihon oyobi nihonjin*, 1915, no. 645, p. 24.
141 Kizaka, op. cit., p. 65.
142 Nakano Seigō, 'Nihon teikoku no shimei', *Nihon oyobi nihonjin*, 1914, no. 639, p. 112, p. 129.
143 Nakano Seigō, 'Kōwa kaigi no shinsō', *Kensei*, 1919, vol. 2, no. 5, pp. 16–20.
144 Nakano especially accuses Chinda for taking this attitude. See Nakano, *Kōwa kaigi o mokugeki shite*, pp. 20–1.
145 Of course, Nakano was not accurate on this point because Britain did support Japan over the Shantung settlement arising out of the secret treaty of 1917. ibid., p. 35; Nakano, 'Kōwa kaigi no shinsō', p. 28.
146 Nakano, *Seijika*, vol. 2, p. 268.
147 Nakano, *Kōwa kaigi o mokugeki shite*, pp. 119–20.
148 ibid., p. 120.
149 Nakano, 'Kōwa kaigi no shinsō', p. 51.
150 Konoe Fumimaro, 'Eibei hon'i no heiwashugi o haisu', *Nihon oyobi nihonjin*, 1918, no. 746, pp. 23–6. For an incisive study of Konoe and this article, consult Nakanishi, op. cit.
151 Nakanishi, op. cit., pp. 230–7.
152 The American government thought that Konoe's thoughts on the race problem were significant. See Morris to Polk, 7 January 1919, SDR 763.72119/3308, *FRUS*, 1919, Paris Peace Conference, vol. 1.
153 Nakanishi, op. cit., p. 238.
154 ibid., p. 240.
155 ibid., p. 244.
156 Konoe Fumimaro, *Sengo ōbei kenkenroku*, Tokyo, Chūō kōronsha, 1981, pp. 33–7.
157 ibid., pp. 137–9.
158 Fukuda was much influenced by the German historical school and advocated 'social policy' (*shakai seisaku*) which promoted a progressive reform of society, placing higher value on the human factor (*jinkaku*) rather than the capital (*bukkaku*). Fukuda Tokuzō, *Seizonken no shakai seisaku*, Tokyo, Kōdansha, 1980, p. 4, p. 197, p. 203.
159 Fukuda Tokuzō, *Reimeiroku*, Tokyo, Daitōkaku, 1920, pp. 282–3.
160 ibid., p. 354.
161 ibid., pp. 286–7, p. 374.
162 Fukuda attacked those who accused him of a pro-German tendency, such as Yoshino Sakuzō, *The Japan Advertiser* and the British press, by claiming that their criticism amounted to the equivalent of intellectual 'lynching'. Fukuda Tokuzō, 'Shōsha wa dare ka', *Chūō kōron*, 1918, no. 364, pp. 31–8.
163 His articles on the peace conference were serialised from 1 to 5 January 1919, entitled, 'Against Economic Imperialism' in *Tokyo nichi nichi shimbun*.
164 Fukuda, *Remeiroku*, pp. 304–5.
165 ibid., p. 300.

166 Fukuda Tokuzō, 'Obeikoku ni taisuru shuchō', 15 November 1918, *Asahi shimbun*.

167 As well as the intellectuals examined above, see Miyake Setsurei, 'Eikyū heiwa no yōken to shiteno jinshu mondai', *Taiyō*, 1919, vol. 25, no. 1; Takahashi Sakue, 'Jinshu sabetsu ni tsuite', *Kokusaihō gaikō zasshi*, 1919, vol. 17, no. 7; Nagai Ryūtarō, 'Jidai sakugo no gaikō', 26 June 1919, *Tokyo nichi nichi shimbun*; Uehara Etsujirō, 'Beikoku kinji no tainichi taido', *Taiyō*, 1919, vol. 25, no. 11.

168 An interesting survey was conducted by a journal, *Taiyō*, which asked one hundred and fifty 'first-rate' academics at the Universities of Tokyo, Kyoto and others to indicate whether they supported the League of Nations. Out of the fifty replies received, thirty-five academics expressed support, eight were opposed, and seven were undecided. This indicates that academics generally tended to share Hara's view. 'Kokusai remmei kanyū no kahi', *Taiyo*, 1919, vol. 25, no. 7, pp. 87–93.

169 Nakanishi says racial equality was Japan's response to 'international universalism' (*sekaiteki fuhenshugi*). Nakanishi, op. cit., p. 240.

3 IMMIGRATION AND THE 'DIPLOMACY OF SAVING FACE'

1 Asada Sadao apparently coined the phrase, 'diplomacy of saving face' (*memmoku gaikō*) to describe Japanese diplomacy over immigration. Asada Sadao, 'Nichibei kankei to imin mondai', in Saitō Makoto *et al.* (eds), *Demokurashi to nichibei kankei*, vol. 2, 1973, quoted from Nakanishi Hiroshi, 'Konoe Fumimaro "Eibei hon'i no heiwashugi o haisu" rombun no haikei', *Hōgaku ronsō*, 1993, vol. 132, pp. 225–58.

2 L.F. Fitzhardinge, *William Morris Hughes: A Political Biography*, vol. 2, Sydney: Angus & Robertson Publishers, 1979, pp. 166–7.

3 Canadian Institute of International Affairs (hereafter CIIA), *Minorities of Oriental Race in Canada*, 8th Conference of the Institute of Pacific Relations, 1942, pp. 15–17.

4 ibid., pp. 15–17; Paul Gordon Lauren, *Power and Prejudice: The Politics and Diplomacy of Racial Discrimination*, Boulder, Colorado: Westview Press, 1988, p. 54.

5 Charles J. Woodsworth, *Canada and the Orient: A Study in International Relations*, Toronto: Macmillan, 1941, p. 48.

6 CIIA, op. cit., p. 7.

7 Memorandum, E. Parkes, 11 December 1920, *PRO*, FO 371/5367, f F3200; CIIA, op. cit., p. 7.

8 K.K. Kawakami, 'Canada as a "White Man's Country"', *Current History*, 1924, vol. 19, no. 5, p. 832.

9 Interestingly, the Canadian press was supportive of the Japanese proposal at the Paris Peace Conference, claiming that it was a just demand and as such its refusal would sow seeds of discontent for the future; *The Citizen*, 29 March 1919 and *Montreal Gazette*, 3 April 1919. Furuya to Uchida, 5 April 1919, 2.4.2.2, *Kokusai remmei: Jinshu sabetsu teppai*, vol. 2, Tokyo, Diplomatic Record Office.

10 CIIA, op. cit., p. 4, p. 7; Kawakami, op. cit., p. 832; Woodsworth, op. cit., p. 67.

11 The Victoria Act 39 of 1855. Australia became a federation on 1 January 1901. Robert A. Huttenback, *Racism and Empire: White Settlers and Coloured Immigrants in the British Self-Governing Colonies*, London: Cornell University Press, 1976, p. 62.
12 ibid., pp. 156–60.
13 Subsequent legislations adopted to the effect were Immigration Restriction Amendment Act 1905, Contract Immigrants Act 1905, Immigration Restriction Act 1908, Immigration Restriction Act 1910, Immigration Act 1912.
14 Act 17 of 1901. Huttenback, op. cit., p. 280.
15 W.K. Hancock, *Survey of British Commonwealth Affairs: Problems of Nationality 1918–1936*, vol. 1, London: Oxford University Press, 1964, p. 173.
16 A.T. Yarwood, *Asian Migration to Australia: The Background to Exclusion 1896–1923*, Melbourne: Melbourne University Press, 1964, pp. 98–9.
17 ibid., p. 78.
18 Gordon Greenwood and Charles Grimshaw (eds), *Documents on Australian International Affairs 1901–1918*, Canberra: Australian Institute of International Affairs, 1977, p. 417.
19 Yarwood, op. cit., p. 100.
20 ibid., pp. 91–2.
21 ibid., p. 82.
22 South Africa had an opposite racial composition from the other Dominions whose white populations outnumbered the non-white; thus, as a Dominion with an indigenous white ruling minority, there was a genuine problem of the racial balance in favour of the non-whites. In the 1921 census, there were 4,699,433 natives, 545,548 mixed and other coloureds, 163,896 Asiatics, and 1,519,488 Europeans in South Africa which demonstrate the extent of the 'colour' problem. Patrick Duncan, 'Race Questions in South Africa', *Foreign Affairs*, 1927, vol. 5, no. 2, p. 293.
23 Cape Colony introduced the Assembly Bill 57 in 1902, Bill to Prevent Introduction of [non-British] Chinese in 1904 and another to amend the law placing restrictions on immigration and providing for the removal from the colony of prohibited immigrants in 1906; Natal produced Act 30 of 1903 to prohibit free Indians. Huttenback, op. cit., pp. 150–2.
24 Buxton to Long, 6 December 1918, *PRO*, FO 371/3817, f 26706.
25 ibid.
26 Greene to Balfour, 27 January 1917, *PRO*, FO 371/2952, f 54930.
27 P. S. O'Connor, 'Keeping New Zealand White, 1908–1920', *New Zealand Journal of History*, 1968, vol. 2, no. 1, p. 44.
28 The earlier restriction acts of 1881 and 1888, Immigration Restriction Act of 1899, Chinese Immigrants Amendment Act of 1907, Immigration Restriction Amendment Act of 1908, Immigration Restriction Amendment Act of 1910, Undesirable Immigrants Exclusion Act of 1919, Immigration Restriction Amendment Bill of 1920.
29 In fact, the difficulty of obtaining the precise figures of Japanese immigrants to New Zealand seems to indicate the minuscule number.

30 O'Connor, op. cit., p. 44. The Imperial government expressed concern that British subjects would face reciprocal treatment in the former German islands in the Pacific, should New Zealand decide explicitly to restrict settlement of Japanese as they had intended to do in Samoa. Under-Secretary of State for Foreign Office to Under-Secretary of State for Colonial Office, 13 March 1918, *PRO*, CO 209/299, f 12886.

31 See Chapter 5 for a discussion of the 'Natal' formula for immigration restriction.

32 Hilary Conroy, *The Japanese Frontier in Hawaii, 1868–1898*, Berkeley: University of California Press, 1953, p. 15.

33 Roger Daniels, *Asian America: Chinese and Japanese in the United States since 1850*, Seattle: University of Washington Press, 1988, p. 115.

34 Roger Daniels, *The Politics of Prejudice: The Anti-Japanese Movement in California and the Struggle for Japanese Exclusion*, Berkeley: University of California Press, 1962, p. 16.

35 Daniels, *Asian America*, p. 112.

36 The paper offered a politically orthodox perspective, owned by a Republican by the name of M.H. de Young. See Daniels, *The Politics of Prejudice*, Berkeley: University of California Press, 1962, p. 25.

37 As a matter of interest, listed below are the objections raised by the League against the Japanese: 'i) We cannot assimilate them without injury to ourselves; ii) no large community of foreigners, so cocky, with such distinct racial, social and religious prejudices, can abide long in this country without serious friction; iii) we cannot compete with a people having a low standard of civilisation, living and wages; iv) it should be against public policy to permit our women to intermarry with Asiatics; v) we cannot extend citizenship to Asiatics; vi) if we permit the Jap to come in, what will . . . become of our Exclusion with China?'; ibid., p. 28.

38 Though Roosevelt was theoretically against Japanese immigration, he continued to pay lip service to Japan, as seen in his address in December 1905; ibid., pp. 35–6.

39 'Japanese immigration into the US: recommendations as to the handling of this problem', doc. 465, reel 25, National Archives Microfilm Publications (hereafter NAMP), M1107; David Starr Jordan to Wilson, 14 April 1913, *Wilson Papers*, vol. 27.

40 Bryan to Chinda, circa 19 May 1913, *Wilson Papers*, vol. 27.

41 Chinda to Bryan, 4 June 1913, *FRUS*, 1913.

42 'Japanese Immigration into the US', doc. 465, reel 25, NAMP, M1107.

43 Chinda to Makino, 16 April 1913, *Wilson Papers*, vol. 27.

44 Wilson to Hiram Warren Johnson and others, 22 April 1913, *Wilson Papers*, vol. 27.

45 Diary of Josephus Daniels, 13 and 16 May 1913, *Wilson Papers*, vol. 27.

46 Press Conference, 19 May 1913, *Wilson Papers*, vol. 27.

47 Confer footnote of Press Conference, 11 April 1913, *Wilson Papers*, vol. 27.

48 Roosevelt to Ray Stannard Baker, 10 November 1911, box 2, *Ray Stannard Baker Papers*, Princeton University Archives.

49 Roger Daniels, *The Politics of Prejudice*, Berkeley: University of California Press, 1962, p. 106.

50 Chinda to Makino, 6 June 1913, *Wilson Papers*, vol. 27.

51 James Duval Phelan was a wealthy banker and real estate dealer of San Francisco, the Mayor of San Francisco 1897–1902, the Wilson leader in California in 1912, and United States Senator for California 1915–1921.
52 Phelan to Wilson, 20 April 1912, *Wilson Papers*, vol. 24.
53 Roger Daniels, *The Politics of Prejudice*, Berkeley: University of California Press, 1962, p.106.
54 This was the preparatory commission set up by Colonel House which produced reports on subjects likely to be raised at the Paris Peace Conference.
55 'Japanese Immigration into the US', doc. 465, reel 25, NAMP, M1107.
56 Roger Daniels and Harry Kitano, *American Racism: Exploration of the Nature of Prejudice*, Engelwood Cliffs, New Jersey: Prentice-Hall, 1970, p. 46.
57 Ambassador Satō entreated that Japan had only wanted the treatment of most-favoured-nation and suggested to improve the present situation by i) concluding an independent treaty for mutual guarantee of most favoured nation treatment or by revising the existing commercial treaty, or ii) American legislation, for instance, constitutional amendment which would restrain any state from discriminating against aliens especially the provision for racial distinction in the federal naturalisation law. House to Wilson, 11 May 1917, *Wilson Papers*, vol. 42.
58 House to Wilson, 6 July 1918, *Wilson Papers*, vol. 48.
59 Daniels, *Asian America*, pp. 103–5.
60 Paul Birdsall, *Versailles Twenty Years After*, Hamden, Connecticut: Archon Books, 1962, p. 90; D.C.S. Sissons, 'The Immigration Question in Australian Diplomatic Relations with Japan 1875–1919', History Section 26/821, Australian and New Zealand Association for the Advancement of Science, 1971, p. 38.
61 Greene to Grey, 15 March 1915, *PRO*, FO 371/2388, f 50192.
62 Katō to Salisbury, 7 October 1897, quoted from Sissons, op. cit., p. 35.
63 On this point I concur with David Sissons, who reaches a conclusion that it was 'essentially a matter of prestige'. Unfortunately, no elaboration is given by him. Sissons, op. cit., p. 38.
64 Makino Nobuaki, *Kaikoroku*, vol. 2, Tokyo, Chūō kōronsha, 1978, p. 85.
65 Shidehara Kijūrō heiwa zaidan (ed.), *Shidehara Kijūrō*, Tokyo, Shidehara Kijūrō heiwa zaidan, 1955, p. 142.
66 Ishii to Gotō, 16 July 1918, doc. 58, 2.4.2.2, *Kokusai remmei: Jinshu sabetsu teppai*, vol. 1; Ishii Kikujirō, *Gaikō yoroku*, Tokyo, Iwanami, 1930, p. 515, p. 522.
67 Uchida Yasuya denki hensai iinkai (ed.), *Uchida Yasuya*, Tokyo, Kajima kenkyūjo shuppankai, 1969, p. 237.
68 Sure enough, when the racial equality proposal was defeated at Paris, the government was accused of a weak-kneed diplomacy by the right-wing press. For example, 'Sabetsu teppai to kokumin no kakugo', *Nihon oyobi nihonjin*, 1919, no. 754, p. 38.
69 Matsui to Uchida, 23 January 1919, doc. 19, *Nihon gaikō monjo*, 1919, part 1, vol. 3; Hankey's Notes of Council of Ten, 22 January 1919, *Wilson Papers*, vol. 54.
70 This prompted Makino to request Tokyo for more discretionary power in the League of Nations negotiation, which was duly granted.

3 February 1919, Hara Keiichirō (ed.), *Hara Kei nikki*, vol. 8, Tokyo, Kangensha, 1950.

71 Note dictated by Balfour on 10 February 1919 on conversation with House, Additional Manuscripts 49751, *Balfour Papers*.

72 Makino, op. cit., vol. 2, p. 85.

73 ibid.

74 Minutes of Diplomatic Advisory Council, 2 December 1918, Kobayashi Tatsuo (ed.), *Suiusō nikki: Itōke monjo*, Tokyo, Hara shobō, 1966.

75 Yoshida Shigeru, *Kaiko jūnen*, vol. 4, Tokyo, Shinchōsha, 1958, pp. 97–8. Yoshida, who later became prime minister, was Makino's son-in-law and acted as his personal assistant at the peace conference.

76 ibid., vol. 4, p. 98.

77 Out of the two, the one in which the Americans showed interest was as follows: 'The equality of nations being a basic principle of the League of Nations, the High Contracting Parties agree that concerning the treatment of aliens in their territories, they will accord them as far as it lies in their legitimate powers equal treatments and rights in law and in fact without making distinction on account of race or nationality.'

78 Makino, op. cit., vol. 2, p. 204.

79 Matsui to Uchida, 2 April 1919, doc. 400, *Nihon gaikō monjo*, 1919, part 1, vol. 3.

80 30 March 1919, *Hara Kei nikki*, vol. 8.

81 'Kenseikai Kiji', *Kensei*, 1919, vol. 2, no. 4, pp. 56–7.

82 Minutes of the Diplomatic Advisory Council, 19 February 1919, *Suiusō nikki*.

83 Onuma Yasuaki, 'Haruka naru jinshu byōdō no risō', Onuma Yasuaki (ed.), *Kokusaihō, kokusai rengō to nihon*, Tokyo, Kōbundō, 1987, pp. 457–9.

84 Niizuma Kōdō, 'Beikoku no han nihon fū', *Nihon oyobi nihonjin*, 1919, no. 756, pp. 35–7; 19 and 22 March, 6 April 1919, *Tokyo nichi nichi shimbun*; 19 March 1919, *Yomiuri shimbun*; 22 March 1919, *Asahi shimbun*.

85 10 and 13 April 1919, *Kokumin*, 17 April 1919, *Chūgai Shōgyō*, in 'Memorandum: Collection of press clippings from certain Japanese papers to April 26, 1919, regarding Japan and the Peace Conference', SDR 894.9111/3, reel 563, NAMP, M820.

86 Address by Katō Takaaki, Phillips to Ammission, 31 March 1919, SDR 185.111/226, reel 321, NAMP, M820.

87 17, 25 April 1919, *Kokumin*, in SDR 894.9111/3, reel 563, NAMP, M820.

88 Nakano Seigō, 'Kōwa kaigi no shinsō', *Kensei*, 1919, vol. 2, no. 5, pp. 16–56.

4 JAPAN'S STATUS AS A GREAT POWER

1 This listing was often referred to by the principal delegations including Britain. Although Japan was originally invited as one of the great powers in the Council of Ten, its status became somewhat ambiguous when the Council of Ten ceased to exist and was replaced by the Council of Four, from which Japan was excluded. This caused national embarrassment for

the Japanese government and an official complaint was lodged. However, it was politely refused on the grounds that Japan would be invited to sit in for discussions affecting its interests. See *FRUS*, vol. 6, p. 32.

2 For the purpose of this study, I have combined the definitions used by Martin Wight and Hedley Bull.

3 In seventeenth- and eighteenth-century Europe, national strength was measured chiefly in terms of population size. Therefore, in spite of the vast territorial possessions of Sweden around the time of the Treaty of Westphalia, it was France, with its far larger population, that was recognised as a formidable power in the European system. See A.D. Osiander, *The States System of Europe, 1640–1990: Peacemaking and the Conditions of International Stability*, Oxford: Clarendon Press, 1994.

4 Martin Wight, *Power Politics*, Leicester: Leicester University Press, 1978, p. 46.

5 Hedley Bull, *The Anarchical Society: A Study of Order in World Politics*, London: Macmillan, 1977, p. 201.

6 Wight, op. cit., p. 50.

7 See for instance, F.S. Marston, *The Peace Conference of 1919: Organisation and Procedure*, Oxford: Oxford University Press, 1944.

8 Bull goes a step further to state that 'great powers are powers recognised by others to have, and conceived by their own leaders and peoples to have, certain special rights and duties'. See his op. cit., p. 202.

9 Bull makes a distinction between the definition of great powers and the role they play. No such distinction is made here; ibid., p. 207.

10 For instance, *nisshin kyōchōron* (Sino–Japanese cooperation), *nisshin dōmeiron* (Sino-Japanese solidarity), *nisshin teikeiron* (Sino–Japanese coalition), *ajia rentairon* (Asian solidarity), *shinkoku kaizōron* (reform China), *shinkan kaizōron* (reform China and Korea), *chōsen kaizōron* (reform Korea), *ajia kaizōron* (reform Asia) come under the umbrella of *ajia shugi*; and *tairiku shinshutsuron* (continental expansion) and *ōbei kyōchōron* (cooperation with the West) come under *datsu-A ron*. It seems that the difference between the number of ways in which *ajia shugi* can be expressed, compared to *datsu-A ron*, is indicative of the importance of identification with Asia in Japanese foreign policy debates in the Meiji period.

11 This is representative of Oka's analysis. See Oka Yoshitake, 'Kokuminteki dokuritsu to kokka risei', *Kindai nihon shisōshi kōza: Sekai no naka no nihon*, vol. 8, Tokyo: Chikuma shobō, 1961.

12 Fukuzawa Yukichi (1835–1901) was a preeminent thinker and educator of the Meiji period. His visits to the United States in 1860 and Europe in 1866 led to the publication of an enormously influential work, *Seiyō jijō* in 1868. He was an ardent advocate of modernisation and Westernisation, as preached in his *Bummeiron no gairyaku* in 1875, and through a vast range of influential books, articles and pamphlets. He founded Keiō University and established *Jiji shimpō* in 1882.

13 Fukuzawa Yukichi, *Fukuzawa Yukichi zenshū*, vol. 10, Tokyo, Iwanami, 1959–60, pp. 221–4.

14 See his introductory chapter, especially pages 12–16, in *Meiji: Shisō no jitsuzō*, Tokyo: Sōbunsha, 1977.

15 After Russia's invasion into Manchuria in 1900, the source of tension in

the Sino–Japanese relationship expanded to include Manchuria which was now regarded to be crucial to Japan's national independence. ibid., p. 172.

16 ibid., pp. 50–4. Oka also mentions that China became Japan's hypothetical enemy after 1883; Oka, op. cit., p. 24.

17 Generally, it is understood that *datsu-A ron* enabled Japan to act as a Western power and to treat China and Korea from a position of strength. Before 1895, however, it was mostly hypothetical as Japan had yet to prove that it was entitled to perceive itself as a member of the West.

18 Banno, op. cit., pp. 16–19.

19 Iriye Akira, *Nihon no gaikō: Meiji ishin kara gendai made*, Tokyo: Chūō kōronsha, 1966, p. 28, pp. 42–3.

20 Konoe Atsumaro (1863–1904), the father of Konoe Fumimaro, was a Meiji politician, an influential figure in the early pan-Asian movement as head of Tōa dōbunkai and Kokumin dōmeikai (Association of National Solidarity) with Inukai Tsuyoshi and the ultra right-wing activist, Tōyama Mitsuru (leader of Genyōsha).

21 Banno, op. cit., p. 107, pp. 116–17.

22 ibid., p. 85.

23 Mamiya Kunio, 'Okuma Shigenobu to jinshu sabetsu teppai mondai', *Waseda daigakushi kiyō*, 1989, vol. 22, p. 222.

24 Jean-Pierre Lehmann, *The Image of Japan: From Feudal Isolation to World Power, 1850–1905*, London: George Allen & Unwin, 1978, p. 149.

25 Iriye, op. cit., pp. 45–7.

26 Ishii Kikujirō, *Gaikō zuisō*, Tokyo: Kajima heiwa kenkyūjo, 1967, p. 186, p. 188.

27 Banno, op. cit., pp. 85–6.

28 ibid., pp. 42–3.

29 Okuma Shigenobu (1838–1922) was a Meiji and Taishō politician, who was Foreign Minister in 1888, during which time he was involved in the revision of the unequal treaties, and again in the Matsukata cabinet in 1896, and formed a coalition government with Itagaki Taisuke in 1898. He was Chancellor of Waseda University in 1907 and returned to politics and formed the second Okuma cabinet in 1914.

30 Mamiya, op. cit., p. 221.

31 ibid.

32 Okuma makes the case also that nations should be judged not in terms of 'standard of nation' (*minzoku hyōjun*) but 'standard of civilisation' (*bummei hyōjun*) because the latter is attainable by all nations regardless of race. Okuma Shigenobu, *Jinshu mondai*, Tokyo: Waseda daigaku shuppan, 1919, p. 76, pp. 88–90.

33 Oka, op. cit., pp. 45–6.

34 S.R. Mehrotra, *India and the Commonwealth 1885–1929*, London: George Allen & Unwin, 1965, p. 33.

35 Oka, op. cit., p. 45.

36 Consult, for example, Michael Weiner, 'Discourses of Race, Nation, and Empire in pre-1945 Japan', *Ethnic and Racial Studies*, 1995, vol. 18, no. 3, pp. 433–56.

37 As it is beyond the scope of this work, no attempt will be made to provide in any great detail the specific events discussed below. Only the most relevant aspects of each of the events will be discussed.

38 Japan gradually absorbed Korea after 1904, starting from signing a protocol in February 1904, then three successive agreements in August 1904, November 1905 and July 1907, and culminating with annexation in August 1910.

39 Munemitsu Mutsu, *Kenkenroku: A Diplomatic Record of the Sino–Japanese War, 1894–1895*, Gordon Mark Berger (ed. and trans.), Tokyo: The Japan Foundation, 1982, pp. 212–3.

40 A.M. Pooley, *The Secret Memoirs of Count Tadasu Hayashi*, London: Eveleigh Nash, 1915, p. 74.

41 In fact, Richard Storry stated that no understanding of Japanese nationalism was possible without understanding the bitterness and humiliation that swept the country in the wake of the Triple Intervention. See Richard Storry, *Japan and the Decline of the West in Asia 1894–1943*, New York: St. Martin's Press, 1979, pp. 29–30.

42 Mutsu, op. cit., p. 254.

43 ibid., p. 250.

44 Pooley, op. cit., p. 81.

45 In 1897, Russia occupied Dairen and Port Arthur on the Liaotung Peninsula. This was followed by a Russian invasion into Manchuria proper in the aftermath of the Boxer Rebellion. The Russian threat became more imminent as a result of these two successive manoeuvrings, leading to the rise of the 'advance north' debate (*hokushinron*) which demanded that both Korea and Manchuria should come under Japanese control.

46 For an authoritative study of the alliance, consult I.H. Nish, *The Anglo-Japanese Alliance: The Diplomacy of Two Island Empires 1894–1907*, London: Athlone Press, 1966, and *Alliance in Decline: A Study in Anglo-Japanese Relations 1908–1923*, London: Athlone Press, 1972. Nish states that the interest in forming the alliance was mutual as Britain also perceived benefit from it.

47 It 'recognised the independence of China and Korea, and the special interests therein of Great Britain and Japan respectively; and bound themselves to maintain strict neutrality in the event of either of them being involved in war, and to come to one another's assistance in the event of either of them being confronted by the opposition of more than one hostile Power', quoted from the Paris Peace Conference Handbook on Japan, March 1919, *PRO*, FO 373/4/15, p 81.

48 Nish, *Anglo-Japanese Alliance*, p. 372; Oka, op. cit., pp. 37–8; Makino Nobuaki, *Kaikoroku*, vol. 1, Tokyo, Chūō kōronsha, 1978, p. 246.

49 Nish, *Anglo-Japanese Alliance*, p. 1.

50 Matsumura Masayoshi, 'Kōkaron to nichiro sensō', *Kokusai seiji*, 1982, vol. 71, p. 40. See also Ian Nish, *Origins of the Russo-Japanese War*, London: Longman, 1985, pp. 238–9.

51 Matsumura, op. cit., p. 44.

52 Oka, op. cit., p. 42.

53 Wight, op. cit., p. 46; Bull, op. cit., p. 201.

54 This is what Iriye calls '*shukanteki gaikō koritsukan*' (the subjective feeling of diplomatic isolation) in op. cit., pp. 49–50.

55 Banno, op. cit., p. 124.

56 Oka, op. cit., p. 47.

57 Banno, op. cit., pp. 126–7.
58 Ironically, it was the Japanese victory in 1905 which jolted the Californians into actively launching an anti-Japanese movement.
59 Paul Birdsall, *Versailles Twenty Years After*, Hamden, Connecticut: Archon Books, 1962, p. 90.
60 Makino, op. cit., vol. 2, p. 85.
61 Birdsall, op. cit., p. 90.
62 Nakano Seigō, 'Nihon teikoku no shimei', *Nihon oyobi nihonjin*, 1914, no. 639, p. 111.
63 This was uttered by Yamagata Aritomo and the Okuma cabinet. Kobayashi Tatsuo, 'Rinji gaikō chōsa iinkai no setchi', *Kokusai seiji*, 1964, vol. 28, p. 55.
64 Nakano Yasuo, *Seijika: Nakano Seigō*, vol. 2, Tokyo, Shinmitsukaku shoten, 1971, p. 244; Oka, op. cit., pp. 52–3; Takamura Naosuke, 'Tenkanki to shiteno daiichiji taisen to nippon', *Kōza nihon rekishi*, part 3, vol. 9, Tokyo, 1985, p. 10.
65 For Prime Minister Okuma's statement of war aims made on 17 August 1914; see Nish, *Alliance in Decline*, p. 124.
66 Technically, the Japanese capture of Shantung constituted a violation of Chinese neutrality which the Chinese government could not defend due to lack of military strength. Chinese Oral History Project, *Wellington Koo Memoir*, part 2, vol. 2, pp. 76–80.
67 The British government sent a message to the Japanese government for the assistance on 7 August 1914, and, within thirty-six hours, the Okuma cabinet decided to go to war in support of Britain. On 23 August, Japan declared war on Germany after the latter failed to respond to the ultimatum.
68 'Points of Contact with Great Britain in the Far East', 29 November 1918, SDR 714.41/24, National Archives Microfilm Publication (hereafter NAMP), M581.
69 Balfour to Milner, 19 January 1918, MS Milner 46, f.3, *Milner Papers*. See also Captain E.H. Rymer, 8 February 1918, *PRO*, FO 371/3233, f 46022; Greene to Balfour, 7 January 1918, FO 371/3233, f 33087.
70 Balfour to Greene, 14 February 1917, *PRO*, FO 410/66, Confidential Print 11301, no 14.
71 Nish, *Alliance in Decline*, p. 256.
72 Greene to Balfour, 23 December 1918, *PRO*, FO 371/3816, f 20038.
73 Greene to Grey, 16 August 1915, *PRO*, FO 410/64, Confidential Print 11282, no 290.
74 Paris Peace Conference Handbook on Japan, Foreign Office, March 1919, *PRO*, FO 373/4/15. As an interesting contrast, this is what it said about China: 'The Chinese are a sober, industrious race, highly endowed with judgment, good sense, and tenacity. Though comprising many types, they are markedly homogeneous, owing to centuries of uniform mental cultivation. The ideals of their intellectual life are not inferior to those in the Western world; and their religion – ancestor worship – tends to bind society together. They are amenable to intercourse; moderation is a virtue with them; and they are accustomed to conduct their own private and local affairs with tact and consideration. By education and temperament they are markedly pacific. They possess the qualities and attributes which

entitle a people to independent existence, and if they are not rapidly inoculated with militarism there is no inherent reason why other nations should fear them or exercise a preventive domination.' Paris Peace Conference Handbook on China, March 1919. FO 373/4/1.

75 Edward Grey, *Twenty-Five Years 1892–1916*, vol. 1, London: Hodder & Stoughton, 1925, p. 100.

76 J.H. Tomes, 'A.J. Balfour and British Foreign Policy: the International Thought of a Conservative Statesman', D.Phil. thesis, University of Oxford, 1992, p. 303, p. 318.

77 Nish, *Alliance in Decline*, pp. 240–1, p. 245, p. 257.

78 The Zimmermann telegram was sent from German Foreign Minister Zimmermann to its minister in Mexico on 19 January 1917 which suggested that if a war were to break out between Germany and the US, then Mexico should mediate between Germany and Japan to bring the latter into the alliance. This was published by President Wilson and produced an irreparable damage to the reputation of Japan. ibid., pp. 212–3.

79 ibid., p. 217.

80 Greene to Balfour, 30 March 1918, *PRO*, FO 371/3234, f 56817; Greene to Balfour, 16 July 1918, FO 371/3234, f 162924; also Nish, *Alliance in Decline*, pp. 247–8.

81 See Lloyd C. Gardner, *Safe for Democracy: The Anglo-American Response to Revolutions, 1913–1923*, New York: Oxford University Press, 1984.

82 Jordan to Curzon, 22 April 1919, *PRO*, FO 405/226, Confidential Print 11604, no. 47; 19 April 1919, *North China Herald*, vol. CXXXI, no. 2697.

83 For instance, Gardner points out that the American ambassador, Paul Reinsch, launched a crusade proclaiming America's concern for China's 'integrity' which, concurrently, had a practical beneficial aspect of enabling American businessmen to seek opportunities in all parts of China as opposed to restricted spheres of influence. See Gardner, op. cit., p. 76.

84 For example, Secretary of State Lansing, when evaluating the Council of Ten at the peace conference, said, 'I know that the United States means to be just and generous and is entirely unselfish in its policies, but I cannot say the same of the other four great powers.' See 'Review of the present condition of the peace conference', 22 January 1919, box 2, vol. 2, *Robert Lansing Papers*, Princeton University Archives.

85 The terms of the Twenty-One Demands which were divided into five groups were as follows: i) China to assent to any future agreement on the disposal of rights to former German Shantung, and also Japan having further commercial rights; ii) extended the Manchuria leases to ninety-nine years, and further rights in Inner Mongolia and South Manchuria; iii) Chinese consent to monopoly rights for an existing Japanese industrial complex in the Yangtze valley; iv) Chinese to promise not to cede to any other power any harbour or bay or island along the coast of China; v) to engage influential Japanese as political, financial and military advisers, etc., bringing China more than halfway under Japan's direct political supervision. It was demand v) that caused international uproar

and was subsequently withdrawn upon intervention by Genrō Yamagata. Storry, op. cit., pp. 108–9.

86 Tokutomi Iichiro (ed.), *Kōshaku Yamagata Aritomo den*, vol. 3, Tokyo: Yamagata Aritomo Kōkinen jigyōkai, 1933, pp. 932–3.

87 Oka, op. cit., p. 57; Kizaka Jun'ichirō, 'Taishōki minponshugisha no kokusai ninshiki', *Kokusai seiji*, 1974, vol. 51, p. 63.

88 Oka, op. cit., pp. 57–8; Ishibashi Tanzan, 'Kakon o nokosu gaikō seisaku', 5 May 1915, in Matsuo Takayoshi (ed.), *Ishibashi Tanzan hyōronshū*, Tokyo, Iwanami, 1986, p. 56.

89 Mitani Taichirō, *Nippon seitō seiji no keisei: Hara Kei no seiji shidō no tenkai*, Tokyo, Tokyo daigaku shuppankai, 1980, p. 236.

90 A. Walworth, *Woodrow Wilson: 2 World Prophet*,New York: Longmans, Green and Co., 1958, p. 126, p. 129. In fact, President Wilson was sufficiently concerned about the deteriorating relationship with Japan that he appointed Roland Morris, his Princeton friend, as ambassador to Tokyo in October 1917 in the hope of improving the relationship.

91 For instance, it was believed that Bryan was seeking a compromise between Japan and China while Lansing and Wilson favoured lodging a complaint but decided against it if Japan contained its interests to Mongolia and Manchuria. Gardner, op. cit., p. 84. Hosoya contends that Bryan and Lansing were more accommodating to the Japanese, whereas Wilson became highly suspicious of Japan. Hosoya Chihiro, *Ryō taisenki no nihon gaikō, 1914–1945*, Tokyo: Iwanami, 1988, pp. 30–5.

92 Gardner, op. cit., pp. 91–3.

93 Lansing to Wilson, 25 September 1917, *Wilson Papers*, vol. 44; Japanese Ambassador to Balfour, 7 November 1917, *PRO*, FO 371/2954, f 212689.

94 Peter Lowe, *Great Britain and Japan 1911–15: A Study of British Far Eastern Policy*, London: Macmillan, 1969, p. 229, p. 254.

95 According to the British, the record of the conversation did not exist. However, there is a record of Grey's conversation with the Japanese Counsellor in London on 9 May 1915 when Grey indicated that Britain would not object to the Japanese demands on the former German settlements in China, should these concessions become part of the negotiation between China and Japan. See box 56, *Davidson Papers*.

96 Nish, *Alliance in Decline*, p. 155.

97 This could be the fruit of a campaign launched by the Japanese government to alleviate the anti-Japanese tendency of *The Times* by inviting its editor, Valentine Chirol, to visit Japan in 1909. However, the Twenty-One Demands were subsequently published by the *Manchester Guardian*. ibid., pp. 9–10.

98 Whereas some in the Army General Staff such as Tanaka Giichi did not take the Americans seriously and considered quashing Chinese opposition internally by using revolutionaries to incite disturbance in China, and internationally by relying on the strength of the Anglo–Japanese Alliance and Russo–Japanese Agreement. Banno Junji, *Kindai nippon no gaikō to seiji*, Tokyo: Kenbun shuppan, 1985, pp. 80–1, pp. 83–4.

99 Most secret memorandum, 22 October 1919, *PRO*, FO 371/3816, f 148769; George W. Egerton, *Great Britain and the Creation of the League of Nations: Strategy, Politics, and International Organisation, 1914–1919*, Chapel Hill, University of North Carolina Press, 1978, p. 83.

100 S.P. Tillman, *Anglo-American Relations at the Peace Conference of 1919*, Princeton: Princeton University Press, 1961, p. 135.
101 Balfour to Milner, 19 January 1918, MS Milner 46, ff.3–4, *Milner Papers*.
102 Frazier and Page to Wilson, 16 March 1918, *Wilson Papers*, vol. 47.
103 D.E. Cronton, *The Cabinet Diaries of Josephus Daniels: 1913–1921*, Lincoln: University of Nebraska Press, 1963, p. 288, p. 295; 'Memorandum on the proposed Japanese military expedition into Siberia,' 18 March 1918, box 2, vol. 1, *Robert Lansing Papers*, Princeton University Archives. Balfour suggested that the Americans were concerned about reviving the memories of the Russo–Japanese War.
104 Lansing to Wilson, 27 February 1918, NAMP, M743.
105 House to Balfour, 4 March 1918, F60/2/45, *Lloyd George Papers*.
106 Confidential summary of correspondence by Ian Malcolm concerning the Allied intervention in East Russia, 21 June 1918, box 71, *Davidson Papers*.
107 The details on the issue of Siberian troop deployment from the Japanese perspective have been extracted from Gaimushō hyakunenshi hensan iinkai (ed.), *Gaimushō no hyakunen*, vol. 1, Tokyo, Hara shobō, 1969, pp. 675–85.
108 Eventually, Motono resigned over the crisis and was replaced by Gotō Shimpei.
109 *Gaimushō no hyakunen*, vol. 1, pp. 681–2.
110 When Lansing protested about the size of the forces in November 1918, Hara immediately reduced the figure to 26,000 by mid-December 1918.
111 Oka, op. cit., p. 54.
112 Inada Shūnosuke, *Jinshu mondai*, Tokyo, Yūrinkaku, 1915, pp. 6–7.
113 Oka, op. cit., pp. 54–5.
114 ibid., p. 55.
115 Iriye, op. cit., pp. 78–9.
116 Oka, op. cit., p. 55.
117 Banno, *Meiji*, pp. 129–30.
118 Banno, *Kindai nippon no gaikō to seiji*, pp. 80–1.
119 Italics are mine. Foreign Office to Colonial Office, 13 January 1919, *PRO*, CO 532/139, f 2719.
120 For example, John Vincent, 'Racial Equality', Hedley Bull and Adam Watson (eds), *The Expansion of International Society*, Oxford: Oxford University Press, 1984.
121 Minutes of Diplomatic Advisory Council, 19 November 1918, Tatsuo Kobayashi (ed.), *Suiusō nikki: Itōke monjo*, Tokyo: Hara shobō, 1966.
122 'Kenseikai Kiji', *Kensei*, 1919, vol. 2, no. 4, pp. 56–7.
123 The Pan African Congress with fifty-seven members from fifteen countries was meeting in Paris to coincide with the peace conference on 19–21 February. This congress included some influential members such as W.B. Dubois, a black American activist, and Blaise Diagne, a Senegalese member of the Assemblée Nationale in France.
124 Ishii recounted a similar tale. Shimomura Hironori, *Nippon gaikō hiroku*, Tokyo: Asahi shimbunsha, 1934, p. 145.
125 Onuma Yasuaki, 'Haruka naru jinshu byōdō no risō', Onuma Yasuaki (ed.), *Kokusaihō, kokusai rengō to nihon*, Tokyo: Kōbundō, 1987, pp. 431–2.

126 ibid., p. 477.
127 The Japanese sources do not necessarily make the categorical distinction between treatment which is equal and that which is racially equal. It is often inferred that 'equal treatment' meant racially equal treatment to the Japanese people.

5 AUSTRALIA OVERWHELMS THE BRITISH EMPIRE DELEGATION

1 D.H.Miller, *Drafting of the Covenant*, vol. 2, New York: G.P. Putnam & Sons, 1928, p. 389.
2 H.V.W. Temperley (ed.), *A History of the Peace Conference of Paris*, vol. 6, London: Henry Frowde and Hodder & Stoughton, 1924, p. 352.
3 Paul Rich terms this as 'racial Anglo-Saxonism', which is 'defined in terms of notions of common Anglo-Saxon racial origins in the colonies of white settlement and the belief that British parliamentary liberties were a product of Anglo-Saxon tribal institutions which had been carried down through centuries and underlay the British imperial mission to spread freedom and justice to other, more backward parts of the world' in his *Race and Empire in British Politics*, Cambridge: Cambridge University Press, 1986, p. 13.
4 Diary, 4 February 1919, Add.51131, f.33, *Cecil Papers*.
5 Miller, op. cit., vol. 2, p. 389.
6 ibid., vol. 2, p. 390.
7 Note dictated by Balfour on 10 February 1919 on conversation with House, Additional Manuscripts 49751, *Balfour Papers*.
8 For an interesting discussion of scientific racism, consult Elazar Barkan, *The Retreat of Scientific Racism: Changing Concepts of Race in Britain and the United States between the World Wars*, Cambridge: Cambridge University Press, 1992.
9 Greene to Balfour, 2 December 1918, *PRO*, FO 608/211, f 475; also similar message in Greene to Balfour, 12 November 1918, CO 532/139, f 4086.
10 Foreign Office to Colonial Office, 13 January 1919, *PRO*, CO 532/139, f 2719.
11 ibid.
12 Max Beloff, *Britain's Liberal Empire 1897–1921*, vol. 1, London: Macmillan, 1987, p. 219.
13 See, for instance, W.K. Hancock, *Survey of British Commonwealth Affairs: Vol. 1 Problems of Nationality 1918–1936*, London: Oxford University Press, 1964, pp. 28–9.
14 ibid., p. 191; S.R. Mehrotra, *India and the Commonwealth 1885–1929*, London, George Allen & Unwin, 1965, p. 65; G. Greenwood and C. Grimshaw (eds), *Documents on Australian International Affairs 1901–1918*, Canberra: Australian Institute of International Affairs, 1977, p. 567.
15 Basically, Dominions were entitled to the status of states with 'special interests' like Belgium and Serbia, on top of being a member of the British Empire delegation. British Empire Delegation Minutes 1, 13 January 1919, F126, *Lloyd George Papers*.

16 Hancock, op. cit., p. 173.
17 Act 17 of 1901. In fact, the Australians thought that they were making a concession in agreeing to this formula because what they really wanted was to specify 'coloured persons'. R.A. Huttenback, *Racism and Empire*, London, Cornell University Press, 1976, p. 280.
18 Hancock, op. cit., p. 173.
19 Huttenback, op. cit., p. 167, p. 282.
20 Bracketed insertion is mine. Grey to Bertie and to Buchanan, 14 January 1915, *PRO*, FO 371/2381, f 5241.
21 Copy of telegram from Greene to Balfour, 12 November 1918, *PRO*, CO 532/139, f 4086; Greene to Balfour, 2 December 1918, FO 608/211, f 475.
22 Also, the Foreign Office was concerned about resolving the problem of Indians in the Dominions prior to making any definitive arrangements with the Japanese, and had asked the Colonial Office to take appropriate initiatives in setting up meetings at the peace conference. Foreign Office to Colonial Office, 13 January 1919, *PRO*, CO 532/139, f 2719; India Office to Foreign Office, 13 January 1919, FO 371/3817, f 6579.
23 Matsui to Uchida, 15 February 1919, doc. 363, *Nihon gaikô monjo*, 1919, part 1, vol. 3.
24 Curzon to Milner, 15 April 1919, Additional Milner Papers, MSS Eng. hist. C699, *Milner Papers*.
25 It must be mentioned that Hughes and his supporters broke away from the Labour Party in 1916 over the conscription crisis and formed a coalition government with the Liberals, calling themselves the Nationalists.
26 William Morris Hughes (1862–1952) dominated Australian politics during the First World War, having acted thrice as attorney-general, and reigned as prime minister 1915–23. He was elected as a Labour member for West Sydney, being a quintessential Labour man. Over the first conscription crisis in 1916, he left the Cabinet together with his supporters, and formed a new coalition government with the Liberals.
27 A.A. Calwell, S.R. Davis, W. MacMahon and L.C. Webb, *The Australian Political Party System*, London, Angus & Robertson, 1954, pp. 56–7; Ian Turner, *Industrial Labour and Politics: The Dynamics of the Labour Movement in Eastern Australia 1900–1921*, Cambridge, Cambridge University Press, 1965, p. xix, p. 22.
28 Calwell *et al.*, op. cit., p. 59.
29 Turner, op. cit., p. 26; L.F. Fitzhardinge, *William Morris Hughes, A Political Biography*, vol. 1, Sydney: Angus & Robertson Publishers, 1964, p. 116.
30 Calwell *et al.*, op. cit., p. 87.
31 The other six were: i) full adult franchise; ii) creation of two Houses of Parliaments; iii) House of Representative to have the sole power of initiating and amending money bills; iv) introduction of a system of non-party government by means of elective ministries; v) direct initiation of legislation by the people, coupled with referendum; vi) payment of members. Fitzhardinge, op. cit., vol. 1, p. 81.
32 Turner, op. cit., p. 53; Calwell *et al.*, op. cit., p. 60, p. 71.
33 Fitzhardinge, op. cit., vol. 1, p. 116.
34 A.T. Yarwood, *Asian Migration to Australia: The Background to Exclusion 1896–1923*, Melbourne: Melbourne University Press, 1964, p. 152.

35 Fitzhardinge, op. cit., vol. 1, pp. 166–7.
36 ibid., pp. 134–6.
37 This was according to Hughes; ibid., p. 136.
38 W.M. Hughes, *The Splendid Adventure: A Review of Empire Relations Within and Without the Commonwealth of Britannic Nations*, London: Ernest Benn Limited, 1929, p. 366.
39 ibid., p. 92.
40 Yarwood, op. cit., p. 93.
41 Neville Meaney, *The Search for Security in the Pacific, 1901–14*, Sydney: Sydney University Press, 1976, p. 46.
42 Turner, op. cit., p. 68.
43 Neville Meaney, *Australia and the World: A Documentary History from the 1870s to the 1970s*, Brisbane: Longman, 1985, p. 14.
44 Lauren makes the point that the only difference between the Japanese and other racially discriminated immigrants was that Japan possessed power. Paul Gordon Lauren, *Power and Prejudice: The Politics and Diplomacy of Racial Discrimination*, Boulder, Colorado: Westview Press, 1988, p. 57; Fitzhardinge, op. cit., vol. 2, pp. 416–7.
45 Meaney, *Australia and the World*, p. 18, p. 23.
46 I.H. Nish, 'Australia and the Anglo-Japanese Alliance, 1901–1911', *The Australian Journal of Politics and History*, 1963, vol. 9, no. 2, p. 211.
47 I.H. Nish, *Alliance in Decline: A Study in Anglo-Japanese Relations 1908–1923*, London: Athlone Press, 1972, pp. 50–1.
48 Meaney, *Australia and the World*, p. 290.
49 Hughes to Lloyd George, 7 October 1919, F28/3/42, *Lloyd George Papers*.
50 Nish, *Alliance in Decline: A Study in Anglo-Japanese Relations 1908–1923*, London: Athlone Press, 1972, pp. 332–7.
51 For details of the conscription crisis, see Ernest Scott, *Official History of Australia in the War of 1914–1918: Vol. 11 Australia during the War*, Sydney: Angus & Robertson, 1936, pp. 292–429.
52 According to E.L. Piesse, who was the Director of the Pacific Branch of the Prime Minister's Office. Fitzhardinge, op. cit., vol. 2, p. 167.
53 This rumour was originated by J.T. Laing and Anstey.
54 Fitzhardinge, op. cit., vol. 2, p. 199.
55 Hughes, op. cit., p. 357.
56 'Australia at the Peace Table', 22 March 1919, *The Argus*.
57 Hughes to Lloyd George, 4 November 1918, F33/1/44a, *Lloyd George Papers*.
58 'Memorandum regarding the Pacific Islands' by W.M. Hughes for the British Empire delegation, 8 February 1919, W.C.P. 116, MS Milner 389, *Milner Papers*.
59 Kerr to Milner, 31 January 1919, Additional Milner Papers, MSS Eng. hist. C700, *Milner Papers*.
60 Nish, *Alliance in Decline*, pp. 144–6.
61 Kerr to Milner, 31 January 1919, Additional Milner Papers, MSS Eng. hist. C700, *Milner Papers*.
62 'Racial Equality', 10 April 1919, *The Argus*.
63 Fitzhardinge, op. cit., vol. 2, p. 12.
64 According to Eggleston who went as a member of the Australian delegation, Hughes 'was working up a newspaper campaign against the British

Government'. W.J. Hudson, *Billy Hughes in Paris: The Birth of Australian Diplomacy*, Melbourne, Nelson, 1978, p. 117.

65 26 June 1919, Senate, *Parliamentary Debates*, (Session 1917–18–19 Second Session of 7th Parliament), vol. LXXXVIII, (18 December 1918 to 6 August 1919).

66 Hughes, op. cit., p. 108.

67 J.G. Latham, *The Significance of the Peace Conference from an Australian Point of View*, Melbourne: Melville and Mullen, 1920, p. 9.

68 Meaney, *Australia and the World*, p. 283.

69 Geoffrey Sawer, *Australian Federal Politics and Law, 1901–1929*, Melbourne: Melbourne University Press, 1956, p. 177.

70 'Peace Conference: The Little Drama of Mr Hughes', 11 April 1919, *The Sydney Morning Herald.*

71 24 January 1919, see also 31 March 1919, *The Argus.*

72 This could have been the result of the news of the peace conference coming from American news agencies.

73 Fitzhardinge, op. cit., vol. 1, p. 194.

74 Scott, op. cit., pp. 365–6.

75 Fitzhardinge, op. cit., vol. 2, pp. 421–2.

76 Colin A. Hughes, *Mr. Prime Minister: Australian Prime Ministers 1901–1972*, Melbourne: Oxford University Press, 1976, p. 62.

77 See for example, 1 September, 15 September, *The Sydney Morning Herald.*

78 10 September 1919, House of Representatives, *Parliamentary Debates*, (Session 1917–18–19 Second Session of 7th Parliament), vol. LXXXXIX, p. 12176.

79 17, 18, 24, 29 September 1919, House of Representatives, *Parliamentary Debates*, (Session 1917–18–19 Second Session of 7th Parliament), vol. LXXXXIX.

80 This involved the reference of powers from the provincial parliaments to the federal government. Robert Garran, *Prosper the Commonwealth*, London: Angus & Robertson, 1958, pp. 279–80.

81 31 October 1919, *The Argus*; 10 December 1919, *Sydney Morning Herald*; Fitzhardinge, op. cit., vol. 2, p. 430.

82 Curzon to Milner, 6 May 1919, Additional Milner Papers, MSS Eng. hist. C699, *Milner Papers.*

83 Hughes, op. cit., p. 108.

6 THE AMERICAN OPPOSITION

1 Speech of Senator James D. Phelan of California in the Senate of the United States, 20 February 1920, SDR 894.00/164–2, National Archives Microfilm Publication (hereafter NAMP), M422.

2 Lansing to House, enclosing a cable from Phelan dated 2 March 1919, folder 2278, box 69, series I, collection group 466, *House Papers*; Phelan to Ammission, 24 March 1919, SDR 185.111/191, reel 321, NAMP, M820.

3 R.E. Hennings, 'James D. Phelan and the Woodrow Wilson Anti-

Oriental Statement of May 3, 1912', *California Historical Society Quarterly*, 1963, vol. 42, pp. 291–300.

4 Tumulty to Newton Diehl Baker with enclosure of letter from Phelan, 5 April 1919, *Wilson Papers*, vol. 57.

5 Charles Seymour (ed.), *The Intimate Papers of Colonel House*, vol. 4, London: Ernest Benn Ltd., 1928, p. 323; D.H. Miller, *Drafting of the Covenant*, vol. 1, New York: G.P. Putnam & Sons, pp. 183–4.

6 H. Foley, *Woodrow Wilson's Case for the League of Nations*, Princeton: Princeton University Press, 1923, pp. 93–4.

7 Onuma Yasuaki, 'Haruka naru jinshu byōdō no risō', Onuma Yasuaki (ed.), *Kokusaihō, kokusai rengō to nihon*, Tokyo: Kōbundō, 1987, pp. 450–1.

8 It is well known that these two groups were not at all cohesive and had several sub-groupings. For a detailed analysis of these groups, consult R. Stone, *The Irreconcilables: The Fight against the League of Nations*, Lexington, University of Kentucky Press, 1970.

9 A group of about thirty Republicans who did not completely oppose the treaty and the League but had strong reservations about the present form as it stood. Their leader was Henry Cabot Lodge.

10 The 'irreconcilables', who were also known as the 'bitter-enders' or the 'battalion of death', consisted of the following members: William Borah (Idaho), Frank B. Brandegee (Connecticut), Albert B. Fall (New Mexico), Bert M. Fernald (Maine), Joseph France (Maryland), Asle J. Gronna (North Dakota), Hiram W. Johnson (California), Philander C. Knox (Pennsylvania), Joseph Medill McCormick (Illinois), George H. Moses (New Hampshire), George W. Norris (Nebraska), Miles Poindexter (Washington), James A. Reed (Missouri-Democrat), Lawrence Y. Sherman (Illinois), Charles S. Thomas (Colorado-Democrat). See Stone, op. cit., p. 1.

11 This group very much wanted the League but not in the form advanced by Wilson.

12 Stone, op. cit., p. 27.

13 ibid., pp. 56–8.

14 Statement of the President, 19 August 1919, part 5, volume 13, section 1, unit 4, *Bernard Baruch Papers*.

15 Inga Floto, *Colonel House in Paris: A Study of American Policy at the Paris Peace Conference 1919*, Princeton: Princeton University Press, 1980, p. 131; see also Henry Cabot Lodge, *The Senate and the League of Nations*, London, Charles Scribner's Sons, 1925.

16 A.L. George and J.L. George, *Woodrow Wilson and Colonel House: A Personality Study*, New York: Dover Publications, 1964, p. 149.

17 J.E. Ingham of Idaho Congregational Conference to Borah, 5 August 1919, container 768, *William E. Borah Papers*.

18 Stone, op. cit., p. 116, p. 133.

19 Intrinsically, the doctrine was isolationist which saw no reason for indiscriminate American involvement in affairs of member states of the League if they were not of direct interest to the United States. Conversely, it dictated the undesirability of others to interfere in the Western Hemisphere, which was considered to be an exclusively American sphere of influence.

20 See, for instance, Borah's speech on 'Americanism' which extols the virtues of an isolationist policy, and urges the United States not to entangle in the European affairs. Speech in the US Senate, 21 February 1919, container 779, *William E. Borah Papers*.

21 25 and 26 March 1919, *New York Times*. Democratic Senator Reed continued to use a racist argument even after the proposal was defeated as a weapon against the League and 'declared that the League would place the destinies of the white race in the hands of ignorant and superstitious nations of black and yellow populations, and charged that many Democrats were supporting it for partisan reasons'. 27 May 1919, *San Francisco Chronicle*.

22 Tumulty to Wilson, 18, 21 and 28 March, 13 April 1919, container 49, *Joseph Patrick Tumulty Papers*.

23 Stephen Bonsal, *Unfinished Business*, London: Michael Joseph Ltd., 1944, pp. 142–3.

24 David Hunter Miller, diary, 18 March 1919, *My Diary: At the Conference of Paris*, vol. 1, New York, privately printed, 1924.

25 Guthrie to Secretary of State, 19 June 1916, SDR 711.94/237, NAMP, M423.

26 R.H. Fifield, *Woodrow Wilson and the Far East: The Diplomacy of the Shantung Question*, New York: Thomas Y. Crowell, 1952, pp. 192–3.

27 Lou Tseng-Tsiang, the chief Chinese plenipotentiary, recalled that the 'policy of friendship' of the United States was very important for China in his *Ways of Confucius and of Christ*, London: Burns Oates, 1948, p. 40.

28 Fifield, op. cit., p. 226; A. Nevins, *Henry White: Thirty Years of American Diplomacy*, New York: Harper & Brothers Publishers, 1930, p. 441.

29 In this study, the *New York Times*, the *San Francisco Chronicle* and the *Los Angeles Times* were surveyed, all of which portrayed a general tendency to view Japan in a negative light during the Paris Peace Conference.

30 A brief history of the Shantung problem is as follows. In November 1897, the Germans landed at Tsingtao in the province of Shantung, and concluded a treaty with China in the following year which bestowed on Germany the lease of Kiaochou and certain associated privileges in the province. When the war broke out in Europe, Japan lost no time in declaring war against Germany and subsequently captured the leased territories in November 1914. The Japanese claimed that they should first have rights and privileges to Shantung which would then be transferred to Chinese sovereignty at a future date. However, the Chinese contended that their involvement in the war had nullified the necessity of an initial transfer to the Japanese. However, the Council of Four, after acrimonious discussions, had ruled in favour of the Japanese. Subsequently, the Chinese dissatisfaction with the Treaty of Versailles resulted in the Chinese abstention from signature. For a discussion of the American involvement in the Shantung settlement, see Fifield, op. cit.

31 Zhang Yongjin, *China in the International System, 1918–1920: The Middle Kingdom at the Periphery*, Oxford: Macmillan, 1991, p. 56; 15 February 1919, *North China Herald*, vol. CXXX, no. 2688; Macleay to Hardinge, 15 February 1919, *PRO*, FO 608/209, f 634/1/4 (no. 1638). The Japanese foreign minister denied this report when asked by Greene.

See 15 February 1919, FO 608/209, f 634/1/1 (no. 2172); Wilson to Lansing, 7 February 1919, container 41, p. 7195, *Ray Stannard Baker Papers*, Library of Congress.

32 Minutes of daily meetings of the Commissioners Plenipotentiary, 5 and 6 February 1919, *FRUS*, 1919, Paris Peace Conference, vol. 11.

33 E.T. Williams to the Commission, 19 March 1919, container 42, p. 7289, *Robert Lansing Papers*, Library of Congress.

34 ibid., Thomas Millard, 6 April 1919, pp. 7337–9.

35 Ray Stannard Baker, *Woodrow Wilson and World Settlement*, vol. 2, London: William Heinemann Ltd., 1923, pp. 225–6.

36 Morris to Lansing, 15 November 1918, SDR 763.72119/2636, reel 387, NAMP, M367.

37 E.T. Williams to the Commission, 19 March 1919, container 42, p. 7289, *Robert Lansing Papers*, Library of Congress.

38 E.T. Williams to the Commissioners, 26 March 1919, SDR 185.111/206, reel 321, NAMP, M820.

39 Williams's view was shared by Thomas Millard, editor of the Shanghai-based *Millard Review*, who considered the Japanese proposal as being too vaguely worded to have any effective threat value; 'Japan, "race equality" and the League of Nations', Thomas Millard, 6 April 1919, container 42, *Robert Lansing Papers*, Library of Congress.

40 ibid., Meeting with Bliss and White on Kiaochou, 29 April 1919, desk diaries of Lansing, reel 2, DM 15,347.

41 The Chinese delegate in the League of Nations Commission, Wellington Koo, supported the racial equality proposal. D.H. Miller, *The Drafting of the Covenant*, vol. 2, New York: G.P. Putnam & Sons, 1928, p. 325, p. 391.

42 In particular, those who supported the theory were suspicious of the perfect timing of the Shantung negotiations which took place immediately after the racial equality negotiations. W. King, *Woodrow Wilson, Wellington Koo and the China Question at the Paris Peace Conference*, Leyden: A.W. Sythoff, 1959, p. 22.

43 6 September 1919, *North China Herald*, vol. CXXXII, no. 2717.

44 ibid.

45 The War Cabinet decided on the following on 12 February 1917: 'The Secretary of State for Foreign Affairs should give an assurance in the terms suggested in the opening sentences of the original Japanese request of the 27 January, with the proviso that the Japanese Government should give a corresponding assurance of support, in the eventual peace settlement, to our claims to the German islands south of the equator, and in our general policy elsewhere' in War Cabinet 63, box 63, *Law (Bonar Law) Papers*.

46 Balfour to Greene, 14 February 1917, *PRO* FO 410/66, Confidential Print 11301, no 14. Greene communicated this message to the Foreign Minister on the same day (FO 410/66, Confidential Print 11301, no 15) and received acknowledgement on 21 February 1917, declaring reciprocal support for British claims as requested (FO 410/66, Confidential Print 11301, no 18).

47 As reported in 21 August 1919, *Le Temps*.

48 Foreign Office confidential memorandum to the Cabinet, 2 February

1917, box 56, *Davidson Papers*; Grew to Polk, 26 February 1919, SDR 893.77/21A, reel 563, NAMP, M820.

49 Zhang, op. cit., p. 58.

50 'No man ever wanted greater publicity than he for the general statements of his position: and few leaders are more secretive when it comes to the discussion of the specific problem. He speaks to the masses in terms of new diplomacy, but he deals with the leaders by the methods of the old.' Diary of R.S. Baker, 8 March 1919, *Wilson Papers*, vol. 55.

51 A.L. George and J.L. George, op. cit., p. 31.

52 Diary of Raymond Blaine Fosdick, 12 December 1918, *Wilson Papers*, vol. 53.

53 According to House, almost as soon as they had first met, 'We found ourselves in such complete sympathy, in so many ways, that we soon learned to know what each was thinking without either having expressed himself', in George and George, op. cit., p. 93.

54 'Colonel House as the President's substitute on the Council of Four,' 8 April 1919, box 2, vol. 2, *Robert Lansing Papers*, Princeton University Archives.

55 Floto, op. cit., p. 163; Balfour to Lloyd George, 20 February 1919, no. 341, F3/4/13, *Lloyd George Papers*.

56 Wilson's dislike of Lansing was blatant as even the private secretary of Mrs Wilson wrote in her diary that ' . . . I think P. heartily dislikes Mr. L. and I am sorry to say he seems to show it in rather a petty way . . . .' in The diary of Edith Benham, 8 April 1919, *Wilson Papers*, vol. 57, and E.B.Wilson, *Memoirs of Mrs. Woodrow Wilson*, London: Putnam, 1939, p. 282. This has been noted much earlier by the British. See Wiseman to Drummond, 20 December 1918, Additional Manuscripts 49741, f.124, *Balfour Papers*; and Harold Nicolson, *Peacemaking 1919*, London: Methuen, 1933, p. 245.

57 'The principal subjects, concerning which President Wilson and I were in marked disagreement, were the following: His presence in Paris during the peace negotiations and especially his presence there as a delegate to the Peace Conference; the fundamental principles of the constitution and functions of a League of Nations as proposed or advocated by him; the form of the organic act, known as the "Covenant", its elaborate character and its inclusion in the treaty restoring a state of peace; the treaty of defensive alliance with France; the necessity for a definite programme which American Commissioners could follow in carrying on the negotiations; the employment of private interviews and confidential agreements in reaching settlements, a practice which gave colour to the charge of "secret diplomacy"; and lastly, the admission of the Japanese claims to possession of German treaty rights at Kiao-Chau and in the Province of Shantung.' Robert Lansing, *The Peace Negotiations: A Personal Narrative*, London: Constable and Company Ltd., 1921, p. 8.

58 This was the reason for preferring to use House rather than the State Department route. Floto, op. cit., p. 63; A.S. Link, *Wilson the Diplomatist: A Look at his Major Foreign Policies*, Baltimore: Johns Hopkins University Press, 1957, pp. 26–7.

59 Thomas J. Knock, *To End All Wars: Woodrow Wilson and the Quest for a New World Order*, New York: Oxford University Press, 1992, pp. 189–90.

60 Bliss, for instance, wrote a memorandum on behalf of the American Commissioners Plenipotentiary to reason with Wilson on 29 April not to support the Japanese demand for Shantung. See Minutes of the daily meetings of the Commissioners Plenipotentiary, 29 April 1919, *FRUS*, 1919, Paris Peace Conference, vol. 11.
61 Arthur Walworth, *Woodrow Wilson: 1 American Prophet*, New York: Longmans, Green & Co., 1958, p. 406.
62 Alfred Zimmern, *The League of Nations and the Rule of Law 1918–1935*, London: Macmillan & Co. Ltd., 1936, p. 179.
63 Wiseman to Reading, (circulated to Milner and the Foreign Office), 19 August 1918, F43/1/14, *Lloyd George Papers.*
64 ibid.
65 See for instance, 'World League is dead letter without U.S. support, says Simonds', 28 February 1919, *San Francisco Chronicle.*
66 For instance, see the diary of R.S. Baker, 30 April 1919, *Wilson Papers*, vol. 58.
67 R.S. Baker, *Woodrow Wilson and World Settlement*, vol. 1, London: William Heinemann Ltd., 1923, p. 235.
68 Arthur Walworth, *Wilson and his Peacemakers: American Diplomacy at the Paris Peace Conference, 1919*, New York: W.W. Norton & Company, 1986, p. 40.
69 Walworth, *Wilson and his Peacemakers*, p. 42.
70 Lansing, op. cit., p. 151.
71 Nevins, op. cit., p. 446.
72 Diary, 8 January 1919, Add. 51131, f.7, *Cecil Papers.*
73 Various schemes were proposed for a league by the Bryce group led by Viscount Bryce, the British League of Nations Society, and the Fabian Society, with counterparts in continental Europe and across the Atlantic. Final Report by the Committee on the League of Nations, 3 July 1918, 'P' (War) Series, *PRO*, CAB 29/1, pp 439–55.
74 Lloyd George to Bonar Law, 20 August 1918, F30/2/41, *Lloyd George Papers.*
75 Both Cecil and Smuts tell of how little practical ideas Wilson had about the covenant. Diary, 19 January 1919, Add.51131, f.18, *Cecil Papers*; Smuts to Gillett, 14 January 1919, no. 193 and 20 January 1919, no. 197, *Smuts Papers*, vol. 22.
76 Diary of Grayson, 6 January 1919, *Wilson Papers*, vol. 53.
77 Diary, 20 January 1919, Additional Manuscript 51131, f.19, *Cecil Papers.*
78 George W. Egerton, *Great Britain and the Creation of the League of Nations: Strategy, Politics, and International Organisation, 1914–1919*, Chapel Hill: University of North Carolina Press, 1978, p. 203.
79 For instance, Clemenceau certainly saw the French support for the League as an important political instrument to secure France's primary objective which was a permanent military guarantee against Germany within the framework of the League. David Stevenson, *French War Aims against Germany 1914–1919*, Oxford: Clarendon Press, 1982, p. 100. Similarly, Lloyd George exploited the American determination to have the Monroe Doctrine to extract concessions on naval armaments. Seth P. Tillman, *Anglo-American Relations at the Peace Conference of 1919*, Princeton: Princeton University Press, 1961, p. 280.

80 Smuts, 'On Policy at the Peace Conference' circulated to the War Cabinet and the King, 3 December 1918, Additional Manuscripts 51076, ff.79–81, *Cecil Papers*.
81 As an analysis of the implications of the League of Nations in the presidential elections is beyond the scope of this work, it would suffice here to say that the American Senate did not ratify the Treaty of Versailles. Wilson lost the elections in 1920, and subsequently suffered heart attacks and died in 1924. Walworth, *Wilson and his Peacemakers*, p. 40.
82 Diary, 19 January 1919, Add. 51131 f.18, *Cecil Papers*.
83 Lodge, op. cit., p. 119; Floto, op. cit., p. 131.
84 Joseph Tumulty to Wilson, 16 March 1919, *Wilson Papers*, vol. 55.
85 Diary, 14 March 1919, binder 5, diaries, series II, collection group 466, *House Papers*.
86 In fact, the religious article was unpopular generally and only gained support from Brazil, China and Roumania. Miller, *Drafting of the Covenant*, vol. 1, p. 268.
87 Diary of Grayson, 6 January 1919, vol. 53, and diary of House, 3 February 1919, vol. 54, *Wilson Papers*.
88 Walworth, *Wilson and his Peacemakers*, p. 313.
89 Italy in particular had antagonistic relations with the United States, Britain, and France mainly due to the uncompromising nature of their demands. J. Blatt, 'France and Italy at the Paris Peace Conference', *International History Review*, 1986, vol. 8, no. 1, p. 37; R. Albrecht-Carrie, *Italy at the Paris Peace Conference*, Hamden: Archon Press, 1966, p. 67.
90 George and George, op. cit., pp. 250–6.
91 As seen in his defence of the unanimity ruling of 11 April. Miller, *Drafting of the Covenant*, vol. 1, p. 464.
92 Britain did not threaten to withdraw over this matter in the speech. ibid., vol. 2, p. 389.
93 ibid., vol. 1, pp. 462–3.
94 D.H. Miller, diary, 11 April 1919, *My Diary: At the Conference of Paris*, vol. 1, New York, privately printed, 1924.
95 Diary of Grayson, 11 April 1919, *Wilson Papers*, vol. 57.
96 It must be noted that Wilson did command considerable respect as chairman as D.H. Miller commented, 'to his final opinions there was an unmistakable deference . . . .' in his *Drafting of the Covenant*, vol. 1, p. 126.
97 ibid., pp. 464–5; Diary, 11 April 1919, Add.51131, f.71, *Cecil Papers*.
98 H.V.W. Temperley (ed.), *A History of the Peace Conference of Paris*, vol. 4, London, Henry Frowde and Hodder & Stoughton, 1924, p. 379.
99 Baker was aware of such discrepancy much earlier as he succinctly summarised that 'He[Wilson] speaks to the masses in terms of new diplomacy, but he deals with the leaders by the methods of the old' in The diary of R.S. Baker, 8 March 1919, *Wilson Papers*, vol. 55.
100 Minutes of the Council of Four, 21 April 1919, *FRUS*, 1919, Paris Peace Conference, vol. 5.
101 Lodge, op. cit., pp. 343–4.
102 According to Lloyd George, Wilson's attitude was, in fact, strongly anti-Japanese. See Floto, op. cit., p. 88. Also House attests that 'Both he

[Wilson] and Lansing lean toward China . . . ' in his diary, 26 April 1919, Seymour, op. cit., vol. 4, p. 467.

103 For instance, Wilson tried to soften the blow of the defeat of racial equality by preparing an explanatory statement on behalf of the Japanese. Of course, he was also concerned about the negative impact this rejection would have on the image of the League. See Miller, *Drafting of the Covenant*, vol. 1, p. 465.

104 Harold Nicolson wrote ' . . . the Japanese had timed their stand upon the Shantung settlement with exquisite cunning. They had chosen the very moment when Italy had abandoned the Peace Conference because of the alleged intransigence of President Wilson' in Nicolson, op. cit., p. 146; Lansing, op. cit., p. 219.

105 Hankey and Mantoux's notes on Council of Four, 22 April 1919, *Wilson Papers*, vol. 57.

106 ibid.

107 As we see in Lansing's note, 'Mr.– (a Chinese delegate) also said that Mr. Baker stated that the President desired him to say that the President was very sorry that he had not been able to do more for China, but that he had been compelled to accede to Japan's demand "in order to save the League of Nations".' in Lansing, op. cit., p. 234. Similarly, Wilson said, 'I am not going to discuss the merits of that question, because it had no merits. The whole thing was bad. . . . We could not ask them (Great Britain and France) to disregard those promises (i.e. the secret treaties with Japan).' Foley, op. cit., p. 108.

108 Tumulty to Wilson, 26 April 1919, container 49, *Joseph Patrick Tumulty Papers*; Tumulty to Wilson, 28 April 1919, *Wilson Papers*, vol. 58.

109 Baker was first the press officer, and then after Wilson's fall out with House became one of his closest confidants. Baker to Wilson, 'Notes on the Japanese–Chinese Question', 29 April 1919, container 30 (reel 29), *Ray Stannard Baker Papers*, Library of Congress.

110 Diary of Grayson, 25 April 1919, *Wilson Papers*, vol. 58.

111 ibid., diary of R.S. Baker, 30 April 1919.

112 Wilson himself admits to this in his Senate Hearings on the Treaty of Peace. See Statement of the President, 19 August 1919, part 5, vol. 13, section 1, unit 4, *Bernard Baruch Papers*.

113 Makino Nobuaki, *Kaikoroku*, vol. 2, Tokyo, Chūō kōronsha, 1978, p. 137.

114 Minutes of the Council of Four, *FRUS*, 1919, Paris Peace Conference, vol. 5; also Seymour, op. cit., vol. 4, p. 467.

115 In fact, Wilson was convinced that the British would side with the Japanese on Shantung. See diary of Grayson, 25 April 1919, and also diary of R.S. Baker, 29 April 1919, *Wilson Papers*, vol. 58.

116 Statement of the President, 19 August 1919, part 5, vol. 13, section 1, unit 4, *Bernard Baruch Papers*.

117 Makino, op. cit., p. 198.

118 Paul Mantoux, *Paris Peace Conference 1919: Proceedings of the Council of Four (March 24–April 18)*, Geneva, Librairie Droz, 1964, p. xvii.

119 One exception was his instruction, given to Miller, on 9 February, to draft an amendment which reflected the 'Equality of Man' clause in the American Constitution. However, it was aborted the following day after

Balfour rejected it on the grounds that it would cause endless problems with the Dominions because of immigration. Miller, docs 362 and 363, *My Diary*, vol. 5; Note dictated by Balfour on 10 February 1919 on conversation with House, Additional Manuscripts 49751, *Balfour Papers*.

120 H. Blumenthal, 'Woodrow Wilson and the Race Question', *Journal of Negro History*, 1963, vol. 48, no. 1, p. 21.

121 ibid., pp. 9–10.

122 Paul Gordon Lauren, *Power and Prejudice: The Politics and Diplomacy of Racial Discrimination*, Boulder, Colorado: Westview Press, 1988, pp. 83–4.

7 CONCLUSIONS AND REFLECTIONS

1 It must be noted that 'the West' and 'the Anglo-Saxons' are used interchangeably in this chapter mainly because that was how the Japanese contemporaries had used the terms.

2 'Jinshu teki sabetsu teppai ni kansuru mondai', 20 September 1921, Tsūshō kyoku, 2.4.2.2, *Kokusai remmei: Jinshu sabetsu teppai*, vol. 3, Tokyo: Diplomatic Record Office.

3 ibid.

4 It was named after Shidehara Kijūrō, who at the time of the Paris Peace Conference was Vice Foreign Minister, then became ambassador to the United States in 1919–21, and subsequently, foreign minister twice in 1924–27 and 1929–31.

5 Chihiro Hosoya, 'Britain and the United States in Japan's View of the International System, 1919–37', in Ian Nish (ed.), *The Anglo-Japanese Alienation 1919–1952*, Cambridge: Cambridge University Press, 1982, p. 5.

6 Conyngham Greene to Balfour, 2 December 1918, *PRO*, FO 608/211, f 475.

7 For a discussion of the 'Shidehara diplomacy', confer Chapter 5 in Akira Iriye, *Japan and the Wider World: From the Mid-Nineteenth Century to the Present*, London: Longman, 1997.

8 ibid., p. 53.

9 For details, consult Iriye Akira and Aruga Tadashi (eds), *Senkanki no nihon gaikō*, Tokyo, Tokyo daigaku shuppankai, 1984; Nish, op. cit.; Erik Goldstein *et al.* (eds), *The Washington Conference, 1921–22: Naval Rivalry, East Asian Stability and the Road to Pearl Harbour*, London: Frank Cass, 1994.

10 D.C. Watt, 'Work Completed and Work as Yet Unborn', in Nish, op. cit., p. 288.

11 Asada Sadao, 'Washinton kaigi to nihon no taiō', in Iriye and Aruga, op. cit., p. 23.

12 ibid.

13 George Kennan criticised this tendency of American statesmen to utter moralistic and legalistic principles without taking into consideration how problems caused by such statements could be pragmatically resolved. In effect, Kennan is critical of the irresponsibility of these utterances, which often did not offer any practical alternative. George F. Kennan, *American Foreign Policy 1900–1950*, New York, Mentor Books, 1951, pp. 44–5.

14 Michael H. Hunt, *Ideology and U.S. Foreign Policy*, New Haven: Yale University Press, 1987, p. 71.
15 Jason Tomes, 'A.J. Balfour and British Foreign Policy: the International Thought of a Conservative Statesman', Doctor of Philosophy Thesis, University of Oxford, 1992, pp. 311–12.
16 Asada, 'Washinton kaigi to nihon no taiō', in Iriye and Aruga, op. cit., pp. 26–7.
17 For the termination of the Anglo-Japanese Alliance, consult Ian Nish, *Alliance in Decline: A Study in Anglo-Japanese Relations 1908–1923*, London: Athlone Press, 1972. What follows is largely taken from his account.
18 ibid., p. 290; Asada, 'Washinton kaigi to nihon no taiō', in Iriye and Aruga, op. cit., pp. 30–1.
19 Nish, *Alliance in Decline: A Study in Anglo-Japanese Relations 1908–1923*, London: Athlone Press, 1972, p. 381.
20 ibid., p. 381, p. 396.
21 Ian Nish, 'Japan in Britain's View of the International System, 1919–37', in his *Anglo-Japanese Alienation 1919–1952*, p. 37.
22 The League called for the cancellation of the Gentlemen's Agreement, exclusion of picture brides, exclusion of Japanese immigrants, Asiatics to be permanently barred from American citizenship, and an amendment of the Federal Constitution that no child born in the US would be given citizenship unless both parents were of the race eligible for citizenship. Roger Daniels, *Politics of Prejudice: The Anti-Japanese Movement in California and the Struggle for Japanese Exclusion*, Berkeley:University of California Press, 1977, p. 85, p. 91.
23 ibid., p. 82, p. 88.
24 Gaimushō hyakunenshi hensan iinkai (ed.), *Gaimushō no hyakunen*, vol. 1, Tokyo, Hara shobō, 1969, p. 873.
25 Daniels, op. cit., p. 106.
26 *Nihon gaikō monjo: Taibei imin mondai keika gaiyō*, Tokyo: Diplomatic Record Office, 1972, pp. 928–33.
27 Daniels, op. cit., p. 101.
28 ibid., p. 101.
29 *Nihon gaikō monjo: Taibei imin mondai keika gaiyō*, pp. 835–6.
30 Kennan, op. cit., p. 46.
31 Masamichi Royama, *Foreign Policy of Japan: 1914–1939*, Westport, Connecticut: Greenwood Press, Publishers, 1973, p. 36.
32 For instance, incidents over Japanese labourers in 1925 in Oregon, in 1926 in California, in 1928 in Washington State. After the Manchurian Incident of 1931, it is not surprising that anti-Japanese sentiment worsened. In fact, the nationality-based immigration quota was not abolished until 1965 under the Johnson Administration. *Gaimushō no hyakunen*, vol. 1, p. 876.
33 Otsuka Takehiro, *Okawa Shūmei to kindai nihon*, Tokyo, Bokutakusha, 1990, pp. 101–4.
34 ibid., p. 114.
35 ibid., p. 183.
36 Wilson states that Kita was 'a non-Marxist or traditional type of right-wing left extremist whose call for the overhaul of social institutions is

clear and direct . . . though he clung always to the traditional Tokugawa neo-Confucian assumption of the organic holism of society'. George M. Wilson, *Radical Nationalist in Japan: Kita Ikki 1883–1937*, Cambridge, MA: Harvard University Press, 1969, p. 93.

37 ibid., pp. 66–7.

38 Quoted from Wilson, ibid., p. 98.

39 Kita was executed for being the brain behind the February 16 Incident of 1936. Okawa was captured but, due to his mental instability, he could not be tried as a war criminal.

40 This association was formally organised in 1928 to defend Japan's rights in Manchuria. Many of its initial members worked for the South Manchurian Railway Company. Sadako Ogata, *Defiance in Manchuria: The Making of Japanese Foreign Policy 1931–1932*, Berkeley: University of California Press, 1964, p. 39.

41 Mark R. Peattie, *Ishiwara Kanji and Japan's Confrontation with the West*, Princeton: Princeton University Press, 1975, p. 141.

42 Kwantung Army memorandum, 'Manmō kaihatsu hōsaku an', January 1932, in Ogata, op. cit., p. 127; Peattie, op. cit., p. 164.

43 Hosoya, 'Britain and the United States in Japan's View of the International System, 1937–41', and Akira Iriye, 'Wartime Japanese Planning for Post-War Asia', in Nish, *Anglo-Japanese Alienation 1919–1952*, p. 187 and p. 57 respectively.

44 Katsumi Usui, 'A Consideration of Anglo-Japanese Relations', in ibid., pp. 77–8.

45 Konoe Fumimaro, *Seidanroku*, Tokyo: Chikura shobō, 1936, p. 263.

46 ibid., p. 253.

47 Matsuoka used the word, 'ijimerareta'. Incidentally, Matsuoka attended the peace conference of 1919 as the principal press secretary of the delegation. Matsuoka Yōsuke Denki Kankōkai (ed.), *Matsuoka Yōsuke: Sono hito to shōgai*, Tokyo: Kōdansha, 1974, pp. 121–2. Also Arita Hachirō has been quoted to have expressed the same sentiment. John W. Dower, *War without Mercy: Race and Power in the Pacific War*, London: Faber and Faber, 1986, p. 59.

48 Gordon Mark Berger, *Parties Out of Power in Japan 1931–1941*, Princeton: Princeton University Press, 1977, pp. 353–4.

49 ibid., p. 354.

50 For instance, Sugimori Yōtarō, *Kokusai gaikōroku*, Tokyo: Chūō kōronsha, 1933, p. 100; Nakano Seigō, 'Kyoryoku seijiron', *Kaizo*, 1933, p. 95; 'Manshū shōnin go no nihon gaikō', *Gaikō jihō*, 1932, no. 668, p. 8.

51 He later become foreign minister under Tōjō and Koiso cabinets. Usui, 'A Consideration of Anglo-Japanese Relations', in Nish, *Anglo-Japanese Alienation*, p. 79.

52 Even the British were reminded by the Japanese in 1941 that they had been the greatest obstacle to 'Japan's natural development', starting with the British Empire delegation's opposition to the racial equality proposal at the Paris Peace Conference. Hosoya, 'Britain and the United States in Japan's view of the international system, 1937–41', in ibid., p. 73.

53 Evidently, the Germans needed to cultivate Japanese friendship with a view to signing an Anti-Comintern Pact. See John P. Fox, 'Japanese Reactions to Nazi Germany's Racial Legislation', *Weiner Library*

Bulletin, 1969, vol. 23, nos 2–3, pp. 46–50.

54 Quoted from ibid., p. 46.

55 Quoted from ibid., p. 50.

56 This is my translation. 'Shōwa tennō no dokuhaku hachi jikan: Taiheiyō sensō no zenbō o kataru', *Bungei shunjū*, 1990, vol. 12, pp. 94–144. This document was discovered in the private papers of Terasaki Hidenari who was one of the closest advisors to the emperor. The 'monologue' was given orally by the emperor in March and April 1946 over five sessions, lasting for eight hours in total.

57 Paul Gordon Lauren, *Power and Prejudice: The Politics and Diplomacy of Racial Discrimination*, Boulder, Colorado: Westview Press, 1988; John Vincent, 'Racial Equality' in Hedley Bull and Adam Watson (eds), *The Expansion of International Society*, Oxford: Oxford University Press, 1984.

58 24 January 1919, Davis to Secretary of State, reel 392, SDR 763.72119/3502, National Archives Microfilm Publication (hereafter NAMP), M367.

59 Memorandum by Quincy Wright, Office of Naval Intelligence, October 1921, on 'Racial Equality', SDR 894.4016, NAMP, M422.

60 David Hunter Miller, *Drafting of the Covenant*, vol. 2, New York: G.P. Putnam's Sons, 1928, p. 390.

61 Naoko Shimazu, 'The Japanese Attempt to Secure Racial Equality in 1919', *Japan Forum*, 1989, vol. 1, no. 1, p. 93.

62 See Arthur de Gobineau, *Gobineau: Selected Political Writings*, London: Cape, 1970.

63 Elazar Barkan, *The Retreat of Scientific Racism: Changing Concepts of Race in Britain and the United States between the World Wars*, Cambridge: Cambridge University Press, 1992, pp. 2–3.

64 ibid., pp. 3–4.

65 ibid., p. 345.

66 For the purpose of this study, 'international society' will be defined using Hedley Bull's definition: 'A society of states (or international society) exists when a group of states, conscious of certain common interests and common values form a society in the sense that they conceive themselves to be bound by a common set of rules in their relations with one another and share in the working of common institutions' in Hedley Bull, *The Anarchical Society: A Study of Order in World Politics*, London: Macmillan, 1984, p. 13.

67 The conditions of great power membership given in Chapter 4 were military strength, 'general interests', peer recognition of its status, and managers of the international system.

68 Martin Wight, *Power Politics*, Leicester: University of Leicester Press, 1978, p. 45.

69 15 January 1919, Hankey's notes of the two meetings of the Council of Ten, *Wilson Papers*, vol. 54.

70 Alfred Cobban, *The Nation State and National Self-Determination*, New York: Thomas Y. Crowell Company, 1969, pp. 62–6.

71 ibid., p. 65, p. 68.

72 H.V.W. Temperley (ed.), *A History of the Peace Conference of Paris*, vol. 4, London: Henry Frowde and Hodder & Stoughton, 1924, p. 429.

73 Edward Mandell House and Charles Seymour (eds), *What Really Happened at Paris: The Story of the Peace Conference, 1918–1919*, London: Hodder & Stoughton, 1921, p. 205; Robert Lansing, *The Peace Negotiations: A Personal Narrative*, London: Constable and Company Ltd., 1921, pp. 85–7.

74 Cobban, op. cit., p. 61.

75 ibid., p. 66.

76 Harold Nicolson, *Peacemaking 1919*, London: Methuen & Co. Ltd., 1943, p. 246.

Bibliography

I DOCUMENTARY SOURCES

1 Official documents

Australia:

Commonwealth Parliamentary Debates (Session 1917–18–19 Second Session of 7th Parliament)

France:

Annales de la Chambre des Députés: Débats Parlementaires: 11me Législature 1919

Annales du Sénat: Débats Parlementaires: Session Ordinaire 1919

Italy:

Ministry of Foreign Affairs, *I Documenti Diplomatici Italiani*, 6th Series, vols 1 and 2.

Japan:

Diplomatic Record Office, Tokyo, Japan:
Gaimushō kōwa jumbi iinkai chōsho
Jinshu mondai ni kansuru zassan
Kakkoku naisei kankei zassan
Kakkoku taigai seisaku kankei zassan
Kokusai heiwa kaigi
Kokusai remmei: Jinshu sabetsu teppai
Pari heiwa jōyaku: Rekkoku no taido oyobi seikyō
Pari heiwa kaigi
Teikoku shogaikoku gaikō kankei zassan
Ministry of Foreign Affairs, Japan, *Nihon gaikō monjo*

Teikoku gikai kizokuin giji sokkiroku, vol. 35, Tokyo, Tokyo daigaku shuppankai, 1981.
Teikoku gikai shūgiin giji sokkiroku, vol. 35, Tokyo, Tokyo daigaku shuppankai, 1981.

The United Kingdom:

Public Record Office, Kew Gardens, London:
CAB 1
CAB 21
CAB 24
CAB 29
CO 42
CO 209
CO 417
CO 418
CO 532
FO 371
FO 373
FO 405
FO 410
FO 425
FO 608
FO 800

The United States:

National Archives Microfilm Publication, National Archives, Washington, D.C.:
M367, Records of the Department of State relating to World War I and its Termination, 1914–1929.
M422, Records of the Department of State relating to Internal Affairs of Japan, 1910–1929.
M423, Records of the Department of State relating to Political Relations between the United States and Japan, 1910–1929.
M424, Records of the Department of State relating to the Political Relations between Japan and other States, 1910–1929.
M581, Records of the Department of State Relating to the Political Relations between the United States and Great Britain, 1910–1929.
M743, Personal and Confidential Letters from Secretary of State Lansing to President Wilson, 1915–1918.
M820, General Records of the American Commission to Negotiate Peace, 1918–1931.
M1107, The Inquiry Documents, 1917–1919.
The US Department of State, *Papers Relating to the Foreign Relations of the United States* (cited as *FRUS*).

2 Private papers

Bodleian Library, Oxford:
Milner Papers
British Library, London:
Balfour Papers
The Cecil of Chelwood Papers
House of Lords Record Office, London:
Davidson Papers
Law (Bonar Law) Papers
Lloyd George Papers
Library of Congress, Washington, D.C.:
Joseph Patrick Tumulty Papers
Ray Stannard Baker Papers
Robert Lansing Papers
Stephen Bonsal Papers
Tasker Howard Bliss Papers
William E. Borah Papers
Manuscripts and Archives, Yale University, New Haven:
The Papers of Edward Mandell House
Frank L. Polk Papers
National Diet Library, Tokyo:
Ijūin Hikokichi kankei monjo (Papers related to Ijūin Hikokichi)
Makino Shinken kankei monjo (Papers related to Makino Shinken)
Terauchi Masatake kankei monjo (Papers related to Terauchi Masatake)
Rare Book and Manuscript Library, Columbia University, New York:
Wellington Koo Memoir, Chinese Oral History Project
Wellington Koo Papers
Seeley G. Mudd Manuscript Library, Princeton University Archives, Princeton:
Bernard Baruch Papers
Ray Stannard Baker Papers
Robert Lansing Papers
University of Cambridge Library:
Smuts Papers (microfilm)
The Papers of Woodrow Wilson, Princeton: Princeton University Press, 1986.

3 Newspapers and periodicals

The Argus, Melbourne, Australia.
Chūō kōron Tokyo, Japan.
Corriere della Sera, Milan, Italy.
Gaikō jihō, Tokyo.
Kaizō, Tokyo.
Kensei, Tokyo.
Kokusai chishiki, Tokyo.
Kokusaihō gaikō zasshi, Tokyo.
The Los Angeles Times, Los Angeles, United States.
Le Figaro, Paris, France.

Le Matin, Paris.
Le Temps, Paris.
Minsei, Tokyo.
The New York Times, New York.
Nihon oyobi nihonjin, Tokyo.
North China Herald, Shanghai, China.
The San Francisco Chronicle, San Francisco.
Seiyū, Tokyo.
The Sydney Morning Herald, Sydney, Australia.
Taiyō, Tokyo.
The Times, London, United Kingdom.
Tokyo asahi shimbun, Tokyo.
Tokyo nichi nichi shimbun, Tokyo.
Yomiuri shimbun, Tokyo.

II PUBLISHED SOURCES

1 Japanese sources

Arita, Hachiro, *Bakahachi to hitowa iu*, Tokyo.

Banno Junji, *Meiji: Shisō no jitsuzō*, Tokyo: Sōbunsha, 1977.

——*Taishō seihen: 1900nen taisei no hōkai*, Tokyo: Mineruba, 1982.

——*Kindai nippon no gaikō to seiji*, Tokyo: Kenbun shuppan, 1985.

Burkman, T.W., 'Sairento pâtona hatsugensu', *Kokusai seiji*, 1976, vol. 56, no. 2, pp. 102–16.

Dingman, Roger, 'Nihon to Wirusonteki sekai chitsujo', Satō Seizaburō and Roger Dingman, eds, *Kindai nihon no taigai taido*, Tokyo: Tokyo daigaku shuppankai, 1974.

Fujimura, Michio, *Nisshin sensō: Higashi ajia kindaishi no tenkanten*, Tokyo: Iwanami shinsho, 1973.

Fukuda, Tokuzō, *Reimeiroku*, Tokyo: Daitōkaku, 1920.

——*Seizonken no shakai seisaku*, Tokyo: Kōdansha, 1980.

Fukuzawa, Yukichi, *Fukuzawa Yukichi zenshū*, vol. 10, Tokyo: Iwanami, 1959–60.

Gaimushō hyakunenshi hensan iinkai, ed., *Gaimushō no hyakunen*, vol. 1, Tokyo: Hara shobō, 1969.

Hara Kei monjo kenkyūkai, ed., *Hara Kei kankei monjo*, 11 vols, Tokyo: Nippon hōsō shuppan kyōkai, 1984.

Hara, Keiichirō, ed., *Hara Kei nikki*, vol. 8, Tokyo: Kangensha, 1950.

Hayashi, Shigeru and Oka, Yoshitake, eds, *Taishō demokurashî-ki no seiji: Matsumoto Gōkichi seiji nisshi*, Tokyo: Iwanami, 1959.

Hayashi, Shigeru and Tsuji, Kiyoaki eds, *Nippon naikaku shiroku*, vol. 2, Tokyo: Daiichi hōki Shuppan, 1981.

Hosoya, Chihiro, 'Makino Shinken to berusaiyu kaigi', *Chūō kōron*, 1965, vol. 80, no. 5, pp. 363–9.

——*Ryōtaisenki no nihon gaikō, 1914–1945*, Tokyo: Iwanami, 1988.

Hosoya, Chihiro and Saitō, Makoto, eds, *Washinton taisei to nichibei kankei*, Tokyo: Tokyo daigaku shuppankai, 1978.

Ikei, Masaru, 'Pari heiwa kaigi to jinshu sabetsu teppai mondai', *Kokusai seiji*, 1962, vol. 23, pp. 44–58.

——'Uchida Yasuya – shōdo gaikō e no kiseki', *Kokusai seiji*, 1976, vol. 56, pp. 1–21.

Imai, Seiichi, *Nihon no rekishi*, vol. 23, Tokyo: Chūō kōronsha, 1974.

Inada, Shunosuke, *Jinshu mondai*, Tokyo: Yūrinkaku, 1915.

Iriye Akira, *Nihon no gaikō: Meiji ishin kara gendai made*, Tokyo: Chūō kōronsha, 1966.

——*Japan and the Wider World: From the Mid-Nineteenth Century to the Present*, London, Longman, 1997.

Iriye, Akira and Aruga, Tadashi, eds, *Senkanki no nihon gaiko*, Tokyo: Tokyo daigaku shuppankai, 1984.

Ishibashi, Tanzan, *Ishibashi Tanzan zenshū*, vol. 3, Tokyo: Tōyō keizai shimpōsha, 1970.

Ishii, Kikujirō, *Gaikō yoroku*, Tokyo: Iwanami, 1930.

——*Gaikō zuisō*, Tokyo: Kajima heiwa kenkyūjo, 1967.

Itō, Hirobumi, *Itō Hirobumi den*, vol. 2, Tokyo: Hara shobō, 1970.

Kikuchi, Gorō and Mizoguchi, Hakuyō eds, *Hara Kei zenden*, 2 vols, Tokyo: Nippon hyōronsha, 1922.

Kikuchi, Takenori, *Hakushaku Chinda Sutemi den*, Tokyo: Kyōmeikaku, 1938.

Kizaka, Jun'ichirō, 'Taishōki minponshugisha no kokusai ninshiki', *Kokusai seiji*, 1974, vol. 51, pp. 59–86.

Kobayashi, Tatsuo, 'Rinji gaikō chōsa iinkai no setchi', *Kokusai seiji*, 1964, vol. 28, pp. 53–71.

Kobayashi, Tatsuo, ed., *Suiusō nikki: Itōke monjo*, Tokyo: Hara shobō, 1966.

Koizumi, Sakutarō, *Saionji Kimmochi jiden*, Tokyo: Kōdansha, 1949.

Kojima, Kazuo, *Ichi rōseijika no kaisō*, Tokyo: Chūō kōronsha, 1951.

Konoe, Fumimaro, *Seidanroku*, Tokyo: Chikura shobō, 1936.

——*Sengo ōbei kenkenroku*, Tokyo: Chūō kōronsha, 1981.

Maeda, Renzan, *Hara Kei den*, 2 vols, Tokyo: Takayama shoin, 1950.

Makino, Nobuaki, *Shōtō kandan*, Tokyo: Sōgensha, 1940.

——*Kaikoroku*, 2 vols, Tokyo: Chūō kōronsha, 1978.

Mamiya, Kunio, 'Okuma Shigenobu to jinshu sabetsu teppai mondai', *Waseda daigakushi kiyō*, 1989, vol. 22, pp. 213–37.

Maruyama, Masao, *Nihon no shisō*, Tokyo: Iwanami shinsho, 1961.

Matsumura, Masayoshi, 'Kōkaron to nichiro sensō', *Kokusai seiji*, 1982, vol. 71, pp. 38–53.

Matsuo, Takayoshi, ed., *Ishibashi Tanzan hyōronshū*, Tokyo: Iwanami, 1986.

Matsuoka Yōsuke Denki Kankōkai, ed., *Matsuoka Yōsuke: Sono hito to shōgai*, Tokyo: Kōdansha, 1974.

Mitani, Taichirō, *Taishō demokurashîron*, Tokyo: Chūō kōronsha, 1974.

——*Nippon seitō seiji no keisei: Hara Kei no seiji shidō no tenkai*, Tokyo: Tokyo daigaku shuppankai, 1980.

Nakanishi, Hiroshi, 'Konoe Fumimaro "Eibei hon'i no heiwashugi o haisu" rombun no haikei', *Hōgaku ronsō*, 1993, vol. 132, pp. 225–58.

Nakano, Seigō, *Kōwa kaigi o mokugeki shite*, Tokyo: Tōhō jironsha, 1919.

Nakano, Yasuo, *Seijika: Nakano Seigō*, vol. 2, Tokyo: Shinmitsukaku shoten, 1971.

Nippon gaikōshi jiten hensan iinkai, ed., *Nippon gaikō jiten*, Tokyo: Gaikō shiryōkan, 1979.

Ohata, Tokushirō, *Nihon gaikō seisaku no shiteki tenkai*, Tokyo: Seibundō, 1983.
Oka, Yoshitake, *Kindai nihon no seijika: Sono seikaku to ummei*, Tokyo: Bungei shunjūsha, 1960.
——'Kokuminteki dokuritsu to kokka risei', *Kindai nihon shisōshi kōza: Sekai no naka no nihon*, vol. 8, Tokyo: Chikuma shobō, 1961.
Okuma, Shigenobu, *Jinshu mondai*, Tokyo: Waseda daigaku shuppan, 1919.
Onuma, Yasuaki, 'Haruka naru jinshu byōdō no risō', Onuma Yasuaki, ed., *Kokusaihō, kokusai rengō to nihon*, Tokyo: Kōbundō, 1987.
Otsuka, Takehiro, *Okawa Shūmei to kindai nihon*, Tokyo: Bokutakusha, 1990.
Saitō, Shizuo, *Nihon gaikō seisaku shiron josetsu*, Tokyo: Shin'yūdō, 1981.
Saitō, Takashi, 'Pari kōwa kaigi to nihon', *Kokusai seiji*, 1958, vol. 6, pp. 105–17.
Satō, Naotake, *Kaiko hachijūnen*, Tokyo: Jiji Tsūshinsha, 1963.
Seki, Shizuo, *Nippon gaikō no kijiku to tenkai*, Tokyo: Mineruba shobō, 1990.
Shidehara, Kijūrō, *Gaikō gojūnen*, Tokyo: Chūō kōronsha, 1987.
Shidehara Kijūrō heiwa zaidan, ed., *Shidehara Kijūrō*, Tokyo: Shidehara Kijūrō heiwa zaidan, 1955.
Shimomura, Hironori, *Nippon gaikō hiroku*, Tokyo: Asahi shimbunsha, 1934.
Shinobu, Seizaburō, 'Taishō gaikōshi no kihon mondai', *Kokusai seiji*, 1958, vol. 6, pp. 1–12.
——*Nihon gaikōshi 1853–1972*, Tokyo: Mainichi shimbunsha, 1974.
Shiroyanagi, Shūko, *Saionji Kimmochi den*, Tokyo: Nippon hyōronsha, 1929.
'Shōwa tennō no dokuhaku hachijikan: Taiheiyō sensō no zenbō o kataru', *Bungei shunjū*, 1990, vol. 12, pp. 94–144.
Sugimori, Yōtarō, *Kokusai gaikōroku*, Tokyo: Chūō kōronsha, 1933.
Takamura, Naosuke, 'Tenkanki to shiteno daiichiji taisen to nippon', *Kōza nihon rekishi*, part 3, vol. 9, Tokyo: Tokyo daigaku shuppankai, 1985.
Takeuchi, Katsumi, *Matsuoka zenken daienzetsu shū*, Tokyo: Kōdansha, 1933.
Tanaka Giichi denki kankōkai, ed., *Tanaka Giichi denki*, vol. 2, Tokyo: Hara shobō, 1981.
Tanaka, Sōgorō, *Yoshino Sakuzō: Nihonteki demokurashî no shito*, Tokyo: Miraisha, 1958.
Tokutomi, Iichiro, ed., *Kōshaku Yamagata Aritomo den*, vol. 3, Tokyo: Yamagata Aritomo Kōkinen jigyōkai, 1933.
Tokyo daigaku kyōyō gakubu nihonshi kenkyūshitsu, ed., *Nihonshi gaisetsu*, Tokyo: Tokyo daigaku shuppankai, 1985.
Uchida Yasuya denki hensai iinkai, ed., *Uchida Yasuya*, Tokyo: Kajima kenkyūjo shuppankai, 1969.
Uchiyama, Masakuma, *Gendai nippon gaikōron*, Tokyo: Keiō daigaku hōgaku kenkyūkai, 1971.
Ugaki, Kazushige, *Ugaki Kazushige nikki*, vol. 1, Tokyo: Misuzu shobō, 1968.
Unno, Yoshirō, 'Pari kōwa kaigi to gaimushō', *Rekishi kyōiku*, 1967, vol. 15, no. 1, pp. 46–53.
——*Kokusai remmei to nihon*, Tokyo: Hara shobō, 1972.
Yabe, Sadaharu, *Konoe Fumimaro*, Tokyo: Yomiuri shimbunsha, 1976.
Yoshida, Shigeru, *Kaiko jūnen*, vol. 4, Tokyo: Shinchōsha, 1958.

2 Western sources

Albrecht-Carrié, René, 'Italian Foreign Policy, 1914–1922', *Journal of Modern History*, 1940, vol. 20, no. 4, pp. 326–39.

——'Italian Colonial Policy 1914–1918', *Journal of Modern History*, 1946, vol. 18, no. 2, pp. 123–47.

——*Italy at the Paris Peace Conference*, Hamden, Connecticut: Archon Press, 1966.

Ambrosius, Lloyd E., *Woodrow Wilson and the American Diplomatic Tradition*, New York: Cambridge University Press, 1987.

Andrew, C.M. and Kanya-Forstner, A.S., 'The French Colonial Party and French Colonial War Aims, 1914–1918', *Historical Journal*, 1974, vol. 17, no. 1, pp. 79–106.

Baker, Ray Stannard, *Woodrow Wilson and World Settlement*, 3 vols, London: William Heinemann Ltd., 1923.

Banton, Michael, *Race Relations*, London: Tavistock Publications, 1967.

——*Racial Theories*, Cambridge: Cambridge University Press, 1987.

Barkan, Elazar, *The Retreat of Scientific Racism: Changing Concepts of Race in Britain and the United States between the World Wars*, Cambridge: Cambridge University Press, 1992.

Barnes, George N., *From Workshop to War Cabinet*, London: Herbert Jenkins Limited, 1924.

Barraclough, Geoffrey, *An Introduction to Contemporary History*, London: Penguin Books, 1967.

Beasley, W.G., 'Japan and Pan-Asianism: Problems of Definition', in *Aspects of Pan-Asianism*, ed., by Janet Hunter, International Studies 1987/II, Suntory Toyota International Centre for Economics and Related Disciplines, London School of Economics and Political Science.

Beloff, Max, *Britain's Liberal Empire 1897-1921*, vol. 1, London: Macmillan, 1987.

Berger, Gordon Mark, *Parties Out of Power in Japan 1931–1941*, Princeton: Princeton University Press, 1977.

Betts, Raymond F., *Assimilation and Association in French Colonial Theory 1890–1914*, New York: Columbia University Press, 1961.

Birdsall, Paul, *Versailles Twenty Years After*, Hamden, Connecticut: Archon Books, 1962.

Blatt, Joel, 'France and Italy at the Paris Peace Conference', *International History Review*, 1986, vol. 8, no. 1, pp. 27–40.

Blumenthal, Henry, 'Woodrow Wilson and the Race Question', *Journal of Negro History*, 1963, vol. 48, no. 1, pp. 1–21.

Boggs, T.H., 'The Oriental on the Pacific Coast', *Queen's Quarterly*, 1926, vol. 33, no. 3, pp. 311–24.

Bolt, Christine, *Victorian Attitudes to Race*, London: Routledge & Kegan Paul, 1971.

Bonsal, Stephen. *Unfinished Business*. London: Michael Joseph, 1944.

Borden, Henry, ed., *Robert Laird Borden: His Memoirs*, vol. 2, London: Macmillan, 1938.

Bourgeois, Léon, *Le Pacte de 1919 et la Société des Nations*, Paris: Bibliothèque Charpentier, 1919.

——*Le Traité de Paix de Versailles*, Paris, 1919.

Brookes, E.H., 'A Far-Seeing International Statesman', in Zelda Friedlander, ed., *Jan Smuts Remembered: A Centennial Tribute*, London: Allan Wingate, 1970.

Brown, Delmer M., *Nationalism in Japan: An Introductory Historical Analysis*, Berkeley: University of California Press, 1955.

Brown, Robert Craig, 'Sir Robert Borden, the Great War and Anglo-Canadian Relations', in John S. Moir, ed., *Character and Circumstance*, Toronto: Macmillan, 1970.

Buell, Raymond Leslie, 'The Development of the Anti-Japanese Agitation in the United States', *Political Science Quarterly*, 1922, vol. 37, no. 4, pp. 605–38.

——'The Development of the Anti-Japanese Agitation in the United States II', *Political Science Quarterly*, 1923, vol. 38, no. 2, pp. 57–81.

Bull, Hedley, *The Anarchical Society: A Study of Order in World Politics*, London: Macmillan, 1977.

Bull, Hedley and Watson, Adam, eds, *The Expansion of International Society*, Oxford: Oxford University Press, 1984.

Butterfield, Herbert and Wight, Martin, eds, *Diplomatic Investigations: Essays in the Theory of International Politics*, London: George Allen and Unwin Ltd., 1966.

Cambon, Paul, *Correspondance: 1870–1924*, vol. 3, Paris: Editions Bernard Grasset, 1946.

Canadian Institute of International Affairs, *Minorities of Oriental Race in Canada*, 8th Conference of the Institute of Pacific Relations, 1942.

Carr, E.H., *International Relations between the Two World Wars 1919–1939*, London: Macmillan, 1947.

Cecil, Lord Robert, *A Great Experiment*, London: Jonathan Cape, 1941.

Clemenceau, G.E., *Grandeur and Misery of Victory*, London: George G. Harrap & Co. Ltd., 1930.

——*Discours de Paix*, Paris: Société des Amis de Clemenceau, 1938.

Cobban, Alfred, *The Nation State and National Self-Determination*, New York: Thomas Y. Crowell, 1969.

'The Colour Question in Politics', *Round Table*, 1922, vol. 13, pp. 38–70.

Connors, Lesley, *The Emperor's Adviser: Saionji Kimmochi and Pre-war Japanese Politics*, London: Croom Helm, 1987.

Conroy, Hilary, *The Japanese Frontier in Hawaii, 1868–1898*, Berkeley: University of California Press, 1953.

Constable, H.J., *From Ploughboy to Premier: A New Life of William Ferguson Massey*, London: John Marlowe Savage and Co. Ltd., 1925.

Crijns, A.G.J., *Race Relations and Race Attitudes in South Africa: A Socio-Psychological Study of Human Relationships in a Multi-Racial Society*, Nijmegen, Academisch Proefschrift, Drukkerij Gebr, Janssen N.V., 1959.

Cronton, David E., ed., *The Cabinet Diaries of Josephus Daniels: 1913–1921*, Lincoln: University of Nebraska Press, 1963.

Crowley, James B., *Japan's Quest for Autonomy: National Security and Foreign Policy 1930–1938*, Princeton: Princeton University Press, 1966.

Currey, Muriel, *Italian Foreign Policy 1918–1932*, London: Ivor Nicholson and Watson, Ltd., 1932.

Daniels, Roger, *The Politics of Prejudice: The Anti-Japanese Movement in*

California and the Struggle for Japanese Exclusion, Berkeley: University of California Press, 1977.

——*Asian America: Chinese and Japanese in the United States since 1850*, Seattle: University of Washington Press, 1988.

Daniels, Roger and Kitano, Harry, *American Racism: Exploration of the Nature of Prejudice*, Englewood Cliffs, New Jersey: Prentice-Hall, 1970.

Davis, L.E. and Huttenback, R.A., *Mammon and the Pursuit of Empire: The Political Economy of British Imperialism, 1860–1912*, Cambridge: Cambridge University Press, 1986.

Dawson, R.M., ed., *The Development of Dominion Status 1900–1936*, London: Oxford University Press, 1937.

Dewey, A. Gordon., *The Dominions and Diplomacy: The Canadian Contribution*, 2 vols, London: Longmans, Green Co., 1929.

Dikotter, Frank, *The Discourse of Race in Modern China*, Stanford: Stanford University Press, 1992.

Dockrill, Michael and Goold, Douglas J., *Peace without Promise: Britain and the Peace Conferences 1919–1923*, London: Batsford Academic and Education Ltd., 1981.

Dockrill, M.L. and Steiner, Zara, 'The Foreign Office at the Paris Peace Conference in 1919', *International History Review*, 1980, vol. 2, no. 1, pp. 55–86.

Donelan, Michael, ed., *The Reason of States: A Study in International Political Theory*, London: George Allen & Unwin, 1978.

Dower, John W., *War without Mercy: Race and Power in the Pacific War*, London: Faber and Faber, 1986.

Dugdale, Blanche E., *Arthur James Balfour*, 2 vols, London: Hutchinson & Co. Ltd., 1939.

Duncan, Patrick, 'Race Questions in South Africa', *Foreign Affairs*, 1927, vol. 5, no. 2, pp. 293–306.

Duncan, W.G.K., ed., *Australia's Foreign Policy*, Sydney: Angus & Robertson, 1938.

Egerton, George W., *Great Britain and the Creation of the League of Nations: Strategy, Politics, and International Organisation, 1914–1919*, Chapel Hill: University of North Carolina Press, 1978.

Ferguson, Ted, *A White Man's Country: An Exercise in Canadian Prejudice*, Toronto: Doubleday, 1975.

Fifield, Russell H., *Woodrow Wilson and the Far East: The Diplomacy of the Shantung Question*, New York: Thomas Y. Crowell, 1952.

Fitzhardinge, L.F., *William Morris Hughes: A Political Biography*, 2 vols, Sydney: Angus & Robertson Publishers, 1964, 1979.

Fletcher III, William Miles, *The Search for a New Order: Intellectuals and Fascism in Prewar Japan*, Chapel Hill: University of North Carolina Press, 1982.

Floto, Inga, *Colonel House in Paris: A Study of American Policy at the Paris Peace Conference 1919*, Princeton: Princeton University Press, 1980.

Foley, Hamilton, compiled by, *Woodrow Wilson's Case for the League of Nations*, Princeton: Princeton University Press, 1923.

Fox, John P., 'Japanese Reactions to Nazi Germany's Racial Legislation', *Weiner Library Bulletin*, 1969, vol. 23, nos 2–3, pp. 46–50.

Fukuzawa, Yukichi, *An Outline of a Theory of Civilisation*, translated by

D.A.Dilworth and G.Cameron Hurst, Tokyo, Sophia University Press, 1973.

Gallagher, Patrick, 'China's Defeat at Paris', *Asia: Journal of the American Asiatic Association*, 1919, vol. 19, no. 7, pp. 633–6.

Gardner, Lloyd C., *Safe for Democracy: The Anglo-American Response to Revolutions, 1913–1923*, New York: Oxford University Press, 1984.

Garran, Robert, *Prosper the Commonwealth*, London: Angus & Robertson, 1958.

Garraty, John A., 'Responsibility Shunned by Lodge; Rebuttal by Henry Cabot Lodge, Jr.', in Ralph A. Stone, ed., *Wilson and the League of Nations: Why America's Rejection?*, New York: Holt, Rinehart and Winston, 1967.

George, Alexander L. and George, Juliette L., *Woodrow Wilson and Colonel House: A Personality Study*, New York: Dover Publications, Inc., 1964.

Gérard, Auguste, *L'Extrême-Orient et la Paix*, Paris: Payot & cie, 1919.

——*Ma Mission au Japon: 1907–1914*, Paris: Librairie Plon, 1919.

——*Mémoires*, Paris: Librairie Plon, 1928.

Glazebrook, G.P. de T., *Canada at the Paris Peace Conference*, London: Oxford University Press, 1942.

Gluck, Carol, *Japan's Modern Myths: Ideology in the Late Meiji Period*, Princeton: Princeton University Press, 1985.

Gobineau, Arthur de, *Gobineau: Selected Political Writings*, London: Cape, 1970.

Gollan, Robin, *Radical Working Class Politics: A Study of Eastern Australia, 1850–1910*, Melbourne: Melbourne University Press, 1960.

Gong, Gerrit W., *The Standard of 'Civilisation' in International Society*, Oxford: Clarendon Press, 1984.

Grayson, Cary T., *Woodrow Wilson: An Intimate Memoir*, New York: Holt, Rinehart and Winston, 1960.

Greenwood, Gordon and Grimshaw, Charles, eds, *Documents on Australian International Affairs 1901–1918*, Canberra: Australian Institute of International Affairs, 1977.

Grey, Edward (Viscount Fallodon), *Twenty-Five Years 1892–1916*, 2 vols, London: Hodder & Stoughton, 1925.

Hancock, W.K., *Smuts*, 2 vols, Cambridge: Cambridge University Press, 1962–1968.

——*Survey of British Commonwealth Affairs: Problems of Nationality 1918–1936*, vol. 1, London: Oxford University Press, 1964.

Hankey, Lord Maurice, *The Supreme Control: At the Paris Peace Conference 1919*, London: George Allen and Unwin Ltd., 1963.

Hennings, Robert E., 'James D.Phelan and the Woodrow Wilson Anti-Oriental Statement of May 3, 1912', *California Historical Society Quarterly*, 1963, vol. 42, pp. 291–300.

Hirai-Young, Katsu and Young, John W., 'Racism and Imperialism: the Issue of Japanese Emigration to 1954', in Alan Rix and Ross Mouer, eds, *Japan's Impact on the World*, Canberra: Japanese Studies Association of Australia, 1984.

Holland, R.F., *Britain and the Commonwealth Alliance*, London: Macmillan, 1981.

House, Edward Mandell and Seymour, Charles, eds, *What Really Happened at*

Paris: The Story of the Peace Conference, 1918–1919, London: Hodder & Stoughton, 1921.

Hudson, W.J., *Billy Hughes in Paris: The Birth of Australian Diplomacy*, Melbourne; Nelson, 1978.

Hughes, Colin A., *Mr. Prime Minister: Australian Prime Ministers 1901–1972*, Melbourne: Oxford University Press, 1976.

Hughes, W.M., *The Splendid Adventure: A Review of Empire Relations within and without the Commonwealth of Britannic Nations*, London: Ernest Benn Limited, 1929.

——*Policies and Potentates*, Sydney: Angus & Robertson, 1950.

Hunt, Michael H., *Ideology and U.S. Foreign Policy*, New Haven: Yale University Press, 1987.

Huttenback, Robert A., *Racism and Empire: White Settlers and Coloured Immigrants in the British Self-Governing Colonies*, London: Cornell University Press, 1976.

Ichihashi, Yamato, *Japanese in the United States: A Critical Study of the Problems of the Japanese Immigrants and their Children*, Stanford: Stanford University Press, 1932.

Ichioka, Yūji, *The Issei: The World of the First Generation Japanese Immigrants, 1885–1924*, New York: The Free Press, 1988.

'The Imperial Conference from an American Standpoint', *Round Table*, 1921, vol. 11, no. 44, pp. 835–47.

Jenks, Jeremiah W., 'Remaking our Far Eastern Policy', *Asia: Journal of the American Asiatic Association*, 1919, vol. 19, no. 9, pp. 886–8.

'Joint Debate on the Covenant of Paris: Henry Cabot Lodge and A. Lawrence Lowell', *League of Nations*, 1919, vol. 2, no. 2, pp. 1–49.

Kawakami, K.K., 'Canada as a "White Man's Country" ', *Current History*, 1924, vol. 19, no. 5, pp. 829–34.

Keith, Arthur Berriedale, *Speeches and Documents on the British Dominions 1918–1931: From Self-Government to National Sovereignty*, London: Oxford University Press, 1932.

Kennan, George F., *American Foreign Policy 1900–1950*, New York: Mentor Books, 1951.

Kiernan, V.G., *The Lords of Human Kind: Black Man, Yellow Man, and White Man in an Age of Empire*, London: The Cresset Library, 1969.

King, Wunsz (Chin Wen-ssu), *Woodrow Wilson, Wellington Koo and the China Question at the Paris Peace Conference*, Leyden: A.W. Sythoff, 1959.

Knock, Thomas J., *To End All Wars: Woodrow Wilson and the Quest for a New World Order*, New York: Oxford University Press, 1992.

Koo, V.K.Wellington, and Cheng-Ting T. Wang, *China and the League of Nations*, London: George Allen and Unwin, 1919.

Lansing, Robert, *The Peace Negotiations: A Personal Narrative*, London: Constable and Company Ltd., 1921.

——*The Big Four and Others of the Peace Conference*, London: Hutchinson, 1922.

——*War Memoirs*, New York: Bobbs-Merrill, 1935.

Lauren, Paul Gordon, *Power and Prejudice: The Politics and Diplomacy of Racial Discrimination*, Boulder, Colorado: Westview Press, 1988.

Lederer, Ivo J., *Yugoslavia at the Paris Peace Conference: A Study in Frontiermaking*, London: Yale University Press, 1963.

Lehmann, Jean-Pierre, *The Image of Japan: From Feudal Isolation to World Power, 1850–1905*, London: George Allen & Unwin, 1978.
Link, Arthur S., *Woodrow Wilson and the Progressive Era 1910–1917*, New York: Harper and Row, 1954.
——*Wilson the Diplomatist: A Look at his Major Foreign Policies*, Baltimore: The Johns Hopkins University Press, 1957.
Link, Arthur S. and Leary, W.M., *The Diplomacy of World Power: The United States, 1889–1920*, Edinburgh: Edward Arnold, 1970.
Lissington, M.P., *New Zealand and Japan 1900–1941*, Wellington: A.R.Shearer, 1972.
Lloyd George, David, *War Memoirs*, vols 4 and 5, London: Ivor Nicholson & Watson, 1934.
Lodge, Henry Cabot, *The Senate and the League of Nations*, London: Charles Scribner's Sons, 1925.
Lou, Tseng-Tsiang, *Ways of Confucius and of Christ*, London: Burns Oates, 1948.
Lowe, Peter, *Great Britain and Japan 1911–15: A Study of British Far Eastern Policy*, London: Macmillan, 1969.
Lower, A.R.M., *Canada and the Far East-1940*, Institute of Pacific Relations, 1940.
Mantoux, Paul, *Paris Peace Conference 1919: Proceedings of the Council of Four (March 24–April 18)*, Geneva: Librairie Droz, 1964.
Marston, F.S., *The Peace Conference of 1919: Organisation and Procedure*, Oxford: Oxford University Press, 1944.
Maruyama, Masao, *Thought and Behaviour in Modern Japanese Politics*, London: Oxford University Press, 1963.
Mayer, Arno J., *Politics and Diplomacy of Peacemaking: Containment and Counterrevolution at Versailles, 1918–1919*, London: Weidenfeld and Nicolson, 1968.
Meaney, Neville, *The Search for Security in the Pacific, 1901–14*, Sydney: Sydney University Press, 1976.
——*Australia and the World: A Documentary History from the 1870s to the 1970s*, Brisbane: Longman, 1985.
Mehrotra, S.R., *India and the Commonwealth 1885–1929*, London: George Allen & Unwin, 1965.
Millar, T.B., *Australia in Peace and War: External Relations 1788–1977*, London: C. Hurst, 1978.
Miller, David Hunter, *My Diary: At the Conference of Paris*, vols 1, 5, 8 and 20, New York: privately printed, 1924.
——*The Drafting of the Covenant*, 2 vols, New York: G.P. Putnam's Sons, 1928.
Miquel, Pierre, *La Paix de Versailles et l'Opinion Publique Française*, Paris: Flammarion, 1972.
Mordacq, J.J.H., *Le Ministère Clemenceau: Journal d'un Temoin*, vol. 3, Paris: Librairie Plon, 1931.
Morton, W.F., *Tanaka Giichi and Japan's China Policy*, Folkestone, Kent: Wm Dawson & Sons, 1980.
Mutsu, Munemitsu, *Kenkenroku: A Diplomatic Record of the Sino–Japanese War, 1894–1895*, edited and translated by Gordon Mark Berger, Tokyo: Japan Foundation, 1982.

Myers, Ramon H. and Peattie, Mark R., eds, *The Japanese Colonial Empire, 1895–1945*, Princeton: Princeton University Press, 1984.
Nevins, Allan, *Henry White: Thirty Years of American Diplomacy*, New York: Harper & Brothers, 1930.
'New Zealand and the Peace Conference', *Round Table*, 1919, vol. 9, no. 35, pp. 637–40.
Nicolson, Harold, *Peacemaking 1919*, London: Methuen, 1943.
Nish, Ian Hill, 'Australia and the Anglo-Japanese Alliance, 1901–1911', *Australian Journal of Politics and History*, 1963, vol. 9, no. 2, pp. 201–12.
——*The Anglo-Japanese Alliance: The Diplomacy of Two Island Empires 1894–1907*, London: Athlone Press, 1966.
——*Alliance in Decline: A Study in Anglo-Japanese Relations 1908–1923*, London: Athlone Press, 1972.
——ed., *Anglo-Japanese Alienation 1919–1952*, Cambridge: Cambridge University Press, 1982.
——*The Origins of the Russo–Japanese War*, London: Longman Group Limited, 1985.
Nitti, Francesco Savarino, *The Decadence of Europe: The Paths of Reconstruction*, London: T. Fisher Unwin Limited, 1923.
O'Connor, P.S., 'Keeping New Zealand White, 1908–1920', *New Zealand Journal of History*, 1968, vol. 2, no. 1, pp. 41–65.
Ogata, Sadako, *Defiance in Manchuria: The Making of Japanese Foreign Policy 1931–1932*, Berkeley: University of California Press, 1964.
Osiander, Andreas, *The States System of Europe, 1640–1990: Peacemaking and the Conditions of International Stability*, Oxford: Clarendon Press, 1994.
Pearce, Sir George Foster, *Carpenter to Cabinet: Thirty-Seven Years of Parliament*, London: Hutchinson, 1951.
Peattie, Mark R., *Ishiwara Kanji and Japan's Confrontation with the West*, Princeton: Princeton University Press, 1975.
Pelcovits, Nathan A., *Old China Hands and the Foreign Office*, New York: King's Crown Press, 1948.
Pooley, A.M., *The Secret Memoirs of Count Tadasu Hayashi*, London: Eveleigh Nash, 1915.
Preiswerk, Roy, 'Race and Colour in International Relations', *The Year Book of World Affairs*, 1970, pp. 54–87.
Rich, Paul, *Race and Empire in British Politics*, Cambridge: Cambridge University Press, 1986.
Riddell, Lord, *Lord Riddell's Intimate Diary of the Peace Conference and After 1918–1923*, London: Victor Gollancz, 1933.
Riddell, Walter A., ed., *Documents on Canadian Foreign Policy 1917–1939*, Toronto: Oxford University Press, 1962.
Rodd, James Rennell, *Social and Diplomatic Memories*, vol. 3, London: Edward Arnold, 1925.
Ross, Angus, 'Reluctant Dominion or Dutiful Daughter? New Zealand and the Commonwealth in the Inter-War Years', in *Collected Seminar Papers on the Dominions between the Wars*, London: Institute of Commonwealth Studies, 1970–1.
Rothwell, V.H., *British War Aims and Peace Diplomacy 1914–1918*, Oxford: Clarendon Press, 1971.

Royama, Masamichi, *Foreign Policy of Japan: 1914–1939*, Westport, Connecticut: Greenwood Press, 1973.

Sawer, Geoffrey, *Australian Federal Politics and Law, 1901–1929*, Melbourne: Melbourne University Press, 1956.

Scott, Ernest, *Official History of Australia in the War of 1914–1918: vol. 11 Australia during the War*, Sydney: Angus & Robertson, 1936.

Seymour, Charles, ed., *The Intimate Papers of Colonel House*, vol. 4, London: Ernest Benn, 1928.

Sforza, Carlo, 'Sonnino and his Foreign Policy', *Contemporary Review*, 1929, vol. 236, no. 768, pp. 721–32.

——*Makers of Modern Europe: Portraits and Personal Impressions and Recollections*, London: Elkin Mathews and Marrot, 1930.

Shimazu, Naoko, 'The Japanese Attempt to Secure Racial Equality in 1919', *Japan Forum*, 1989, vol. 1, no. 1, pp. 93–100.

——'The Racial Equality Proposal at the Paris Peace Conference', in *Japan and the First World War*, International Studies Discussion Paper, IS/95/291, 1995, The Suntory Centre, STICERD, The London School of Economics.

Shotwell, James T., *At the Paris Peace Conference*, New York: Macmillan, 1937.

Sissons, D.C.S., 'The Immigration Question in Australian Diplomatic Relations with Japan, 1875–1919', History Section 26/821, Australian and New Zealand Association for the Advancement of Science, 1971.

Smuts, J.C, *Greater South Africa: Plans for a Better World: The Speeches of J.C. Smuts*, Johannesburg: Truth Legion, 1940.

——*Jan Christian Smuts*: London: Cassell, 1952.

Snelling, R.C., 'Peacemaking 1919: Australia, New Zealand, and the British Empire Delegation at Versailles', *Journal of Imperial and Commonwealth History*, 1975, vol. 4, no. 1, pp. 15–28.

Spiller, G., ed., *First Universal Races Congress Held at the University of London 26–29 July 1911*, London: P.S.King, 1911.

Steiner, Zara S., *The Foreign Office and Foreign Policy, 1898–1914*, Cambridge: Cambridge University Press, 1969.

Stevenson, David, *French War Aims against Germany 1914–1919*, Oxford: Clarendon Press, 1982.

Stone, Ralph, *The Irreconcilables: The Fight against the League of Nations*, Lexington: The University of Kentucky Press, 1970.

Storry, Richard, *A History of Modern Japan*, London: Penguin, 1960.

——*Japan and the Decline of the West in Asia 1894–1943*, New York: St. Martin's Press, 1979.

Tardieu, André, *The Truth about the Treaty*, London: Hodder & Stoughton Ltd., 1921.

Taylor, A.J.P., *English History 1914–1945*, Harmondsworth, Middlesex: Penguin Books, 1970.

Taylor, G.P., 'New Zealand, the Anglo-Japanese Alliance and the 1908 Visit of the American Fleet', *Australian Journal of Politics and History*, 1969, vol. 15, no. 1, pp. 55–76.

Temperley, H.V.W., ed., *A History of the Peace Conference of Paris*, 6 vols, London: Henry Frowde and Hodder & Stoughton, 1924.

Thorne, Christopher, *Allies of a Kind: The United States, Britain and the War against Japan, 1941–45*, London: Hamish Hamilton, 1978.

Tilley, John and Gaselee, Stephen, *The Foreign Office*, London: G.P.Putnam's Sons Ltd., 1933.

Tillman, Seth P., *Anglo-American Relations at the Peace Conference of 1919*, Princeton: Princeton University Press, 1961.

Tinker, Hugh, *Race, Conflict and the International Order: From Empire to United Nations*, London: Macmillan, 1977.

Tomes, J.H., 'A.J.Balfour and British Foreign Policy: the International Thought of a Conservative Statesman', Doctor of Philosophy Thesis, University of Oxford, 1992.

Turner, Ian, *Industrial Labour and Politics: The Dynamics of the Labour Movement in Eastern Australia 1900–1921*, Cambridge: Cambridge University Press, 1965.

Twitchett, Denis and Fairbank, J.K., eds, *The Cambridge History of China*, vols 12 and 13, Cambridge: Cambridge University Press, 1983.

Underhay, F.C., 'Sir Robert Borden and Imperial Relations', *Dalhousie Review*, 1931, vol. 10, pp. 503–17.

Walworth, Arthur, *Woodrow Wilson*, 2 vols, New York: Longmans, Green and Co., 1958.

——*Wilson and his Peacemakers: American Diplomacy at the Paris Peace Conference, 1919*, New York: W.W. Norton & Company, 1986.

Weiner, Michael, 'Discourses of Race, Nation, and Empire in Pre-1945 Japan', *Ethnic and Racial Studies*, 1995, vol. 18, no. 3, pp. 433–56.

Weston, Rubin Francis, *Racism in U.S. Imperialism: The Influence of Racial Assumptions on American Foreign Policy, 1893–1946*, Columbia, South Carolina: University of South Carolina, 1972.

'White Australia', *Round Table*, 1921, vol. 11, no. 42, pp. 312–38.

'A White New Zealand and Restrictions on Immigration', *Round Table*, 1920, vol. 11, pp. 221–4.

Wight, Martin, *Power Politics*, Leicester: University of Leicester Press, 1978.

Wigley, Philip G., *Canada and the Transition to Commonwealth: British-Canadian Relations 1917–1926*, Cambridge: Cambridge University Press, 1977.

Wilson, Edith Bolling, *Memoirs of Mrs. Woodrow Wilson*, London: Putnam, 1939.

Wilson, George M., *Radical Nationalist in Japan: Kita Ikki 1883–1937*, Cambridge: Massachusetts, Harvard University Press, 1969.

Wilson, Woodrow, *A History of the American People*, 5 vols, New York: Harper and Brothers, 1902.

Wood, F.L.W., *New Zealand in the World*, Wellington: Department of Internal Affairs, 1940.

Woodsworth, Charles J., *Canada and the Orient: A Study in International Relations*, Toronto: Macmillan, 1941.

Yarwood, A.T., *Asian Migration to Australia: The Background to Exclusion 1896–1923*, Melbourne: Melbourne University Press, 1964.

Zhang Yongjin, *China in the International System, 1918–1920: The Middle Kingdom at the Periphery*, Oxford: Macmillan, 1991.

Zimmern, Alfred, *The League of Nations and the Rule of Law 1918–1935*, London: Macmillan, 1936.

Index

Note: REP = racial equality proposal

77662185R00150

Made in the USA
Middletown, DE
24 June 2018